To my husband, Seymour, for his forty years of love, support, and encouragement

TREATING
COUPLES

THE JOSSEY-BASS LIBRARY OF CURRENT CLINICAL TECHNIQUE

IRVIN D. YALOM, GENERAL EDITOR

TREATING COUPLES

A VOLUME IN THE JOSSEY-BASS
LIBRARY OF CURRENT CLINICAL TECHNIQUE

Hilda Kessler, EDITOR

Irvin D. Yalom, GENERAL EDITOR

Jossey-Bass Publishers • San Francisco

Substantial discounts on bulk quantities of Jossey-Bass books are available to corporations, professional associations, and other organizations. For details and discount information, contact the special sales department at Jossey-Bass Inc., Publishers. (415) 433–1740; Fax (800) 605–2665.

For sales outside the United States, please contact your local Simon & Schuster International Office.

 Manufactured in the United States of America on Lyons Falls Pathfinder Tradebook. This paper is acid-free and 100 percent totally chlorine-free.

Library of Congress Cataloging-in-Publication Data

Treating couples/Hilda Kessler, editor.
    p.   cm.—(A volume in the Jossey-Bass library of current clinical technique)
Includes bibliographical references and index.
ISBN 0-7879-0205-5 (alk. paper)
    1. Marital psychotherapy. I. Kessler, Hilda, date. II. Series: Jossey-Bass library of current clinical technique.
RC488.5.T716 1996
616.89'156—dc20   95-42119
                                                  CIP

FIRST EDITION
PB Printing 10 9 8 7 6 5 4 3 2 1

CONTENTS

FOREWORD

At a recent meeting of clinical practitioners, a senior practitioner declared that more change had occurred in his practice of psychotherapy in the past year than in the twenty preceding years. Nodding assent, the others all agreed.

And was that a good thing for their practice? A resounding "No!" Again, unanimous concurrence—too much interference from managed care; too much bureaucracy; too much paper work; too many limits set on fees, length, and format of therapy; too much competition from new psychotherapy professions.

Were these changes a good or a bad thing for the general public? Less unanimity on this question. Some pointed to recent positive developments. Psychotherapy was becoming more mainstream, more available, and more acceptable to larger segments of the American public. It was being subjected to closer scrutiny and accountability—uncomfortable for the practitioner but, if done properly, of potential benefit to the quality and efficiency of behavioral health care delivery.

But without dissent this discussion group agreed—and every aggregate of therapists would concur—that astounding changes are looming for our profession: changes in the reasons that people request therapy; changes in the perception and practice of mental health care; changes in therapeutic theory and technique; and changes in the training, certification, and supervision of professional therapists.

From the perspective of the clientele, several important currents are apparent. A major development is the de-stigmatization of psychotherapy. No longer is psychotherapy invariably a hush-hush affair, laced with shame and conducted in offices with separate entrance and exit doors to prevent the uncomfortable possibility of patients meeting one another.

Today such shame and secrecy have been exploded. Television talk shows—Oprah, Geraldo, Donahue—have normalized psychopathology and psychotherapy by presenting a continuous public parade of dysfunctional human situations: hardly a day passes without television fare of confessions and audience interactions with deadbeat fathers, sex addicts, adult children of alcoholics, battering husbands and abused wives, drug dealers and substance abusers, food bingers and purgers, thieving children, abusing parents, victimized children suing parents.

The implications of such de-stigmatization have not been lost on professionals who no longer concentrate their efforts on the increasingly elusive analytically suitable neurotic patient. Clinics everywhere are dealing with a far broader spectrum of problem areas and must be prepared to offer help to substance abusers and their families, to patients with a wide variety of eating disorders, adult survivors of incest, victims and perpetrators of domestic abuse. No longer do trauma victims or substance abusers furtively seek counseling. Public awareness of the noxious long-term effects of trauma has been so sensitized that there is an increasing call for public counseling facilities and a growing demand, as well, for adequate treatment provisions in health care plans.

The mental health profession is changing as well. No longer is there such automatic adoration of lengthy "depth" psychotherapy where "deep" or "profound" is equated with a focus on the earliest years of the patient's life. The contemporary field is more pluralistic: many diverse approaches have proven therapeutically effective, and the therapist of today is more apt to tailor the therapy to fit the particular clinical needs of each patient.

In past years there was an unproductive emphasis on territoriality and on the maintaining of hierarchy and status—with the more prestigious professions like psychiatry and doctoral-level psychology expending considerable energy toward excluding master's level therapists. But those battles belong more to the psychotherapists of yesterday; today there is a significant shift toward a more collaborative interdisciplinary climate.

Managed care and cost containment is driving some of these changes. The role of the psychiatrist has been particularly affected as cost efficiency has decreed that psychiatrists will less frequently deliver psychotherapy personally but, instead, limit their activities to supervision and to psychopharmacological treatment.

In its efforts to contain costs, managed care has asked therapists to deliver a briefer, focused therapy. But gradually managed care is realizing that the bulk of mental health treatment cost is consumed by inpatient care and that outpatient treatment, even long-term therapy, is not only salubrious for the patient but far less costly. Another looming change is that the field is turning more frequently toward the group and family therapies. How much longer can we ignore the many comparative research studies demonstrating that the group therapy format is equally or more effective than higher cost individual therapies?

Some of these cost-driven edicts may prove to be good for the patients; but many of the changes that issue from medical model mimicry—for example, efforts at extreme brevity and overly precise treatment plans and goals that are inappropriate to the therapy endeavor and provide only the illusion of efficiency—can hamper the therapeutic work. Consequently, it is of paramount importance that therapists gain control of their field and that managed care administrators not be permitted to dictate how psychotherapy or, for that matter, any other form of health care be conducted. That is one of the goals of this series of texts: to provide mental health professionals with such a deep grounding in theory and such a clear vision of effective therapeutic technique that they will be empowered to fight confidently for the highest standards of patient care.

The Jossey-Bass Library of Current Clinical Technique is directed and dedicated to the frontline therapist—to master's and doctoral-level clinicians who personally provide the great bulk of mental health care. The purpose of this entire series is to offer state-of-the-art instruction in treatment techniques for the most commonly encountered clinical conditions. Each volume offers a focused theoretical background as a foundation for practice and then dedicates itself to the practical task of what to do for the patient—how to assess, diagnose, and treat.

I have selected volume editors who are either nationally recognized experts or are rising young stars. In either case, they possess a comprehensive view of their specialty field and have selected leading therapists of a variety of persuasions to describe their therapeutic approaches.

Although all the contributors have incorporated the most recent and relevant clinical research in their chapters, the emphasis in these volumes is on the practical technique of therapy. We shall offer specific therapeutic guidelines, and augment concrete suggestions with the liberal use of clinical vignettes and detailed case histories. Our intention is not to impress or to awe the reader, and not to add footnotes to arcane academic debates. Instead, each chapter is designed to communicate guidelines of immediate pragmatic value to the practicing clinician. In fact, the general editor, the volume editors, and the chapter contributors have all accepted our assignments for that very reason: a rare opportunity to make a significant, immediate, and concrete contribution to the lives of our patients.

Irvin D. Yalom, M.D.
Professor Emeritus of Psychiatry
Stanford University School of Medicine

INTRODUCTION

Hilda Kessler

We are living in times of dynamic social transformations in which couples are being challenged to respond to rapidly evolving cultural forces confronting and changing relational expectations. The issues clients are likely to bring to therapists reflect these macrocosmic social pressures as well as their personal microcosmic struggles.

Therapists too are being challenged to meet the ever-mutating needs of our clients. Simultaneously, and in response to the same social forces affecting our clients, we are being presented with a multiplicity of new ideas, theories, and techniques, each insisting that we conceptualize and treat our clients' problems in a specific way or direction. In addition, governmental demands as to what to treat and managed care direction about how and when to treat are presenting new and, at times, frustrating challenges to us all.

Both clients and therapists are perpetually being bombarded by a plethora of self-help books, workshops, television programs, and videos purporting to teach how, with a minimum of effort, to achieve *the* ideal relationship. These approaches invariably introduce and legitimize new sets of expectations couples should have of one another or new relational demands therapists should make of their clients. Unfortunately, this frequently muddies rather than clarifies the expectations couples have of each other and of therapy. The impact on the therapist is often confusion and the undermining of confidence.

This book is meant for therapists searching for help through the contemporary labyrinth of couples therapy and aims to promote the use of their wisdom and creativity in treating clients. The therapists whose contributions are included in this book come from a variety of theoretical positions and represent some of the best current thinking about couples; all are united in their respect for the integrity of their clients.

My starting point in editing this volume, based on more than twenty-five years of clinical work with individuals and couples, is that there is no single answer or approach to treating couples. I strongly argue for therapeutic flexibility, even though this requires increased responsibility of the therapist as well as greater sophistication in order to fit the treatment to the client rather than to follow a predetermined recipe. The reward of flexibility is greater effectiveness and patient satisfaction, and the enlivening of clinical practice.

DEFINITIONS

Before proceeding further, it may be useful to clarify the definition of *couple* used in this volume. The defining characteristic of a couple resides in the nature of the *commitment* they have made to one another. A couple has the intention of remaining together for the foreseeable future. They may or may not crown that commitment in a formal manner, such as through marriage, but they have made a promise that their partner will be the singular and primary focus of their attention. The term *marriage* is often used throughout this volume in recognition of that commitment. A couple consists of two adults capable of understanding and accepting the seriousness and meaning of such a commitment. The uniqueness of the couple dyad is distinct from the family unit or from casual precommitted relationships.

The definition of couples therapy also requires some attention. One might define such therapy by the number of people occupying your office at a particular moment. On the other hand, one might define it on the basis of the focus of attention, purpose, and goal you and your clients give to the therapy.

In my view, to think of couples therapy as requiring both partners always to be present straightjackets the therapist and the therapeutic process. If the purpose of the therapeutic experience to which all parties have agreed is to assist a couple to deal more effectively with the problems in the joint enterprise of their lives, then the number of persons in your office at any given moment becomes irrelevant. Once this position is accepted, it becomes possible either to work with the couple conjointly or to see them separately if that is what's needed, in your opinion. It may be more efficacious at times, as Arnold Lazarus has suggested, to see the members of a couple separately—for example, to instruct them on the simple basics of relating—and postpone joint sessions with a focus on their interactive processes for later on in the therapy. Regardless of how you structure an individual hour, if your purpose, function, and goal is directed toward the couple, you are doing couples therapy.

A Brief History of Couples Therapy

Couples therapy is a relative newcomer to the mental health field. It originated in the context of pastoral counseling and as part of the family guidance movement. Its early purpose was to help steer married couples through troubling times. When it began to be conceived psychotherapeutically, it had no coherent unifying theory. Nevertheless, in its short history, it spurred a profusion of practices.

Couples therapy, as we know it, bears the imprint of two main sources: first, individual clinical treatment derived from behaviorism, cognitive psychology, and psychodynamics and, second, family systems-oriented practice. The latter source has been particularly influential on the development of couples therapy.

Couples therapy received its first big boost with the introduction by Gregory Bateson and his colleagues of cybernetics and systems ideas into the treatment of families. These latter theories evolved largely outside of traditional academic and clinical psychology and borrowed concepts from philosophy, engineering, and other sources. Their introduction into therapy established a precedent that has made couples therapy particularly available to and absorbent of nonpsychological influences and inclinations. Sociopolitical and cultural trends invariably find a waiting home there.

Initially the classical psychodynamic schools of therapy had antipathy toward couples therapy. Over time, however, this enmity melted and ways were sought to expand and alter therapeutic assumptions in order to accommodate work with units larger than that of the individual. Object relations and control mastery theories, for example, contain interpersonal perspectives and, consequently, are adaptive for couples work. Although these theories are intrapsychically based, they nevertheless view the actions on the internal stage of the individual's mind as being populated by an interacting array of actors representing vital historical personages. Concepts such as reenactment, projective identification, and defensive maneuvers account for the specific actions, giving color and force to the scenery on stage.

In contrast to their predecessors fifty years ago, contemporary couples therapists have a vast array of theoretical constructs and a large bag of potentially beneficial tricks from which to choose in working with their clients. Separating the wheat from the chaff and the valuable approaches from the fashionable ones has become an important issue in the field. The need for scientific scrutiny and outcome studies of couples therapy is widely apparent. Without the benefit of extensive studies comparing and contrasting the various forms of couples therapy currently practiced, therapists are left on their own to decide which form of therapy to use with which particular couple and with which issue. Some observers, such as John Gottman, suggest that little if any of our theory and practice is founded on empirical scientific research.

Practitioners of couples therapy make up a heterogeneous group ranging from psychiatrists to marriage and family counselors and pastoral ministers, representing differing levels of psychological education and with a varying knowledge of pertinent research skills and findings, clinical experience, and auxiliary information. These notable differences may alter the style and spin each professional division may bring to the therapeutic situation even as each attempts to achieve similar goals.

One's professional affiliation may influence one's theoretical position, but if theory is adhered to blindly, one may become trapped in a cul-de-sac that distorts one or more essential features of the therapeutic territory and directs our attention away from our clients' core issues. A central premise of this book is that theory may guide you in your therapeutic endeavor, but it cannot give you the answers. Only the couple can do that.

THE APPROACH TAKEN IN THIS BOOK

As I pointed out earlier, the need for therapeutic flexibility is a paramount consideration in conducting couples therapy, and this is a point that several contributors will underscore in their respective chapters. Flexibility can come only when dogmatic approaches are eschewed. Thus, this book expresses a nondogmatic, eclectic viewpoint in which treatment is shaped to particular persons and problems.

In working with individual couples, considerable ingenuity and creativity is frequently required. This book encourages the therapist to be creative but, at the same time, to be mindful of ethical considerations and the need to monitor and evaluate one's efforts. In particular, I believe therapists need to engage their thinking faculties when working with couples and, in an ongoing way, to use the clinical functions of evaluation, assessment, judgment, and hypothesis formation and testing. Thinking requires data gathering both from our clients and from existing clinical research about couples therapy and psychology in general.

My particular emphasis on engaging our thinking processes in doing couples therapy is motivated, in part, by what I see as a need to counter the current overemphasis on feelings as a guide to therapeutic behavior. Feelings, like children, are delightful, but also erratic, uncontrollable, and often excessive. When feelings guide our behavior or that of our clients, without the intervention of wisdom, knowledge, and cognitive processes, it is tantamount to placing a well-intentioned child in control of the family. Not a very good idea! On the other hand, using the data contained in feelings or emotions together with cognitively derived information and incorporating both into the therapeutic process positions the therapist for creativity, the effectiveness of which can be monitored and evaluated.

Another point of emphasis here is the importance of contextualizing the couple's situation in a larger historical and social framework. This broader viewpoint, I believe, provides greater understanding and appreciation of our clients and their relationships. More important, it protects us from the conceit of believing that we have all the answers to the human enterprise of living together as a couple. The multiplicity of forms marriage has taken in response to differing historical trends and pressures and in various cultural milieus humbles us in recognition of the malleability and adaptability of the human psyche.

The broader context of our clients' personal histories as well as the history of their relationship provide the meaning they give to their perceived problems and to the remedies acceptable or not acceptable to them. Couples therapy has tended to operate in an ahistorical framework, thereby missing important nuances and, consequently, impeding successful treatment.

PERSPECTIVES ON MARRIAGE

Our concept of marriage is integral to and parallels social, economic, and cultural structures—it fits the zeitgeist. A broad historical perspective allows the observer to note parallel yet related trends between social movements, the status of marriage, and the psychological structure of the individual.

By recorded ancient times, marriage and the family were recognized as cornerstones of society. The family was seen as the central means to fulfill society's goals, transmit culture, and ensure its continuity. Therefore, it was endowed with ritual, rules, and restrictions that were enforced by religious and other institutions. Marriage, marital satisfaction—socially defined expectations of the "good enough" marriage—and individual satisfaction in marriage were all subordinated to these goals.

If one looks at divorce as a barometer of marital expectations, it becomes apparent that in periods when divorce was restricted, marriage was not expected to provide much in the way of personal satisfaction. On the other hand, when the rules regarding divorce were lax (as they are today), personal expectations of marriage ran high, and the psychological and emotional demands placed on the individual spouse became enormous.

Before the Industrial Revolution, when divorce was essentially prohibited, affectional ties between mates were tenuous at best. Husbands and wives tended to occupy, generally, same-gender, separate worlds. Low levels of marital satisfaction were balanced by the low levels of expectations spouses had of one another, thus ensuring family stability.

Whereas in the Middle Ages community affiliations and institutions provided most of the social-emotional needs of individuals and also served to support the family as a whole, by the early industrial society the family was forced to become more self-reliant and demanding of its members. This required radical changes in relational expectations and practices among spouses in which enhanced affectional ties between family members were demanded to keep the unit together. The notions of romantic love and companionship between marital partners developed as a response to these needs and to compensate for the breakdown of the community as a source of emotional satisfaction. The Industrial Revolution also saw the rise of the idea of individualism, which, eventually, had a profound impact on our concept of marriage. By the early nineteenth century it became apparent that imbalances existed between the individual's pursuit of personal pleasure and autonomy and the family's need for personal subordination for the good of the whole. These conflicts foreshadowed our current preoccupation with individualism versus family values. Nevertheless, on the whole, marriage was based more on duty and self-sacrifice rather than on the idea of personal satisfaction.

As a result of industrialization and the concomitant centralization of social, governmental, and economic structures, additional pressures on marriages arose, namely, social dislocation, alienation, and the cult of the "self-made man." These pressures left many feeling inadequate and less prepared to cope with a world that was now perceived as inhospitable. The concept of the *family as a safe haven*—a place to which one could escape and receive solace and comfort—developed and gave rise to increasing psychological demands on couples and family members alike.

As we entered the twentieth century, the forces set in place earlier, coupled with the conversion to a consumer, pleasure-driven economy, increased pressure on the family. A new marriage code evolved in which the home became a shrine of the "good life" in addition to being a safe haven. An unbounded psychological expansiveness promised newlyweds true love and a future of happiness, bliss, and excitement.

Marital stress and disappointment were inevitable as expectations exceeded the emotional and psychological capacity of men and women. Those who couldn't adapt divorced at ever-increasing rates—although by recent standards still low—and for new reasons, such as the lack of personal or sexual satisfaction.

Marriage and the family were expected to compensate fully for the breakdown of community support and social alienation by providing spouses with companionship, romantic love, protection, intimacy, and emotional support in addition to the gratification of sexual and personal needs and, as if that was not enough, the enhancement of their own growth and development as a whole person. A tall order!

The currently high divorce rate suggests that couples simply cannot fulfill all of what is being asked of them. The task is too exhausting. It is no wonder that after a few years of marriage couples find their emotional bank account empty and feel depleted as individuals.

On a recent program on National Public Radio, "Our Retreat from Marriage," experts and laypeople alike expressed the belief that marriage as an institution may have lost its social purpose, a victim of the "legitimization of self-fulfillment." Several commentators pointed out that a consumption-oriented society is antithetical to the person's ability to postpone gratification, the psychological requirement and the very factor needed for good family membership and long-term relationships.

What bearing do these perspectives have on couples therapy? A great deal. Therapists are part of and, in many instances, agents of the culture of consumerism and over the last several decades have actively contributed to the concept of self-fulfillment at the expense of communal needs.

We have encouraged our clients not to be *uptight*, meaning not to be motivated by moral or ethical constraints, to *let go*, or not to be bound by the past and to embrace the present. We have denigrated the ideas of self-sacrifice and duty. We have shifted away from the Victorian emphasis on the superego and are in the process of shifting from an emphasis on ego-based cognitive functions to the emotionally driven id requirements for immediate pleasure and gratification necessary for a consumer society. Psychotherapy, as it is currently practiced, may unwittingly be abetting the sociocultural forces that contribute to marital disturbances. The irony is that clients frequently come to us for help to save their marriages, and if the underlying philosophy guiding our work emphasizes the primacy of the individual, then how can we honestly hold ourselves out as neutral, dispassionate professionals?

In my view, therapists may play an increasingly important role in helping couples overwhelmed by the conflicting and confusing demands placed on them as individuals and as members of a social unit. But in our own minds we need to be clear what notions of psychological health and of marital satisfaction we adhere to and would like to support in our therapeutic work. We cannot help our clients if we share their confusions, and clients are certainly entitled to know in advance where we stand.

Helping our clients improve or save their marriages means reminding them that relationships require the ebb and flow of give-and-take. There are times when the self is subordinated for one's mate, if for no other reason than to make sure that one does not deplete one's partner. Couples need to be helped to articulate not only what they want out of their relationship but also what they are willing to put into it. They, as well as therapists, need to become aware of their beliefs about couplehood and assess how well these beliefs fit the reality of a life together. I view this as the way to resist cultural messages destructive to marriage.

Therapists see couples who do not share or are uncomfortable with contemporary Pepsi-generation cultural requirements. Some clients believe that self-sacrifice for one's mate and children is a noble idea. We hope therapists will experience such clients as a breath of fresh air rather than as psychological aberrations.

OVERVIEW OF THE CONTENTS

In recognition of the universals or similarity between all couples, the first chapter is devoted to traversing the basic therapeutic stance distinguishing couples therapy from individual or family therapy. The emphasis is on the therapeutic aspects rather than on the particular couple's issues. Strategies are described to help the therapist move across the terrain of couples therapy over time as well as how to navigate through a particular session. Therapists are encouraged to engage their clients actively while maintaining appropriate boundaries.

The usefulness of evaluation, assessment, and goal setting is described as a key aspect of the initial stage of therapy. Emphasis is placed on understanding and conveying to one's clients how differing linguistic codes, the differentiation of meanings, and differing expressive styles may either enhance or impede conflict resolution and the satisfaction of needs. Practical suggestions such as the use of "staff meetings" are described. Also, attention is given to how to manage the possible end points of treatment, under optimal, moderate, and poor conditions.

Chapter Two deals with some of the common myths clients and therapists have about couples therapy. Couples therapy is particularly prone to the absorption of nonpsychologically derived concepts and psychobabble. Thus, Dr. Margaret Thaler Singer and I attempt to highlight how fiction may become "fact" and how these supposed truths influence what couples bring to therapy and how we work with them. We argue that it is important for therapists to differentiate between fads and fashion on the one hand and more enduring and useful psychological concepts on the other.

Unfortunately, therapists are as prone to accept myths as truth as laypersons are. In fact, *therapeutic shared delusions* are not unknown in the history of psychotherapy. For example, Freud's elaborate explanation of female hysteria blinded psychotherapists for years from understanding the effects of sexual abuse on female sexual anxiety. These myths or shared delusions often interfere with competent, adequate, and successful psychotherapy. Furthermore, some myths have such power that believing therapists are likely to impose them on their innocent, unsuspecting clients. This bears on the issue of countertransference.

Obviously, we cannot compile a complete list of myths clients and therapists hold. They are simply too numerous. Some of the contributing chapters, however, contain additional instances of myths. For example, Dr. Jack Schiemann and Dr. Wendy L. Smith describe the myth of "coming out"—that is, that one cannot be a "whole" person unless one publicly exposes one's sexual orientation, a belief prevalent among homosexual men and women.

Increased mobility and the loosening of ties to one's identified reference group have raised the prevalence of "mixed marriages" in which couples with diverse racial, religious, cultural, ethnic, regional, or economic backgrounds attempt to make a life together. Often, only after the bloom is off the rose, they discover that the romance of opposites can sometimes lead to frustrations and misunderstandings. Dr. Joel Crohn highlights their particular set of problems and gives specific practical suggestions to help you help them in Chapter Three.

His chapter points out the importance of not dismissing or underestimating the problems encountered in bringing together mates who find each other's backgrounds mystifying and confusing. The couples therapist is not expected to be an expert on every group or subgroup likely to be encountered in clinical practice, but naivete or inexperience is not an excuse for failing to explore the significance and meaning the differences between partners may pose for your clients.

Dr. Crohn's chapter gives insights into the major areas therapists should be aware of, including conflicts with the family of origin, the issues of separation and rejection, personal and family religious and affiliative identities, and conflicting cultural codes.

Cultural codes are a complex and largely invisible set of beliefs and behaviors that permeate almost every aspect of a relationship. They include, among other things, sex roles, emotional expression, the placement of physical-spacial boundaries, the nature of familial ties, and attitudes about child rearing. When mixed couples assign very different meanings and importance to one or more of these areas, they are likely to be dismayed and hurt. What was once experienced as quaint and charming in the partner may now be viewed in a much more negative light.

In his chapter, Dr. Crohn discusses the impact of ethnic diversity on modern marriage and its effects on psychotherapeutic practice. For instance, an Indian therapist described a couple as "disengaged," while her American counterpart described the same couple as "enmeshed." The same phenomenon appeared quite different when viewed through one's cultural lenses. This example also illustrates what happens when subjective standards replace objective norms, an issue discussed in greater detail in Chapter Two.

In Chapter Four, Dr. Schiemann and Dr. Smith deal with the issues relating to the treatment of gay and lesbian couples. As society relaxes its prohibition on homosexual relationships and recognizes their legitimacy, the number of such unions are becoming more prevalent and openly evident. Gay and lesbian couples are as likely to run into difficulty in their relationships as are heterosexual couples, perhaps more so. The authors point out that in the absence of precedence, such couples have the additional task of forging new sets of rules and roles to fit their distinctive situation. Their continued experience of stigmatization undoubtedly adds to the difficulties they face in forming and maintaining their partnership.

In larger cities, where homosexuality is more prevalent, gay and lesbian couples have the option of working with a couples therapist who shares their sexual orientation. In smaller communities, however, that choice may not be available. Also, some homosexual couples may prefer to see a "straight" therapist in order to maintain a greater sense of privacy, boundaries, the non-politicalization of their personal concerns, and for many other reasons. Practicing couples therapists, regardless of their sexual orientation, need to be prepared to provide acceptable and suitable treatment for this population.

Drs. Schiemann and Smith's chapter goes a long way in guiding us toward that end by underscoring issues that arise over the course of a long-term homosexual relationship. They also focus on problems around maintaining boundaries, monogamy, gender-role stereotypes, the issue of coming out, creating a family, and living with AIDS, all of which should be useful and edifying for all therapists.

In Chapter Five, Dr. Seymour Kessler deals with health issues in couples therapy. The interplay between physical and psychological conditions is being increasingly recognized by both physicians and psychotherapists alike. Dr. Kessler shows how health issues can play a significant role in the life of a couple as well as in couples therapy. Health issues may not only influence personality development, but they sometimes also become the kernel around which a couple shapes their dynamics and adaptation to each other. As such, ignoring this issue, when relevant, may impede the therapist's ability to assist clients.

This chapter describes the various routes by which concern about one's own or one's partner's past or present physical functioning interacts with the couple's dynamics. Emotional investment and meaning assigned to illness and body image may differ widely between mates and arouse conflict and confusion. Acute or chronic illness may strike either partner or their offspring unexpectantly. These events may test the couple's strength, pulling them together or driving them apart.

When faced with an overwhelming health crisis, couples may come into therapy, sometimes at the suggestion of their physician. At other times, they may not be aware of the effect health issues may be having on their relationship. In such situations the therapist may be the first to point it out and to help them elucidate its meaning and their particular style of coping.

Covert somatic issues, such as the gradual bodily changes with aging or the use of bodily concerns as a means of attaining the gratification of emotional needs, may be easily overlooked by therapists, given that many of us are not trained to take notice of physical factors in a couple's interactions. This chapter addresses that missing aspect of our education and alerts us to the interplay of physical and psychological factors.

Dr. Steven A. Foreman deals with the difficult couple in Chapter Six. Such couples are the bane of the couples therapists' existence and are often referred to as "couples from hell." While many couples may be difficult at times, these couples represent a clear and identifiable group characterized by their engaging in severely disturbed or abusive behaviors. Almost invariably such couples come from families that may have been abusive, neglectful, or traumatic. One or both partners may display major psychological illnesses. Invariably these couples are identifiable by the exhaustion, hopelessness, helplessness, guilt, or anger engendered countertransferentially in the therapist.

Difficult couples may also display cultural, health, substance abuse, and other problems. However, most of these issues cannot be approached because these couples are particularly resistant to change. In some cases, difficult couples may overlap with those Dr. Susan Hanks describes later as showing Type I violent behavior. When violence is present, one should treat that first before proceeding to work on entrenched interpersonal issues.

How to help these couples uncouple themselves from the repetitive reenactment of past family relationships is the focus of Dr. Foreman's chapter. In your office, they tend to "cast a spell," inviting you to join them in their distorted beliefs about themselves, their partners, and, in general, how the world works. They engage in high-level blaming, pulling for you to take sides in order to judge the partner as responsible for all their joint difficulties. Each partner sees themselves as blameless. The seriousness and persistence of their efforts to enlist your alliance are cues to recognizing their dilemma. Helping them truly hear one another is an important first-level intervention.

Dr. Foreman suggests that you slowly and patiently turn the tables and invite the couple to join you in reframing and challenging their distorted beliefs, often around issues of responsibility, worry, and guilt. They need your permission to differentiate from their families of origin in order to achieve a healthier relationship with one another; otherwise they may feel doomed to repeat the past endlessly. Furthermore, it is necessary to identify what each partner is fighting about, what their "hot buttons" are, and what leads to misunderstandings. Difficult couples may also require practical tools to help them disengage from arguments, listen to each other, and convey important information.

Countertransferential issues with these couples are particularly challenging for the therapist. Dr. Foreman shows how countertransference might be used productively to understand

and empathize with your couple since such reactions provide "a window into the past," allowing the therapist to see what the partner's childhood experience might have been like. Your emotional and behavioral responses, unlike theirs, allows them to discover that other responses are possible to similar sets of circumstances. Such couples watch you closely at times because they are trying to learn and to emulate your system of emotional management.

In working with difficult couples, it is important that the therapist not misinterpret their often disdainful, aggressive, and provocative behavior toward each other as an indication that they want out of the relationship. Your belief in their capacity to improve and behave more positively is often the thread of hope they hang onto during therapy.

In Chapter Seven, Dr. Susan E. Hanks focuses attention on the problem of domestic violence in couples therapy. When couples engage in violent behavior toward each other, the therapist needs to be particularly adroit in knowing how to respond appropriately. Therapeutic mistakes in this context are less tolerable since the safety and security of the parties are at stake. We may not have the opportunity or the luxury of indulging ignorance or of transferring the couple out to another therapist.

Domestic violence is not a psychiatric diagnosis; rather, it is a phenomenological reality describing a cluster of *behaviors* in which physical force, restraint, or threats of force are used to compel the other to do something against his or her will. Therapists cannot remain neutral in the face of violence and in working with couples in whose relationship violence occurs should make the stopping of violence their first and primary goal.

Dr. Hanks points out that not all battering behavior is similar and not all persons engaged in such behavior constitute a single cohort. Thus, she provides a typology by means of which violent behavior and types of violent couples might be differentiated. The typology includes the acute, situational reaction; the chronic, cyclical expressive affective storm; the habitual, repetitive instrumental kind; and, lastly, acute and chronic secondary violence. Each category is discussed, and their clinical and treatment implications are elucidated.

Dr. Hanks rightly recognizes that couples therapy is not an appropriate treatment modality for all couples in which violence occurs. Her typology helps to differentiate when therapy might be useful and when it is contraindicated. Her chapter also offers insights into treatment procedures and pitfalls once the clinician decides that couples therapy is warranted.

Couples who engage in violent behavior do not necessarily identify themselves as such at the onset of therapy. It might be their secret and may not emerge until they feel safe and have established a sense of trust with the therapist. Not infrequently, the secret is divulged during a session in which the partners are separated. If you suspect violent behavior is occurring, it may be useful to see the couple separately and confront each partner. The couple needs to know that while you do not condemn them, you take the violence seriously and do not condone it. You provide the message that you condemn the behavior and are willing to work with the couple to help them learn to put an end to the use of violence.

Finally, in Chapter Eight, Dr. Vicky A. Johnson deals with parenting issues in couples therapy. She points out that the unspoken assumption that if the kids are in trouble it reflects trouble in the parental unit is not always true. Often couples seek therapeutic help because they encounter difficulties in their parenting functions that affect their relationship, and not the other way around. Many well-functioning couples begin to flounder when they become parents, especially if one of them had a particularly difficult childhood. We tend to privately assess our own and our partner's merit by the quality of the parenting skills. A father who ignores his children or a mother who is overly impatient is likely to be judged negatively by his or her mate and engender negative feelings in the other. These feelings are likely to spill over into the couple's relationship.

When children are part of the picture, therapists need to think of their clients in terms of mates as well as parents. Dr. Johnson's chapter reinforces the notion that parenting is a vital aspect of a couple's life together. She emphasizes that children function as a psychological asset rather than as a burden, as parents sometimes may initially feel.

Parenting may also arise as an issue in couples therapy as couples struggle with the decision to raise a family. In the current cultural milieu, the overemphasis on the self as the ultimate entity of significance may make it more difficult for adults to make commitments, especially those in which the giving of the self for a relatively long period of time is required. Therapists can assist clients by helping them elucidate their acquired beliefs and feelings pertaining to parenting and childhood. Such explorations may expose differences between the mates and long-held misconceptions and fears, thereby allowing them to gain confidence in their ability to parent well.

UNIFYING THEMES

The various chapters included in this volume have several unifying themes. First, several contributors use a developmental model to provide a context for their therapeutic focus and interventions. The latter are inevitably shaped by the particular stage in which a couple is engaged.

Couples generally pass through similar developmental stages punctuated by major life cycle events. Their relationship begins with the *getting-to-know-you* and *honeymoon* stages, accompanied by a sense of an expansive future. During this period their unity and family are frequently created. Disillusionment almost inevitably follows as their differences begin to loom larger than their similarities. Successful navigation through this period often leads to the harvest years, ending inevitably with the stages of loss and death. Several chapters offer specific suggestions relevant to a particular developmental stage in the life cycle of a couple.

Second, the issues that bring couples into therapy often show a common thread. Frequently, the couples we see are caught in their personal, separate, defensive structures that limit their ability to understand, adapt to, and cope with their mates. Living behind such a structure also inhibits their capacity for self-understanding as well as the adequate expression of their thoughts and needs. All of the contributors describe the mechanisms by which a once loving partner becomes transformed into an undermining and sabotaging "enemy." The intrusion of old scripts learned in one's family of origin is recognized as playing a major role in many of these situations.

The couples we see in treatment often reveal a remarkable capacity not to hear each other. This leads to confusion, blaming, and misunderstandings. Dr. Crohn's description of cross-cultural miscuing might easily be applied to couples who come from ostensibly similar backgrounds but whose personal ghosts from a private past inhibit them from understanding their mate.

Third, all the contributors pay considerable attention to the therapist's role. Regardless of the population with which they deal, they all recognize that their task is to help their clients identify and disengage from past ghosts and to relate to their mates in terms of current realities. They all try to deal with reality.

In their role as therapists, they often act as elucidators, translators, and interpreters of one partner to the other. Their stance is one in which they have an active engagement with their clients. They do not hesitate to offer practical suggestions to their clients, and all try to model good emotional management skills.

To accomplish their therapeutic tasks, the contributors may focus on one partner at a time, while the partner remains passive and observant, absorbing new information and eliciting empathy. A willingness to alter the standard couples therapy format by allocating separate time for each partner is practiced by several of the contributors. The catchwords to describe their work seem to be flexibility and creativity.

The words of I. Hoshii from his book *Sex and Marriage* best express the sentiment I wish to convey in this volume:

> No marriage can be an ideal marriage but every marriage can
> be an honest and joyful attempt to live up to the challenge of
> life in common.

Although the institution of marriage has undergone major changes in the course of history, it has survived in one form or another. This resiliency may be a function of our human need to bond with others. To paraphrase Thornton Wilder, we are meant to go through life two by two.

As social animals with a biological function to raise our young, no other human institution is likely to serve that function quite as effectively as marriage. Our basic need to belong, I believe, will also overcome the pressures pulling couples apart even though the form that marriage takes in the future may be quite different than it is today or was in the past.

ACKNOWLEDGMENTS

My thoughts about couples and couples therapy have been shaped and honed over two decades of work with many couples who entrusted me with their fears and hopes as we struggled together to help them remain united. I thank them all for being my teachers and hope that I have been a worthy student.

The opportunity to further develop and describe what I know about couples therapy was graciously given by Dr. Irv Yalom, and I am deeply grateful for his support.

Each contributor was asked to focus on what was most useful in working with their particular population without regard to current fads or the demands for political correctness. They have all done so with courage, honesty, and wisdom and with a depth of understanding that will outweigh and outlast by far current shibboleths. I also wish to thank the contributors for being willing to set aside the time in their very busy lives to work with me to meet tight deadlines.

From the start, Alan Rinzler, my editor at Jossey-Bass, provided me with space to develop the structure and focus of the book while guiding and supporting me when I needed it. He was there throughout the process of developing this volume from genesis to completion, and I wish to express my gratitude.

Discussions with colleagues have helped me clarify my thoughts, and I especially wish to acknowledge Elizabeth Richards for her inspiring thoughts and insights about difficult couples. Also, I thank my many friends for their patience, for helping me stay my course, and for being there for me.

Lastly, I wish to thank my two sons and their wonderful wives. Their lives as couples underscore my faith that marriage and family life continue to have the capacity to nourish and support this and future generations.

NOTES

P. xv, *It may be more efficacious . . . in the therapy:* Lazarus, A. (1992). When is couples therapy necessary and sufficient? *Psychological Reports, 70,* 787–790.

P. xv, *Couples therapy . . . treatment of families:* Korchin, S. (1978). *Modern clinical psychology.* New York: Basic Books.

P. xvi, *Initially the classical . . . on the internal stage:* Wile, B. (1981). *Couples therapy: A nontraditional approach.* New York: Wiley.

P. xvi, *projective identification:* Catherall, D. (1992). Working with projective identification in couples. *Family Process, 31,* 355–367.

P. xvi, *scientific scrutiny . . . therapy currently practiced:* Jacobson, N. S., & Addis, M. E. (1993). Research on couples and couple therapy: What do we know? Where are we going? *Journal of Consulting and Clinical Psychology, 61,* 85–93.

P. xvi, *Some observers . . . scientific research:* Gottman, J. (1994, May/June). Why marriages fail. *Networker,* pp. 41–48.

P. xviii, *By recorded ancient times . . . cornerstones of society:* Hoshii, I. (1986). The world of sex. In *Sex and marriage* (Vol. 2). Kent, England: Norbury.

P. xix, *If one looks at divorce . . . personal satisfaction:* Goody, J. (1983). *The development of family and marriage in Europe.* Cambridge, England: Cambridge University Press.

P. xix, *Whereas in the Middle Ages . . . demanding of its members:* Goldthorpe, J. E. (1987). *Family life in western societies.* Cambridge: Cambridge University Press.

P. xix, *The notions of romantic love . . . emotional satisfaction:* Stone, L. (1977). *The family, sex and marriage in England 1500–1800.* New York: Harper Torchbooks.

P. xix, *The Industrial Revolution . . . concept of marriage:* MacFarlane, A. (1986). *Marriage and love in England: Modes of reproduction 1300–1840.* New York: Blackwell.

P. xix, *imbalances existed between the individual's . . . personal satisfaction:* Tufte, V., & Myerhoff, B. (1979). Introduction. In V. Tufte & B. Myerhoff (Eds.), *Changing images of the family.* New Haven, CT: Yale University Press.

P. xx, *The concept of the* family as a safe haven . . . *family members alike:* Demos, J. (1979). Images of the American family, then and now. In V. Tufte & B. Myerhoff (Eds.), *Changing images of the family.* New Haven, CT: Yale University Press.

P. xx, *A new marriage code evolved . . . personal or sexual satisfaction:* May, E. T. (1980). *Great expectations: Marriage and divorce in post-Victorian America.* Chicago: University of Chicago Press.

P. xx, *The currently high divorce rate . . . depleted as individuals:* Baumeister, R. (1991). *Escaping the self.* New York: Basic Books.

P. xxi, *marriage as an institution . . . long-term relationships:* Malthus, D. (1995, January 17). Sex in America: Our retreat from marriage (Radio broadcast). *All things considered,* National Public Radio.

P. xxiii, *Freud's elaborate explanation . . . sexual anxiety:* Miller, A. (1984). *Thou shalt not be aware.* New York: Farrar, Strauss, Giroux.

P. xxxi, *The couples . . . not to hear each other:* Richards, B. (1995). Personal communication.

P. xxxii, *No marriage can be an ideal marriage:* Hoshii, I. (1986). *op. cit.*

P. xxxii, *Our basic need to belong:* Steinhauer, J. (1995, January 10). Big benefits in marriage. *New York Times,* p. A8.

1

Basics of Couples Therapy

Hilda Kessler

We are not often challenged to formulate and articulate what we actually do during a couples therapy hour, let alone how we think about such therapy overall. I shall attempt this task here.

My approach to couples therapy is an integration and explication of several theories, both clinical and academic, that shed light on interpersonal human behavior. I also draw upon anthropology, sociology, and history to provide a larger contextual framework in which to place interpersonal psychological phenomena. Clinically, I have been nurtured by family systems and psychodynamic theories. I rely heavily on knowledge derived from cognitive, developmental, and learning theories to validate, augment, and enrich clinical structures. Taken together, these various sources provide me with ways of knowing, seeing, and doing that distinguish my approach to couples therapy.

My style of working has evolved over many years and countless therapy hours with all types of couples. I have developed some helpful approaches that not only produce good results but also give me a way of navigating through the therapeutic process, hour by hour as well as over its course. I hope they will be as useful to others in the field as they have been for me.

In this chapter, I will discuss three stages of couples therapy and what I believe needs to occur in each stage as a preparation for the succeeding one. I will also provide a navigational map to guide the therapist through the therapy hour. Lastly, some specific therapeutic strategies will be presented as well as suggestions as to how to avoid obstacles to successful outcomes.

ACT ONE: GETTING STARTED

Couples therapy challenges the therapist in ways quite different from those of individual therapy. Being together in an office with a couple in conflict creates a state of dissonance into which you are ineluctably drawn. Each partner invariably pushes and pulls to get you to ally yourself with him or her rather than with his or her partner. As you experience these forces, you struggle to keep your balance as well as your neutrality. Your task is to find a way to navigate through waters that can be fairly choppy at times. You need to be extremely alert for shifts in the wind and changes in the underlying currents. Because you need to be so much on your toes, you may find yourself much more fatigued by the end of an hour with a conflicted couple than you might in individual work. On the bright side, you might also feel much more challenged and stimulated.

Establishing a Working Alliance

Establishing and maintaining a good therapeutic relationship simultaneously with two separate, disparate individuals is the first challenge facing you as couples therapy begins. You need to gain the trust and confidence of each partner, which may be tricky since each may require and respond to different, possibly opposite, initiating overtures. The one partner, for example, may respond to a rational approach, while her mate may require an indication of emotional availability and warmth. Or a partner may be forward and demanding, requiring that you take charge immediately, while the wife may be frightened of people she perceives as being high-powered and may experience your charge taking as a threat.

Your task is to size up your couple quickly and modulate your behavior so that you establish the beginnings of a working alliance. An approach that fits each partner requires that you be not only flexible but also nimble-footed, as you move comfortably back and forth between two possibly opposite approaches.

If you are markedly more comfortable with one partner rather than the other, the latter is likely to feel left out and may sabotage your efforts. You might find yourself feeling more sympathetic to one partner; his or her style of being may be more in line with your own. Or you may sense a closer cultural, intellectual, or professional connection with that person. You might feel that he or she is psychologically more available or has greater insight and is more flexible in thinking or behavior. For example, a foreign-born wife of one couple was very distrustful of the therapeutic process. She stonewalled me for the first few sessions, softening up only after many reassurances that I did not dislike her. Her husband, who was accustomed to the culture of therapy, was much easier to like, and it was easier to be sympathetic to his situation. A partner who displays paranoid characteristics or is very competitive with you may also challenge your ability to form an adequate alliance. Some clients, on the other hand, are so eager to be liked and so adept at charming others that they may succeed in tipping you over to their side. Awareness of disparities in how you respond to partners individually can be grist for the proverbial therapeutic mill. However, you may never get to use your awareness unless you establish a way of relating to both partners that is comfortable for everyone.

Put in other terms, your primary task is to develop a positive transference with both partners. If you have a positive transference with one and a negative transference with the other, all of your transactions will reflect this imbalance and create tension for both you and them.

The Empathetic Stance: Overcoming the Therapist's Resistance

Empathy goes hand in hand with doing therapy of any kind. In couples work, it is especially essential. It is one of those beautiful human capacities that bridges the gap between ourselves and others. Empathy is the connection that makes it possible to find a way of accepting our clients and their current state by reducing our resistance to them.

Take the time to relate empathetically to the less attractive partner. Try to understand that person's feelings and his or her situation, position, struggles, desires, and frustrations. In doing so, you are likely to transmit the required verbal and nonverbal messages of compassion and acceptance that partner may need to form an alliance with you. In working with the couple mentioned earlier, I made sure to address many of my comments to the foreign-born wife, despite her silence. I tried to understand how frightened she might be in my office, not knowing the therapy protocol and not knowing how to relate to me, in addition to the confusion she must feel in many of her other daily dealings in this foreign country. It was important to her that I verbalize my empathy for her situation. By doing so, I was able to feel closer to her and find her behavior completely appropriate.

There are times, try as you might, when you are not able to empathetically attach to your clients. Something in them touches something in you that says, "Keep your distance." When that happens, get a consultation or transfer the client to someone else. Blaming the client or yourself doesn't help anyone, but altering the situation does.

The Empathetic Stance: Overcoming the Client's Resistance

The testing ground on which couples therapy tends to succeed or fail often concerns how therapists deal with their clients' shame and guilt. Couples come into treatment with an abundance of these feelings: shame for having made a mess of their relationship and guilt for having failed to live up to their promise to one another (that is, for letting themselves and their mates down). If they are also parents, these feelings probably extend to their children. They often experience shame and guilt because they know that their marital difficulties are causing pain and hardship for them too. Unless these feelings are dealt with, therapeutic progress will often be impeded. As the first order of business, therefore, we have to lessen their sense of guilt and shame. Successful execution of this task goes a long way toward the establishment of a working alliance with our clients.

For example, a couple whose sex life had almost totally disintegrated after a twenty-year marriage needed reassurance that they were not "freaks." I suggested to them that they may still have a great deal of affection for one another and a purpose to their relationship despite their sexual anxieties. Indeed, I pointed out that their sexual difficulties were not altogether that unusual and may in fact be serving a very useful purpose. By placing their sexual behavior into a different context, I allowed them to feel less ashamed of themselves. This approach opened up an examination of their sexual behavior under a new set of assumptions.

Sometimes I help couples reduce their sense of shame or guilt by reminding them that contemporary couples are trailblazers, given the rapid social, economic, and other changes in relationships they need to deal with. Couples today are forging a new path without adequate preparation and without a clear sense of what tomorrow will bring. As pioneers they are allowed to get lost and yet remain heroic figures. Such simple approaches, employing empathy, helps create a *trusting* relationship between me and my clients.

Setting Goals and Agendas: Conveying Respect

Setting goals and establishing agendas serve many functions in the beginning stage of couples therapy, not the least of which is that by doing so, you convey your respect for the couple's maturity, autonomy, and identity. Assigning them the responsibility for establishing the goals and agendas of their therapy also conveys our willingness to accept them where they are with their definition of marriage, whatever it is, traditional, gender imbalanced, or containing extramarital relationships. By encouraging couples to set their therapy agenda, we acknowledge that our clients make many adaptations that work for them but that may make us uncomfortable.

For example, I saw a young couple who were together for seven years but who neither were formally married nor intended to have children. Their initial complaint was a lack of "good communication," a frequent euphemism for a whole host of difficulties. Now, I strongly believe in the importance of making commitments permanent and in building family as a way of developing and enlarging the relationship. But they did not come to see me about those issues. Those were *my* issues, not theirs. My function was to focus on what troubled them.

The first stage of therapy was devoted to concretizing and elucidating the specific area of communication that was causing their distress. They had not been able to satisfactorily resolve their "good guy–bad guy" competition. The female partner feared that since she was the one who voiced demands in the relationship, she was placed in the role of the "heavy." From her viewpoint, her partner took the moral high ground, since he appeared self-sacrificing. In their own way, they were telling me that they needed to establish greater emotional equality before they could consider formalizing their relationship. Parenthetically, when their rather short-term therapy ended, they began talking about having children. I am convinced that had I brought up the issues of commitment and children prematurely, they would never have been able to reach it on their own and might have had a negative therapeutic experience.

Empowering our clients to set their goals and agendas also keeps us from yielding to the temptation of fixing what they do not consider broken. Sometimes we are sorely tested in this regard, as the following example illustrates.

A female client whom I had seen in individual therapy had informed me about sexual abuse when she was a child. She had never informed her husband of the fact, and, for some very personal reasons, she did not have any intention of doing so. Several years later, they called me for some couples counseling around some unrelated family issues. Respect in this case meant that she had to rely on me to adhere to her decision not to inform her husband of this childhood experience. If I held the position or belief that she *had to tell, in order to be cured,* then I would have been disrespectful of her wishes and boundaries and replicated her abusive childhood experience. It would have been not only therapeutically injurious but also disrespectful of her wishes.

The couples' sessions focused on the active issues that needed resolution, primarily dealing with problems with his children from a previous marriage. The wife's unspoken agenda included her need to receive acknowledgment that I saw her as an equal in her adult roles as wife and mother. I was ever mindful for any sign that she may want to use the couples work as an occasion to inform her husband of her childhood experience. None appeared.

Establishing goals and agendas also serves other useful functions. First, they can be used diagnostically and prognostically. Are the couple's goals specific or vague and global? Are they presented as a united or disunited set of goals? Is the disparity narrow or wide? Are the goals realistic within the confines of their circumstances and personalities? If they present specific, realistic, and uniform goals, they are probably a fairly well-functioning couple, and therapy should probably be short-term. If, on the other hand, their goals are vague, unrealistic, and widely disunited, then you should expect longer-term, more difficult, troubling therapeutic progress.

Second, establishing goals and agendas provides you and the couple with reference points by which progress can be assessed over time. When either you or your clients become discouraged and feel that "We are not getting anywhere," these reference points become very useful to keep spirits from failing.

Third, goals and agendas often change during the course of therapy. When that happens, earmark the event, for it may be that you are tackling new and more difficult issues as you progress in therapy.

There is always one goal that you, the therapist, are responsible for alone, and that is maintaining a sense of hope. You do this by allying yourself with the couples' underlying, unspoken wish to be loved, respected, accepted, and nurtured by the partner.

Secret Agendas: The Bane of Therapy

Secret agendas are the anathema of couples therapy. They create an undercurrent that pulls you further out to sea and leaves all parties feeling disoriented.

Basically there are two different types of secret agendas: *outcome* agendas and *defensive* agendas. When a partner has privately predetermined what the status of the couple's relationship will be at the completion of therapy ("We will be together, separated, or divorced"), you are confronted with an instance of a secret outcome agenda. For example, one partner may secretly intend to end the marriage and may have already committed themselves to a future mate. However, this partner may need to go through the motions of having "tried" couples therapy as a way of assuaging feelings of guilt. Some individuals also want to be sure that they have "parked" the rejected spouse safely in the hands of another caretaker, the therapist, before moving on.

The ultimate signal, alerting you to the presence of a secret agenda, is the sabotage, such as when interventions that might be right on the button are undermined by the exiting partner. When you suspect that a spouse is harboring a secret agenda, confrontation in the presence of the other spouse will often provoke vigorous denial or further sabotaging of the sessions. If you are not wedded to seeing the couple together, an individual session at this point might be useful. In the absence of the about-to-be-rejected partner, the saboteur is much more likely to come clean and tell all. After assessing the irreversibility of the agenda, you will then need to work out a strategy for informing the naive partner.

The most common type of secret agenda is guarding one's defenses with multiple disguises. Defensive agendas can be identified by the intransigence of the person's behavior even though the behavior is disruptive to the couple's functioning. Thus, these behaviors are tenaciously maintained, despite their cost, because they serve defensive purposes such as keeping secret the person's shame, sense of inadequacy, dependency, or other fears and anxieties. Generally, the person feels that if the secrets were made public, he or she would no longer be loved and respected. If the partner knew how dependent or frightened the person really was, that person would be rejected and shamed for harboring such feelings.

For example, a middle-aged couple were engaged in a long-term committed but troubled marriage. Deeply damaging fights seemed to erupt over superficially insignificant disagreements. Therapeutic interpretations had as much impact on reducing these blow-ups as trying to sweeten the ocean with a cube of sugar. But in the course of therapy, their destructive pattern began to dislodge its secret. The husband triggered an eruption each time the wife made any move toward independence. The wife, on the other hand, triggered an eruption each time the husband spent quality time with one of their children.

He was terrified of abandonment and terribly ashamed of his dependency. In order to camouflage his fears, he attacked her whenever she attempted to differentiate or separate from him. His attack only abated when, emotionally exhausted, she made overtures toward reconciliation. This was a signal (for him) of her subordination and a return to the "safety" of being a dependent wife. The wife turned to the children rather than her husband for emotional support and presented herself as the ultimate self-sacrificing "mother hen," representing his role as that of being an ogre. When her position of superiority was threatened, she attacked her husband. Once her hegemony over the children was reestablished, she resumed her loving behavior toward him. Neither partner was willing to expose their individual strategy for fear that if the other learned of their dependency, subterfuge, and alliances, they would be rejected and unloved.

Therapists can identify defensive behavior by the self-righteous language the person uses that enhances his or her position at the expense of the other's. For example, "I'm right, you're wrong" statements and such put-downs designed to throw the partner off-track as "How could you be so dumb? Everyone makes advance preparations" are common indicators of defensive agendas.

Couples invariably come into conflict when the defensive structure of one partner is at variance with the defensive structure of the other. A case in point is the couple about to leave on a much wanted vacation. Travel evokes anxiety in each partner. Both are aware of but ashamed of their anxious feelings. Neither tells the other about how they feel; rather, each begins to mobilize their personal anxiety-reducing strategies. Her response to her anxiety requires minute, compulsive preparations in the hope of warding off unknown catastrophes. His response, in contrast, is to avoid all preparations until the very last minute. He is an avoider; she is an anticipator. Their respective needs clash. Compromise is futile. It is not difficult for us to imagine the angry words, hurt feelings, and power struggle that precede their vacation. Once on vacation they calm down, but the damage has already been done. One couple forswore future vacations as the only solution they could come up with, one that seriously limited the pleasure of the marriage.

When you suspect defensive secrets are interfering with the couple's ability to accommodate to one another, a gentle and compassionate exposure of these secrets allows the couple to confront their beliefs and experience empathy instead of rejection. Premature exposure of secrets, before you have established trust and credibility, will invariably be met with angry reactions or threats of terminating therapy.

Being Active and Engaged

Couples therapy requires therapists to take an active and engaged position vis-à-vis their clients. Couples *need* you to be involved for several reasons. Many have acquired destructive patterns of interaction that they are unable to stop. Inevitably, they repeat these patterns in your office, both to show you what they do and to elicit your assistance in learning less harmful patterns. They need you to guide them, to show them the way to more harmonious interactions. Just as a movie director has to be "up close and personal" in order to guide the actors' performance, a therapist has a parallel task. Therapeutic involvement allows you to engage in activities that are helpful to your clients, namely, teaching them new interactive skills and helping them sort out their dirty linen. For example, from a distance, I would not have been able to teach clients how to de-escalate arguments, how to hold "staff meetings" (described later), how to give and take information about each other, or how to switch off the blame game, to name a few skills clients often need to learn.

Second, therapeutic distance increases the danger that the client will experience you as being judgmental and disdainful. Distance gives the erroneous impression that you want to avoid getting yourself soiled by the couple's mess. Thus, remaining passive and distant may inadvertently escalate their sense of guilt and shame and increase the probability of negative projections and transference. Couples therapy, unlike individual therapy, leaves much less room for you to interpret and make good use of your clients' projections. Negative transference should be avoided if at all possible.

Third, therapists need to be able to move clients off their present stuck position skillfully. The right touch, gentle yet firm, present yet nonintrusive, requires a position that conveys a sense of engagement to clients. Our clients come to us wounded and figuratively bruised, wanting us to touch and accept them. From an engaged position, we are much more sensitive to their emotional state and the nuances of their emotional shifts. We are thus able to move our clients with soothing and comforting words rather than brutal and demeaning ones. From an engaged, involved, and respectful position we can be honest without being harsh.

Fourth, from an involved position, you inform the client that you are interested in them and are willing to be the "good friend," who with wisdom, insight, and intelligence is ready to give a helping hand.

A word of caution: if you get too emotionally close, you may become vulnerable to overidentifying with your clients, lose your sense of boundaries and observational perspective, and are liable to project your own issues onto them. I am reminded of a case I supervised in which the therapist overwhelmed his clients by confessing that his own marriage was presently coming apart at the seams. He was trying to tell them that he could empathize with their situation because he was in a similar one. They experienced his confession as a demand that they support him emotionally rather than that he would be available for them. They lost confidence in him; if he couldn't keep his relationship together, how would he be able to help them? They faked a quick recovery and terminated therapy.

This therapist's behavior can be explained, in part, by his inexperience, although experienced therapists have been known to make similar demands on their clients by getting too close and familiar with them. Fortunately, we can tell when we are therapeutically positioned well. There is a comfort, an ease, a sense of trust and a grace to the atmosphere and to the interactions in the room, no matter how painful or difficult the subject under discussion may be. You may have worked very hard in the session, but you are not exhausted. If you begin to feel exhausted during the session, try changing your emotional position, move back a bit. Does that help? If not, move forward, increase your engagement. Keep track of your energy barometer. If it is too low, you are too far away. If it is too high, you are too close. Remember, clients bring their climatic atmosphere with them to our offices, and you will need to adjust your position so that it fits with theirs. No one position fits all.

Evaluation: Functional and Diagnostic

In the process of developing a working relationship and setting goals, your are simultaneously engaged in the process of evaluation and assessment of the couple's strengths and limitations. A thorough evaluation takes time, emerging after several sessions in which you have an opportunity to interact with the couple and observe their interactions with one another. It is a good idea to make sure that the goals set are compatible with your evaluation of the couple's abilities.

Evaluation has two prongs: one is functional and the other is diagnostic. Functional evaluation focuses mainly on the interactive qualities of the relationship, that is, on how the couple gets along together. Diagnostic evaluation focuses on the personality structure of each partner. Functional evaluation asks the following questions (which may vary from couple to couple):

- What keeps this couple together? What is the glue?
- What is pulling them apart?
- What external resources are available to each partner that might enable them to compromise?
- When do they get into conflict? Is there a pattern to their conflicts, and what seems to trigger them?
- What function do their conflicts seem to serve?
- What is the power structure of the relationship, both overt and covert?
- How do their personalities fit together? Where are the points of friction?

You will note that these are functional questions, pertaining to who, what, how, and when, avoiding *why* questions. The latter are often stalling tactics engaged in by the therapist or by the couple in order to maintain the status quo. While interesting, they do not necessarily stimulate change. From a functionalist perspective, engaging in *why* analyses would only be useful if it enhances forward movement.

Diagnostic evaluation provides a quick map of the couple's respective personality structures. It also lets you know what defensive maneuvers each is likely to adopt, their overall rigidity or flexibility, as well as their strengths and weaknesses. If you know, for example, that you are dealing with a paranoid personality, you will not expect much flexibility in thinking. If you are dealing with a narcissistic personality, you might find empathetic understanding beyond his or her capability. Some of the questions to ask in diagnostic evaluation are as follows:

- What is the personality structure of each partner?
- What are their characteristic defensive maneuvers?
- Which ego skills are likely to be weak or strong?
- What internal resources are they able to draw on?
- What are their bottom lines, the areas of rigidity below which they cannot compromise?

In your evaluation, it is also important to ascertain what qualities and behaviors are either missing or distorted in the couple's relationship. Among the most significant diagnostic features you will want to know about are the couple's capacity to hear one another empathetically, to engage in generous behavior toward the other, and to gain an understanding of the other as their relationship progresses. When either one or both mates are lacking in one or more of these traits, the couple is probably starving for affection.

Some individuals must be taught how and when to be generous and thoughtful. For example, one such couple, who were married twenty years and had three children, were clearly lacking in simple kindness and generosity toward one another. The wife, an artist, was caught up in her own world, not noticing that her husband, who was also extraordinarily self-absorbed, was beginning to wander far from home for his affectional fixes. Neither was able to apprehend the connection between their complaints about the other and their own behavior. Nor were they aware of their lack of empathy for the other's suffering.

My task was to teach him simple generosity in the form of showing interest in her world, a willingness to assist her in tasks around the house, and a fuller sharing of his economic resources. As he practiced these new skills, she began to soften up and show more affection to him. It was slow work, reeducating him to function in an adult role of father and husband and both protector and provider. He was a willing student, given that basically he was a generous person. I heavily rewarded him with praise for his efforts. The wife learned to do likewise as she modeled herself after me.

One final note regarding evaluation. Are all couples psychologically capable of benefiting from couples therapy? The couple entering our office has defined themselves as wanting this form of treatment. Must we always agree with them, or might some other form of treatment, such as individual or group therapy, be more beneficial?

Arnold Lazarus, in a provocative paper, points out the difficulty of doing couples therapy when one or both partners lacks the psychological sophistication or the capability to adjust to or to adopt new and necessary behaviors. It has been the assumption of strategic, systems, or structural family therapy that the psychological requirements of any of the parties is irrelevant. The assumption has been that if one changes the circumstances, or the structure of the couple's situation, behavioral changes will follow. Lazarus disagrees and presents a useful set of criteria to determine whether a couple is likely to benefit from couples therapy.

ACT TWO: THE MIDDLE PHASE

You have now established a working, trusting, and respectful relationship with your clients. Having set the agenda and goals, you know where you are going. You have a fair evaluation of your clients, their personality constructs, as well as their defensive styles. You are now ready to get into the heart of therapy.

In the course of making your functional and diagnostic evaluations, you have formulated hypotheses and associated therapeutic strategies in your mind, which now have to be empirically tested, perhaps reformulated and honed.

Moving the Drama Forward

An empirical attitude on the part of the therapist provides a way of moving through the therapy hour and applying a longer-range strategy. Once you have formulated a hypothesis about a particular aspect of your clients' functioning, you need to gather data and determine how well they fit your hypothesis.

For example, I worked with a couple who defined their problem around sexual issues. The husband complained about a lack of sexual intimacy, blaming his wife for the situation. The wife said she did not want to become pregnant and thus was sexually disinterested. I hypothesized that the wife's sexual disinterest was related to the husband's disfigurement following a serious household accident years previous. His shame prevented discussion of the effects of the accident on either partner. Her so-called fear of pregnancy protected his shame and her reluctance to encroach on it. At an appropriate point, I tested my hypothesis by opening a discussion of the accident and consequent disfigurement when he (predictably) complained about the lack of sexual intimacy in their relationship. This time, I prompted her to tell him how she felt about his body. When I did so, I could feel the tension in the room. In a very simple sentence, she said, "When I look at your body it's hard for me to become sexually aroused." He was shocked and almost fell off his seat. Immediately he tried to interrupt her, and he sputtered something deflective and critical about her.

From this single interaction, I had important information and confirmation of part of my hypothesis: her sexual disinterest was fueled by his disfigurement. This was a sore spot for him. His reactive attempt to shift the action away from him revealed his distress. He appeared wounded by the disclosure, probably because it reawakened his original sense of being injured. Most important, however, the secret was out in the open.

I had a choice at this point either to support her for being honest or to support him in his pain. The choice was made on the basis of two things: who needed the greater support and who, if not supported, might undermine the hour. I focused on him and empathetically acknowledged his hurt and how difficult a topic this had been to talk about. His musculature relaxed as he accepted the empathy. This suggested that my shift to him was the right move. He replied, "Yes, it is," as if exhausted by the many years of false bravado. My hypothesis was now completely confirmed. He too had paid a high price for his deflections, in that it denied him needed empathy and support.

But my work in the session was only half done. I kept half an eye on her, watching to see her reactions. She seemed both relaxed and anticipatory, curious but not frightened. This suggested that I could continue to focus on him.

Now that the sore spot has been exposed, I asked myself, what is the best way to deal with it? I formulated another hypothesis, namely, that they both lacked a safe arena in which to air their feelings. I suggested that they were afraid to talk about the accident for fear of further injuring the other and out of fear of being rejected. I was aware of the importance of ensuring that I address both with my voice, eyes, and posture. I needed to convey my acceptance of their struggle and not condemn them. They spontaneously started to talk about how terrible a time it was for them, their guilt and shame, and their decision to put on a good face for the public. Unfortunately, they forgot to remove the mask when they talked to each other. His body, during this discussion, became more erect rather than slouched. The crisis had passed, but, I wondered, could they talk about the event without my being present to provide safety and empathy? This was my next hypothesis. I suggested that they try to continue the conversation at home. To myself, I knew that the next session, when I inquired if they talked about it, would give me new data.

Timing, Timing, Timing

The timing of your interventions is as critical as their content. I'm sure you have all had the experience of a client complaining, "You should have told me so-and-so sooner—now it's too late."

Good timing is very tricky. You can be damned for being too cautious as well as too premature. There are two useful ways to confront the question of timing. First, lay the groundwork. Second, state your thoughts in *seemingly* tentative statements.

Laying the groundwork consists of making a series of approximate statements, as if tilling the ground, softening it up for the planting of a seed. Timing requires patience and a plan of action on the part of the therapist.

For example, one couple, both of whom were alcoholics by anyone's standards, came to see me after they had exhausted the patience of several highly regarded therapists. Neither partner was willing to acknowledge the destructive role alcohol played in their relationship. If, in the initial sessions, I told them to gain control of their drinking, they would have been out the door. If, on the other hand, I ignored the problem, then I would be colluding with them, which I was not willing to do. Each session, I asked them about their drinking, drawing the connection between that behavior and the occurrence of arguments. After the fifth session, I directly asked them whether they connected their drinking with the issues they were dealing with in their marriage, family, and work. Once they were able to acknowledge the connection, I inquired whether they had given any thought to controlling their drinking. After another few sessions, I laid out their options: either they took steps to control their drinking, or they were wasting my time and their money, because it didn't matter which therapist they saw—they were drowning their efforts in alcohol. They claimed that none of their previous therapists had laid out their options so clearly to them. It didn't matter whether that was the case or not; what did matter was that through a series of successful approximations of the main interpretation, they had become ready to hear and accept it.

The strategy of stating your thoughts as if you are being tentative allows you to test the waters, to find out whether the client is ready for the interpretation or intervention. I like to use such expressions as "I have a hunch that . . ." or "Something tells me that. . . . What do you think?" or "Let's try testing the hypothesis that. . . ." All of these statements leave lots of room for your client to disagree, add or subtract, or just to try it on for size. I try to say things in such a way so as to avoid placing clients into a situation in which they must either accept what they may not be ready to accept or to reject what may be useful to them. My approach gives them time to consider the interpretation.

Being thoughtful and considerate with your timing of interventions also models how to deal more effectively with a difficulty clients frequently experience in their relationship. Couples often have timing problems and need to be taught how to time their interactions, especially those in which some a delicate subject must be broached.

Good timing presupposes that one is capable of repressing the impulse to say what's on one's mind. The husband who just needs to tell his wife about his upsets as soon as she returns home from a difficult day at work or the wife who insists on withholding painful information until her husband is about to fall asleep are engaging in impulsive or aggressive behavior. Learning how to time communication requires the application of judicious emotional control. In a marriage, couples have the task of repressing their sexual and aggressive behavior as well as controlling their impulsive verbal and nonverbal emotional behavior. Timing presupposes that one is capable of planning, which, in turn, presupposes that one is capable of controlling one's anxieties. The therapist, whose timing is planned and careful, indirectly teaches by modeling for their clients how it is done.

Linguistic Codes

Language, words, verbal communication are the bread and butter of all psychotherapy. Although we and our clients speak in a common language, we do not necessarily encode and decode meanings in the same manner. We may not understand our clients' verbal communications, and we shouldn't assume that our clients understand us or each other, even though we may be all using the same words.

Deborah Tannen has done a magnificent job of elucidating the differences between male and female communication styles and between the interpersonal effects each gender wants to achieve with their ways of organizing their communications. There are other varieties of verbal styles that therapists should also consider. For example, some people use language primarily as an expressive medium to convey feelings, while others use it to convey rational thoughts and factual information. These two linguistic functions cannot be neatly divided into feminine or masculine styles since they appear to run across gender lines.

Expressive Versus Rational Styles.   An expressive style conveys color, mood, feeling, and sentiment. It is brimming with exaggerations and superlatives, such as *never, always, worst, best,* or such phrases as "I've told you that a thousand times."

The rational, factual linguistic style, on the other hand, insists on precision, neatness, and an exactness devoid of emotional overtones. Its purpose is to convey facts, primarily relating to external reality, in the hope that everyone can agree about that reality and thus avoid conflict.

It is useful to point out these stylistic differences to the clients and to teach them to translate meanings from one system into the other. For example, when the husband says to his wife, "You never throw out the garbage" and the wife retorts, "Oh, yes, I do—I did it yesterday," they are missing each other's point. An accurate translation is as follows:

> *Husband:* I wish you would remember to throw out the garbage more often. I hate to have to remind you. It makes me feel as if you don't care about what is important to me.
>
> *Wife:* Just tell me when you want it done. I can't read your mind. I don't mean to hurt you, but you hurt me when you ignore the efforts that I do make to please you.

A less obvious example caught my attention during a session with another couple. The wife told her partner, with a sense of great satisfaction, that she felt *distanced* from him. He immediately became crestfallen and dejected. Not getting the response she expected, she felt let down, assuming that he was not supportive of her. This was a case of proverbial ships passing in the night, leaving everyone, including myself, confused. What happened?

Upon inquiry, we discovered that she had meant *separate*, as in more psychologically bounded, and not distant, as in far away. Once that meaning became clear, it was not only acceptable to him but also brought a sigh of relief, given how burdensome he experienced her dependency. He, in turn, was able to be pleased for her.

Of course, therapists also have their linguistic style, which may be more akin to one partner than the other. Be aware of your style. If it is out of kilter with your client's linguistic style, translate when necessary. Make sure that your meaning is being equally understood by both partners.

Linguistic Differentiation. Clients often verbalize thoughts, feelings, needs, and hopes in global undifferentiated constructs. Depression and sadness may be labeled as "feeling down." "Feeling bad" may signify anger, rage, irritation, frustration, annoyance, as well as guilt or shame, excitement, and anxiety, blurring the significant difference between these various states. Mislabeling may also lead to a failure to differentiate between sexual arousal and the wish for physical affection. A partner may indicate their wish for the latter by acting coquettishly, and then be surprised and upset when their mate responds sexually. Or a mate may hug and kiss their partner in a sexual manner, when trying to signal their intention to end an argument. Likewise a statement indicating that one "feels close" to their partner may mean they are sexually aroused, wanting to give or receive affection, or prepared for an intimate communication. Inaccurate, global labeling generally leaves the transmitter of information confused, because they don't understand why they often do not receive the right response back. It also confuses the receiver, whether they are aware of it or not, because he or she is not sure what the appropriate response might be in a particular situation.

Linguistic Confusion: Needs, Wants, and Wishes.   Needs, wants, and wishes are classes of gratifications, forming a hierarchy of intensity of requirement. For example, an infant's need to be fed derives from an organic instinct for survival. Wants, higher up on the hierarchy, are constructions derived from a sense of well-being rather than from survival. Wishes are furthest removed from survival, arising from a desire for pleasure only. For example, I might *need* transportation, *want* a car, and *wish* for a Mercedes. Wishes *should* be frustrated at times. Wants *may* be frustrated at times. Needs, because their frustration is experienced as very threatening to the self, should only be frustrated when it is unavoidable to do otherwise. One of the major tasks of parenting is teaching the child to delay gratification and to deal with consequent frustration. In this regard, the successful acquisition of an appropriate repertoire of responses to frustration depends on whether parents have taught the child to make important distinctions between the frustration of needs, wants, and wishes.

Some of our clients have not learned to make these distinctions and may experience the frustration of their wishes with the same emotional intensity and urgency as they do when their wants or needs are frustrated. Thus, they may not have learned how to handle differing degrees of frustration and may respond to frustration in an undifferentiated way. Such clients often use "If you love me, you would . . ." statements in their demand for gratification, generally with a whine in their voice. They frequently lack understanding of and insight into the give and take of relationships. In couples therapy these clients need to be taught to distinguish between needs, wants, and wishes and how to acquire essentials successfully. It is a way of teaching them to stop crying "wolf" so frequently.

Mental Likert Scale:
Giving Numerical Values

Husbands and wives who use differing linguistic styles, who engage in linguistic confusion, and who do not know how to translate the meaning of their mates communications accurately often find themselves arguing (in vain) about reality. Also, seemingly small misrepresentations or mistranslations sometimes lead to large hurts over a period of time. This occurs because partners fail to distinguish between what's truly significant from what's trivial for their mate and thus, inadvertently, keep stepping on the other's toes without realizing they are inflicting injury or, for that matter, that the mate is injured.

One way I deal with such problems is to introduce the concept of a mental Likert scale, from one to ten, signifying the increasing importance a client gives to a particular event, word, need, and so forth. Ask your client how important a particular need is for them and to quantify it on the scale. In one instance, a couple reported that neither mate greeted the other in a welcoming, respectful, and affectionate manner when reuniting after a long hard day. He would come home and immediately isolate himself, needing to recover from his daily grind. The wife, needing immediate connection, tended to bombard him with a detailed description of her activities during the day. Both were frustrated by the seeming incapacity of the mate to respond to their respective needs. These daily mutual frustrations escalated, leaving each to wonder whether they had married the right person.

I asked them to quantify their respective needs on a scale from one to ten. The husband was able to identify his need for a short respite on coming home as a ten on the scale. His wife was shocked when she realized how intrusive she had been. But her need for a welcoming hello and kiss on the cheek was likewise on the upper reaches of the scale. He thought that she just liked to chatter at his expense. Once the misunderstanding was cleared up, they were able to work out a simple satisfactory routine.

Special Strategies

Couples often need specific strategies to help them through areas of entanglement or stuck places. Therapists should not assume that if couples achieve emotional competence, they would also naturally evolve workable, everyday management systems. It is not unusual for a successful business person to regress to an incompetent child as soon as he crosses the threshold of his home. The following strategies are meant to encourage partners to employ their competent ego functions at home as well as at work.

Staff Meetings. A useful concept I introduce to many couples is that of holding staff meetings in which personal and management issues are separated. Many couples' battles over mundane, day-to-day operational decisions are displacements of subtler struggles. In the workplace, these same individuals may have enormous responsibility and may make and carry out major decisions. At home, however, they may turn the simplest task into a nightmare. Who takes care of arranging for the baby-sitter? Doing the family shopping? Paying the bills? Arriving at answers to such questions may become a mud-fest of accusations or stonewalling sabotage. One solution I find helpful is to encourage such couples to adopt a home management strategy I call a staff meeting.

   For example, a married professional couple could not agree on how to divide or assign family chores equitably. Attempts to discuss this issue generally ended up frittering away their precious time on disputes, leaving essentials undone. In contrast, other important decisions relating to their children were conflict-free. Both partners came from families in which one parent arbitrarily assumed the role of leader and decision maker and the other parent tended to acquiesce. Given their avowed belief in egalitarianism, this model would not work for them. While they wisely chose a relatively safe arena to enact their struggle to differentiate, it nonetheless left them depleted and wondering what was wrong with their marriage. Their self-observation fell short of their standard for a healthy marriage. Thus, they assumed they were poorly matched and wondered whether the marriage had a future.

I suggested that they meet regularly at a designated time and place for a specified amount of time when interference could be kept to a minimum. A rotating chairperson helped prevent problems of dominance. Careful, continuous note taking, not unlike organizational minutes, ensured accountability and avoided disagreements about what was said and who said it. Each partner could include agenda items for discussion.

One attends staff meetings with one's ego functionally intact, prepared to focus on purposeful planning, prompt execution of agenda items, and the suppression of secret agendas. Each partner expects to be held accountable. During the learning phase, it is useful to remind them to exclude personal feelings, grudges, and emotions from the meetings. The purpose of the meetings is to deal with task-related matters.

Many couples are surprised at how well it works. They quickly get the idea and learn that they can make decisions quite easily, if they stick to the facts and stay objective and issue oriented. Couples discover that if they do not undermine the process with unrelated issues, their everyday lives flow smoothly. In attributional terms, by shrinking the areas of conflict and enlarging the areas of satisfactory, problem-solving interactions, they observe themselves as compatible and cooperative rather than as incompatible and antagonistic. They are more likely to assess themselves as a well-matched couple.

Staff meetings incorporate an additional side benefit. Couples acquire the cognitive structure that allows them to focus externally on the issue or task at hand rather than on the doer of the task, their mate. The issue, for example, is preparing dinner rather than the mate's past performance or one's own anxieties stemming from inadequate parenting in childhood.

In time, the neutrality of staff meetings also allows mates to confess feelings of inadequacy that surround certain gender-identified activities. One husband, for instance, finally found the courage to confess to his wife that he hated to interact with most home maintenance people and would prefer that the wife take responsibility for obtaining bids on their home painting project. She was more than pleased to take over that task if he, in turn, traded with her by taking over the laundry duties she disliked. They discovered that when they did tasks they enjoyed as opposed to those they thought they should perform, they were both more effective and cooperative. Once day-to-day functioning is separated from emotionally charged issues, therapists and clients are freer to focus on the latter.

I do not mean to suggest that staff meetings by themselves are all that may be needed to get couples back on track. But this tool, or others like it, that has the effect of freeing a significant area of their interactions from conflict and hostility helps change the emotional valence of relationships, which allows couples to confront deeper, more personal, and emotionally charged issues with some hope of success and with the experience of empathy.

Between Sessions: Homework. A troubled relationship is like a house in disrepair. It needs lots of fixing and sprucing up. It can't all be accomplished in one hour a week. It needs directed attention and focused energy between sessions. That is where the concept of homework comes into play. It gives the couple the message that they can take some responsibility for repairing their own situation, and it prepares them with tools to do so after the therapy session is over. The weekly staff meeting is an example of homework and of the tools to help couples stay on track. However, many couples, especially at the beginning of therapy, are not ready for something as sophisticated and requiring a degree of cooperation as staff meetings. But, they may be ready for other simpler types of homework. The following is a list of some assignments I have found useful:

- Prepare lists of:
  What you like about your partner, and what you don't like
  about your partner
  Enjoyable things you like doing with together
  Enjoyable things you prefer to do apart

   The particular list I assign emanates from discussions during
the therapy hour. Its function is to shift the partners' awareness
away from complaints and blaming behaviors to focusing on specific pleasurable or unpleasurable behaviors.

- Keep a log:
  Arguments: ascertain when during the day or week they are
  most likely to occur—morning, evening, midweek, weekend,
  when kids are home or absent.
  Energy levels, eating, drinking, sleeping, and other health habits.
  Some people become cranky when they are fatigued. At such
  times they have a short fuse and become easily irritated and
  argumentative. Couples can learn to recognize down times and
  learn to deal with these times better.

- Construct and safeguard valuable time together in which differences of all types are avoided. Labeling pleasure as homework sidesteps obstacles that couples may put in their way.

- Read. For some couples, information is a valuable means by
  which new constructs of interaction and an acceptable definition of marriage can be created. For example, *Sex in America*,
  by Robert Michael and his colleagues, has helped many couples view their sexual relations in a new light. Make sure that
  you have read the material first and that it is appropriate for a
  particular couple.

   Use your imagination when devising homework. Keep it
within the level of the couple's current relationship, and make it
simple and doable.
   A couple's response to homework is often a useful diagnostic
tool. Those who take it seriously and work at it are most likely

ready to make improvements in their relationship. Couples who habitually avoid the assignment might harbor a secret agenda or have some reason why they wish to undermine their therapeutic progress.

ACT THREE: CONCLUDING PHASE

There are three possible scenarios pertaining to the completion of therapy. First and most ideal, the couple has reached their stated goals and together are ready to resume their relationship with renewed enthusiasm and greater skillfulness.

Second, but still acceptable, the couple has gone as far as they can at this point, falling short of their goal but able to limp along. One or both are willing to enter individual therapy to alleviate some of the strain on the relationship that originates from their own psyche and history. They are left with a feeling of hope and promise, if not with a sense of completion.

The third scenario is less optimistic. Therapy, at least from your perspective, has been prematurely ended, the couple has not achieved its goals, and no one is feeling particularly hopeful. The therapy has ended because somebody has run out of energy, you or the couple. There seems to be nowhere else or go. They might or might not stay together.

Note that in outlining the scenarios earlier I have not used the terms *success* or *failure of therapy*; rather, I have focused on the achievement of the couple's goals. Staying together or separating as the criteria of successful or unsuccessful therapy only makes sense in relation to the couple's overt or covert agenda. I find that using the couple's agenda and goals, both those emerging early in the therapy and those developed in its second stage, is a much better yardstick for determining the outcome of the therapy.

Therapy might be evaluated on objective and subjective grounds. Objective evaluation consists of asking the following types of questions:

- How close did we get to reaching the stated goals?
- What still remains to be done?
- What interfered with achieving the desired goals?
- Were the goals realistic in the first place? If not, was the couple able to redefine their goals more realistically?
- Are they more skillful in dealing with disagreements?
- Are they more empathetically understanding and tolerant of each other?
- Has the quantity of positive interactions increased?

On a subjective level, evaluation may consist of how the couple feels about their therapeutic experience. The following questions might be asked:

- Was it a positive experience for them? Would they be willing to use therapy again, if needed?
- Are you, the therapist, feeling satisfied with your work?
- Most importantly, are they feeling more optimistic about their future?

Your task at the end of therapy will depend on which of the three scenarios best describes the therapeutic encounter. If it is the first scenario, your task is to help the couple maintain and build on their achievements. If it is the second one, your task is to encourage them to remain hopeful, red flag future trouble spots, and help them identify what to do when those arise. If it is the third scenario, the task is to paint a brighter picture for the future than the couple is able to envision at this point. Of course, you may never get the opportunity to offer anything, if they end the therapy without much notice.

Maintenance

Marriage, like a house, requires constant maintenance and repair. It cannot be taken for granted and survive over a long period of time. It is important to teach that message to clients before they end therapy, otherwise they will become disappointed when the next conflict or crisis emerges.

What constitutes maintenance? Scheduled periodic reviews, requiring time together to find out how the other guy is doing. Are partners experiencing dissatisfaction and about what? Are they OK? Identify trouble spots and learn how to talk to each other about them. Use the tools learned in therapy to deal with problems. Review sessions should be scheduled in advance, on a weekly basis, if possible. Don't go longer than a month between sessions. It's easier to clear up recent misunderstandings than ones that get stale and fester. Make reviews pleasant, organizing them around a pleasurable activity, such as dinner out, a nature walk, or some other activity when you are likely to be relaxed and receptive.

One of the things I try to teach couples in therapy is that they need to spend time alone and restore their relationship. A common problem today is that, with all the other demands on a person's time and energy, it is difficult to find the time to be together unless a conscious effort is made to allocate such time. Couples with relationships that work frequently are those who make the time to devote to their relationship. When they do so, they are able to identify trouble spots ahead, such as anticipating a major change in a job, difficulties with children or parents, and so forth. Anticipating allows them to plan how they want to respond as a couple. This, in turn, helps them feel that they are working as a unit, with mutual confidence.

The Check-Up

It is important to convey to couples—especially those who ended couples therapy before completeing all their therapeutic work (as in Scenario Two)—that it is acceptable to use therapy as a resource when they reach an impasse.

I avoid using the term *termination* to describe the end point of therapy, because it has the unfortunate connotation that a process has reached a final state of completion. The life of a couple is fluid and dynamic. Not even divorce, if a couple has children, terminates their relationship. If therapy has been at all useful for a couple, they should be encouraged to use it as an available resource in the future, should the need arise. It is important to emphasize that it is not a sign of failure to return for another round of sessions. When couples feel that they have a fallback position, a fail-safe point, they are less fearful about ending therapy knowing that they have not yet reached some ideal state in their relationship.

It is useful to use positive terms when presenting the possibility of a return for additional couples work. I put it in terms of a *check-up* or consultation, or as an aspect of prevention to get to problems before they cause deterioration. It is also important to establish agreement that either partner can call for an appointment with the expectation that the other will honor it.

Red Flagging

Helping couples identify issues likely to crop up in the future is particularly helpful for couples who end therapy in a less than optimal way. They may not have learned the necessary skills to deal with certain types of conflicts and may be less equipped to anticipate them when they find themselves in trouble again. If you red flag these possible difficulties, you are not creating a self-fulfilling prophesy. Rather, you help the couple be prepared to know what actions to take should these problems arise. In such situations, they are less likely to judge themselves or their mates as failures or to feel as defeated as they might otherwise have.

After the Conclusion of Therapy

It is not uncommon for a couple's therapist to be asked to continue seeing one of the partners in individual therapy after the couple's work is ended. Indeed, individual treatment may have been recommended during the course of therapy for many different reasons. How should you respond to such a request?

When is it appropriate to say yes, and when to say no? If you have formed a good working relationship with the couple, transitioning to individual therapy may interfere with your working with the couple in the future. If you have raised red flags and encouraged the couple to think of returning in the future, you have essentially identified yourself as their common therapist. It is difficult to wear two hats at the same time. You are either their joint therapist or an individual therapist to one of them. Future couples work might leave one of them out in the cold or create inequality in your relationship with the couple. In either case, that is not a good proposition. Shifting to individual work should therefore only be undertaken if it is made clear to both partners that you would no longer be available as their couples therapist. If all freely agree, then you can carefully make the transition.

The watchword here is caution. The nature of individual therapy and the relationship between therapist and clients is so different in both instances that one should be very careful when switching roles.

There are times when couples therapy is used as an entrée to individual therapy by one of the partners. They may have been too frightened to see someone alone and used their mate as a transitional object to ease their way into therapy. If that is the case, you are often made aware of that fact during the first stage of therapy. The couples phase is then usually short-term, and the therapeutic agenda tends to be constructed in individual terms. The sooner the transition to individual work is made, the easier it is on all concerned.

Couples therapy, for most therapists, is a major challenge. Having to relate to two separate individuals, each with their separate dynamics, while simultaneously focusing on their status as a unit, requires a fair amount of mental gymnastics. The potential for countertransference issues is compounded, arising from your personal history, marital, and relational experiences.

Frequently our success in treating couples depends on our ability to be creative and to shape the therapy around the needs of the particular client. What may work for one couple may not work for another.

The outline, suggestions, techniques, and maps presented here are meant to assist you in thinking about how to do couples therapy without getting lost in either the couples' or your own dynamics. It is by no means an exhaustive exposition. Rather, it is hoped that you will be stimulated to think about what, how, and why you do what you do, as a couples therapist.

NOTES

P. 5, *goals and agendas . . . definition of marriage:* Nunnally, E. (1993). Solution focused therapy. In R. A. Wells & V. J. Giannetti (Eds.), *Casebook of the brief psychotherapies.* New York: Plenum.

P. 13, *Diagnostic evaluation . . . strengths and weaknesses:* Snyder, D. K., Mangrum, L. F., & Wills, R. M. (1993). Predicting couples' responses to marital therapy: A comparison of short- and long-term predictors. *Journal of Consulting and Clinical Psychology, 61,* 61–69.

P. 15, *partners . . . capability to adjust:* Lazarus, A. (1992). When is couples therapy necessary and sufficient? *Psychological Reports, 70,* 787–790.

P. 20, *differences between male and female communication styles:* Tannen, D. (1990). *You just don't understand.* New York: Morrow.

P. 21, *Clients often verbalize . . . global undifferentiated constructs:* Willi, J., Frei, R., & Limacher, B. (1993). Couples therapy using technique of construct differentiation. *Family Process, 32,* 311–321.

P. 27, *Read:* Michael, R., Gagnon, J., Laumann, E., & Kolata, G. (1994). *Sex in America.* Boston: Little, Brown.

P. 30, *What constitutes maintenance?:* Carlson, J., & Sperry, L. (1993). Extending treatment results in couples therapy. *Individual Psychology, 49*(3–4), 450–455.

2

MYTHS IN COUPLES THERAPY

Hilda Kessler and Margaret Thaler Singer

In this chapter, we will examine and debunk myths that couples hold about how couples should be, myths about what couples therapy can do, and myths that therapists believe. All of these myths interfere with the therapeutic process.

A *myth* is a popular fable whose source is not verifiable but is passed on as a traditional notion explaining nature, customs, or folkways. The purpose of a myth is to cast a particular implication or essence on an event rather than to depict the event accurately. Thus we criticize myths that get into the therapy process because they either maintain unsubstantiated notions or turn our clients and ourselves away from our ability to deal with reality issues.

Couples come to therapy searching for help to learn more about how to make their lives work. Many are in a quagmire complicated by myths they hold about one another, about married life, and about therapy itself. If their beginning assumptions are based on faulty notions, they inevitably run into predicaments that interfere with their ability to cope and work together.

As therapists, we are expected to wade through this fictional morass, to help them sift through distortions and myths and find the reality of who each is and how to accommodate to one another. Perhaps we are often called *shrinks* because the public views us as being able to shrink the fabric of fiction down to the core elements of truth. When therapists believe the same myths as couples do or, worse, when they begin implanting their own myths into the therapy, they abandon their skills of professional observation and become not therapists but soothsayers, magicians, builders of cultic beliefs, or just plain old quacks.

Each partner enters therapy with many personal myths, learned during their formative years, including shared cultural and ethnic myths. No matter their source, many myths have such an aura of truth that they are accepted without question. After the therapist adds to these some of the professional myths that are the current shared delusions of our profession, the threesome may be off on some unrealistic wanderings in therapy. For example, in the 1950s, the belief that schizophrenogenic mothers existed took on mythic characteristics. In the 1960s the myth of "let it all hang out" became a professional shibboleth.

In their emerging states, myths in the form of shared professional delusions are difficult to identify. It is only in retrospect that they become apparent, much to our mutual embarrassment. During the period in which myths are accepted as truth, therapists tend to harm their patients, either by being blind to the truth or by advancing suggestions, directions, or recommendations that are not necessarily in the patient's best interest. Paul McHugh, chief of psychiatry at Johns Hopkins Medical School, artfully refers to similar notions as "therapeutic misadventures."

In this chapter we will identify some of the contemporary myths held by clients as well as therapists, regarding couples and couples therapy.

MYTHS COUPLES TRY TO LIVE BY

In this section we explore two of the most prominent myths couples espouse: real love would make everything all right, and I give more than I get.

Love

Therapists hear the first myth voiced as "If she really loved me, she would be willing to do what pleases me without my having to ask for it in the first place." The same theme is rendered, with varying degrees of intensity, by summoning up the image of "true love." "If he *truly* loved me, he would. . . ." Some partners up the ante and call for "unconditional love," as in "If her love were *unconditional*, she would. . . ." The ultimate declaration calls for "true unconditional love." "If his love were *true and unconditional*, he would. . . ."

Underlying all of these statements are the assumptions that love, in all its variations, should:

- Enable the lover (or husband or wife) to be a mind reader
- Motivate the other to be a ready and willing gratifier

The passion of the believer and the force of the myth's emotional appeal give it a ring of truth and tend to convince the listener of its accuracy. Furthermore, since it's easy to feel guilty for withholding love—or whatever it is that is being requested—one hardly has the audacity to examine or question the logic underlying such premises.

The endowment of love with these mythic powers arises from a failure to distinguish between emotions and behavior. Emotions create a personal state of arousal and orient one toward or away from the object of the emotion. Love is an emotion that tells us how we feel about another person and orients us toward the object of our love.

Confusion inevitably arises when the emotion of love is equated with specific, expected behavior. Behavioral expressions of love are learned and vary greatly, depending on one's familial, cultural, and personal experiences. One wife may express love for her husband by cooking his favorite dishes, while another wife may plan small, personal outings for the two of them. One husband may express love for his family by showering them with money, whereas another man may express it by being a strong disciplinarian. Romance literature is replete with examples of love that is never expressed as well as of love that is dramatically demonstrated. Unless one clearly perceives the difference between the *feeling* of love and the *behavioral expression* of love, then disappointment is likely to follow since the behavioral expectations are based on unrealistic grounds. It is as if the partner says, "I must control the exact way you express your love; otherwise it is not love."

The mythic belief that love should produce desired actions is probably tied to early childhood experiences, particularly the longing for the perfect unity of mother and child. Whereas in reality, the parent/child relationship may have been less than minimally adequate, the fantasy may assume enormous wish-fulfilling characteristics. The portrayal of the idealized parent-child bond is reminiscent of Raphael's *Madonna and Child* in which the child is shown adored by a totally giving, submissive mother, a willing source of nurturance and protection. When adults expect such total, selfless giving from those who love them, they are yearning for an imagined, idyllic world of infantile narcissism.

Contemporary popular culture reinforces the mythic belief that love should produce desired actions. For example, the feeling of "entitlement" or the belief that one "deserves" such and such without needing to do anything in return is a widely held myth. Although love is not generally invoked to support why one deserves something in these instances, nonetheless, what inspires such ideas is the underlying belief that like an infant, one should receive just because one is.

Clients often express their adherence to mythic love when they complain that their mate does not love or understand them, using as proof the lack of gratification of any number of wishes. You might notice the naive, almost childlike, supplicating voice and body posture assumed by the client and the total sense of disbelief and betrayal that occurs when the unspoken wish is not gratified. Often it becomes necessary to correct a client's belief in an idealized but nonexistent world and to point out to him that his mythic beliefs are based on the wish that goodness will come as a result of being "truly or unconditionally loved" or by merely being "understood."

Not infrequently, no matter how gently and compassionately it is done, tampering with a person's dreams engenders hostility or even rage. The client's emotional reactions act as a barometer to gauge the benefit expected from the myth, how vital a role it plays in their system of procurement of needs, and how disappointments are experienced. This myth seems to be held most tenaciously by those who have a rather limited repertoire of strategies for satisfying their needs. They may feel quite helpless and at a loss as to how to find new ways of getting what they want.

The Doctrine of Fairness

The underlying metamessage in the fairness myth is "I'm not getting what I deserve" or "I'm being cheated." The person senses an inequity between what he perceives he "gives" and what he "gets" in return.

The doctrine of fairness is often invoked in the service of the belief that all rewards, benefits, entitlement, advantages, compensations, and other desirable goodies should be awarded equally. Equality in such instances is subjectively determined or based on such "objective" Marxian criteria of "To each according to his or her need."

While the myth of love is grounded in early childhood experiences, the myth of fairness is based on sibling rivalry and its variant, the playground. Believers in the myth of fairness generally hold that they are always being shortchanged and that the grass is always greener somewhere else. Driving these beliefs are the feelings of envy and jealousy and, sometimes, greed.

The green-eyed monster of jealousy resides in an internal, hidden cave, goading its owner to want what the other has. For example, a professional man in his mid-fifties married a rather wealthy widow. In the name of fairness and equality, he insisted that she include him as an equal partner in all of her financial holdings and that she rewrite her will making him the sole beneficiary, to the exclusion of her children. Overtly, he justified his greed, using the moral injunction that marriage partners should have equal economic status. Covertly his message expressed jealousy ("You have so much, and I have so little") and a demand for recompense for having suffered in childhood relatively more than she did. He appealed to her sense of morality in the hope of arousing her guilt and, consequently, her compliance, a ploy commonly used by adherents of the fairness myth. Needless to say, the marriage did not last long, ending in a messy divorce, despite their prenuptial agreement.

The invoker of the fairness myth tends to express his complaint in a childlike, whiny voice, assuming that everyone knows precisely what he means by his often vague demand. Or the person tries to appear as a rational adult and might even admit that she knows that the world is not fair, *but* her case is invariably different. She may also engage in a personal form of accounting to prove the "unfairness" of her mate or the disadvantage into which she has been placed.

The doctrine of fairness may be the major device used by some clients to assure the gratification of their wishes. Without it they are at a loss as to how to obtain desired gratification. Attempts to demythologize their beliefs are often met with the accusation that you, the therapist, are also being unfair and taking the partner's side. Likewise, they may respond by pouting or arguing their case in a manner worthy of the best defense lawyer.

The myth of fairness has undergone a powerful resurgence lately in the form of gender equality. For example, a couple described how they argued about whose turn it was to change the baby's diaper, while the child howled in discomfort. The wife felt that it wasn't fair that she had to change the baby's diaper more often than her husband just because she was home during the day. Therefore, it followed that it was his turn to change it in the evening. "Why should women have to do all the dirty work," she cried, "while men get to go out and have fun?"

Virulent forms of beliefs in "gender equality" insist on a daily accounting of who did what for whom. Recompense for any imbalance must be immediate. Such a formula omits a long-term perspective. In the lengthy journey a couple takes together, the balance of effort and reward keeps shifting and changing. No amount of daily accounting or reimbursements can alter that reality.

The myth of fairness sometimes comes cloaked in rather sophisticated costumes. In one instance, a highly successful professional woman, forty-six years old, complained that her husband was much too compliant and lacked backbone dealing with his boss. Though his behavior did not directly impact her, nonetheless it made her furious and tended to generate conflict in the marriage. In describing the husband's behavior, she invoked the myth of fairness, protesting that his behavior ultimately placed an unfair burden on her. She feared that if he is "weak," he will not be able to support her in the way she fantasized. The myth of fairness represented her wish to rely and be dependent on her husband. It was unfair, in her judgment, because she felt she was giving more than she would eventually receive.

The fairness myth is often invoked when one partner feels that, on the whole, he is putting out more energy than he is receiving. By doing so, couples often circumvent the more difficult process of exploring their habits of give-and-take and how these habits are experienced by themselves and their partner.

You have no doubt come across other myths and beliefs that clients bring into therapy in your own work with couples. Such myths are particularly difficult to unseat because they are invoked to satisfy rather urgently felt needs. Clients are often at a loss as to how to proceed in their relationships without such myths. Yet, unless attention is given to changing the belief systems inherent in these myths, progress in the relationship may be impeded.

MYTHS COUPLES HAVE
ABOUT PSYCHOTHERAPY

Couples bring to therapy multiple beliefs about the process of therapy and the role of the therapist in that process. These are myths that place the therapist in the role of a judge who is to resolve the conflicts between them, or a seer who will announce that they have a "fatal" problem, or a fixer of their problems. Also, these are the myths that communication cures everything or that therapy is antimarriage. Couples who hold these beliefs often view therapy solely in terms of remediation of faulty communication or the dissolution of the relationship.

The Therapist as Judge

Couples who are preoccupied with mutual fault finding and search for the most blameworthy party in their marital dissatisfaction are most likely to expect the therapist to be a judge. That stance may be so vital to their sense of personal integrity that they truly believe that your function is to judge which one of them is responsible for the current state of affairs. They have little interest in actually doing anything to change individually or to see their own role in their relational conflicts. If you refuse to enter such a contract with the couple, they may decide to discontinue therapy and blame you for being unprofessional.

In one case, a women became annoyed at her therapist for not blaming her husband for being unwilling to father a second child with her. She refused to acknowledge that her husband, who was seventeen years her senior and entering early retirement, was worn and weary from an arduous career and the raising of five children from his previous marriage. She was convinced that if the therapist judged him to be in the wrong, that he would then willingly acquiesce to her demands. The therapist's refusal to play this role and to impose the wife's will as a verdict confused and angered her. It was her last resort in a desperate battle of coercion. She threatened to discontinue therapy many times. As the therapist quietly stood her ground and continued to define her role not as judge, arbitrator, mediator, lawyer (or feminist), but as the bearer of psychological understanding of the needs and positions of both of them, she gradually allowed the therapeutic process to work its effect.

We may mistakenly think that better-educated or more sophisticated clients will have a greater appreciation of the role of the couple's therapist. Alas, such is not the case. Recently a couple, who between them had one and a half Ph.D.'s, entered treatment. The wife was certain that the only reason the husband badgered her for years to see a therapist with him was because he had decided to leave her. Furthermore, she was certain that any therapist would side with him and would confirm that she indeed was an insufferable person and that he had a "right" to find a better mate. She entered therapy expecting the therapist to pronounce her as good as divorced. Her fear permeated the whole of the first session. It was not until the therapist understood her terror and was able to reassure her that a therapist was not a judge that she was able to relax enough to engage in the process of therapy. (They neither divorced nor did they walk happily into the sunset. Life is often lived in the in-betweens.)

Is the Diagnosis Fatal?

Not infrequently, a couple begins therapy with a sense of fear and foreboding, similar to the experience of visiting a doctor and expecting to hear that they have an incurable disease. Couples sometimes assume that merely admitting to having marital difficulties is tantamount to being beyond help and that their relationship is beyond repair. They may also fear self-exposure, that is, that the therapist will uncover their fatal flaws both as individuals and as a couple. The myths underlying these concerns are "We should be perfect. We should be able to solve our own problems. Couples therapy will not help. It is an admission of failure."

Couples who hold such beliefs may be reluctant to seek therapeutic help in a timely fashion and may indeed enter therapy beyond the point of no return, when one of the partners has already decided to end the marriage. Thus the belief becomes a self-fulfilling prophesy.

The Fix-My-Mate Myth

The therapist may also be led into the role of "the doctor who will fix my mate." Such a partner sees the sole cause of the marital difficulties in the partner. The person enters therapy with the injunction "Doctor, you fix him!" Parents may bring their children into therapy with the same expectation.

A man once brought his fiancée to therapy with the request that she be "cured" of her bad habits. These consisted of phoning him at home at any hour of the night, whenever she became anxious about his fidelity, and raising her voice when she feared he was not paying attention to her. He wanted the therapist to act as a surgeon who would excise his fiancée's bad habits. He did not see himself as part of the couple's problems. He believed that if the therapist did her job right, she would get rid of the fiancée's "undesirable" behaviors.

In another case, a husband brought his wife to therapy asking that she be cured of her excessive smoking and eating. He had tried for years to persuade her to do so without success but heard that therapy was useful. He was sure that a professional would succeed where he failed. In such cases therapists have to disabuse the person of the myth that they "fix" partners to satisfy the other and have to educate the couple to view their situation as one to which both contribute. In so doing therapists simultaneously educate the couple about what therapy can and cannot achieve. Most clients, although disappointed at first, stay for the more difficult task of "fixing" their own relationship under the guidance of the therapist.

The Supremacy of Communication

Given the fact that we are in the "information age," with the information superhighway hovering on the horizon, it is not surprising that many couples have bought into the mythic belief that all their woes as a couple are due to poor communication. On the surface, invoking the *communication* myth gives the impression that both partners are taking some responsibility for their relational troubles. However, this myth generally translates into the belief that "If I only explained myself better, and if my partner listened better, then my partner would give me what I want." By focusing on the process, form, and style of communication, the validity of the content of the request is left intact.

Couples are likely to believe that the main function of couples therapy is to clear up their "communication" problems. The hook for the therapist in this particular myth (as in others) is that we ourselves may hold the same belief. Therapists do teach their clients to make "I" statements, to give equal air time to each partner, to state requests more succinctly and assertively—all useful communication skills. However, no matter how useful they may be, teaching such skills is not the main or only function of couples therapy.

How couples communicate may interfere with their ability to address their problems, but couples therapy needs to deal at least equally with the content of their disagreements and conflicts. For example, a couple married for thirty years came into therapy with a "communication" problem, as they put it. According to the husband, the wife was having difficulty understanding why his current three-month affair was in fact her fault, given that she had failed to provide him with adequate sexual pleasure. For her part, the wife was distraught; she could never get a word in edgewise, given the husband's propensity for long-winded harangues. They were both using their "communication" problem, genuine as it was, as a displacement for much deeper personal and marital difficulties. Their couples therapist bought into the communication myth, all the while their marital situation deteriorated. The couple learned to state their case using all the appropriate "I" sentences, and so forth, but neither said much about what was really troubling them. Therapeutic movement finally commenced when the therapist altered his strategy and began focusing on their fears and anxiety about aging.

Couples Therapy Is Antimarriage

Couples may be reluctant to seek therapeutic help because they believe the myth, rightly or wrongly, that "couples therapists are in the business of breaking up marriages." The coincidence of an increase in the number of divorces coupled with a dramatic increase in the number of couples therapists may have helped fuel this myth.

To the extent to which couples therapists have bought into the new cultural beliefs that undermine the institution of marriage, they may have unwittingly contributed to the myth's substantiation. Given this situation, it may be important to state one's position about marriage and divorce early on in a couple's therapy, namely, that such important decisions belong to the couple and that your role is dedicated to helping them help themselves and not splitting them apart.

Your honesty will be a great relief, even if it does not coincide with the couple's goal, and could ward off a client's defensive maneuvers. One couple, who came to therapy on the advice of their physician, was particularly guarded and defended. It was only after they were asked whether they thought therapy was going to "break them up" that they confessed their assumption that all couples therapists had that unstated goal. It was a goal that they definitely did not share. The therapist's reassurance that they, not the therapist, would make that kind of decision went a long way in establishing a working relationship. Divorce was never again mentioned during the course of therapy.

MYTHS THERAPISTS HAVE OF COUPLES

The history of clinical practice is full of examples of myths held by therapists about how couples should act. These myths sometimes become intertwined with the therapeutic process and interfere with the therapist's ability to guide couples out of their painful situation. Our clients may hold the same myths, however; if *we* base our work on myths rather than on reality, we may betray not only the couple but the trust the public has of us as helping professionals. Myths held by therapists have the potential of serving their personal needs rather than those of clients and thus contain the seeds of potential insidious harm. Also, by substituting new myths for old ones, we do not help couples struggling to find ways to accommodate to the reality of their lives.

Therapists' Personal Myths

Therapists, like everyone else, base their lifestyle choices on personal needs, circumstances, and current societal patterns. But some therapists treat their own choices as the only ones, not only for themselves but for others as well. When this happens, the therapist is likely to use clinical authority to validate his or her own choices and situation. Thus, the lonely, divorced therapist may use therapy to create other lonely, divorced people as if to say, "My lifestyle is superior. Since I'm divorced, other people should be divorced, especially *you* since *your* marriage looks a lot like mine used to." Or a depressed, unfulfilled therapist may convince depressed, unfulfilled clients that this is about as good as life gets.

The more therapists regard their personal myths as absolute *truth*, the more likely they may impose them on their clients. Additionally, when therapists' mode of working reduces the clients' choices, and the choices they do encourage resemble their own preferences and myths, couples may be subjected to considerable harm.

For example, a divorced marriage counselor acted out her personal negative myth about marriage by alienating troubled marital partners from one other. First, she altered the therapy contract from couples to individual work, choosing the more vulnerable, manipulatable partner, in this case the wife, for individual treatment with her while sending the other partner to a junior therapist whom she supervised.

Second, both therapists worked to dichotomize the couple into a victim and a victimizer. The husband was blamed for all of the marital difficulties by the wife's therapist, and the husband's therapist cast the wife as the sole cause of the discord. Having been instructed not to discuss their sessions at home, the couple had no opportunity to round out the one-sided picture promoted by the therapists. They consequently acted out their respective frustrations, becoming increasingly more irritated with one another.

Third, the senior therapist encouraged the wife's dependency on her, seeing her thrice weekly, and presented herself as rescuing the innocent wife from a failing marriage. Dependency was further reinforced by placing the wife in a twice-weekly group she led consisting of other "rescued, innocent, victimized marital partners." The wife became so psychologically dependent on this therapist that she was unable to join her husband when his job required a transfer to another state.

Fourth, in due time the therapist convinced the wife that divorce was the only viable solution to their long-standing marriage. And fifth, the divorce lawyer, who was handpicked by the therapist, was not in a position to give the client independent counsel since the former was part of the same network as the therapist.

By the use of undue influence, a tight net was spun around the unsuspecting clients one after another. The therapist's life choices were imposed through therapy on her clients, and her myth that divorce was good for people was put into action.

Other similar cases have occurred in which the husband was the more vulnerable partner. A senior executive who was retiring—a trying time in life—went into couple's therapy with the hope of improving his marriage and family life. The therapist, himself recently divorced, isolated the husband from his wife by placing him in individual and group therapy. In both treatment situations, the wife was identified as his enemy. By way of contrast, the therapist presented himself as his only true ally. Not unexpectedly, he became dependent on the therapist, seeing him almost daily. He was encouraged to file for divorce, which predictably ensued but which, contrary to the therapist's prediction, did not solve all his problems. His independent lawyer, noticing his ambivalence about the filing for divorce as well as his obvious depression, suggested that he see another therapist before proceeding. After an unbiased couples therapist worked with them jointly, the couple reunited.

Gender-Related Issues

Certain political, social, and quasi-philosophical positions held by therapists can infiltrate their attitudes toward men and women seen in couples therapy. Publicly debated positions on feminism, gender, sexism, sexual harassment, and other politicized topics cause some therapists to lose track of their ethical mission as therapists. They slip into propagating their own highly charged political biases via their interpretations of the behavior of men and women in couples therapy and project their own political agendas and biases onto unsuspecting clients.

The myths involving gender are too numerous to specify. We will focus on the central myth involving the basic evil nature of men (or women). The nebulousness of such concepts as sexism and its derivatives, when applied outside the sociopolitical arena, promote a mythic status and power to one or another gender.

In couples therapy, for example, a female therapist may encourage a woman client to act out the therapist's politicized agenda against her male partner. Conversely, a male therapist, because of his personal agenda, may encourage a male client to assert his masculinity and control his "uppity" female partner. Male bashing and female bashing result.

One hears mythical statements about the "testosterone-driven behavior of men," as if this provides a sufficient explanation of the behavior of a specific individual. One female therapist, who became convinced that men are dangerous for women's health, questioned a colleague about her long-term marriage. Men are by nature so oppressive, how could a therapist treat women if she remained under the dominance of a man? Having been swept up in the women's separatist movement, this therapist lost all objectivity.

In another instance, a female client described her husband's behavior after he attended a "warrior weekend," on the suggestion of their couple's therapist, a strategy meant to boost his self-esteem. This formerly rather mild-mannered husband strutted about the house insisting that his wife obey his orders for sex, food, and the like, on demand. At first she thought this was some fraternity-style prank and went along with the act. After a few more warrior weekends, she became concerned, feeling that the stability of her marriage was being threatened. The couple's original agenda in couples therapy, to sort out problems arising from creating a blended family, was subverted by the therapist into his politically driven goals.

Sexism, by which the domination of women by men is implied, has also been implicated as a major inhibitor of marital intimacy. For example, it has been argued recently that sexism contributes to a women's diminished self-esteem within a marital context, leading to a loss of intimacy. Unfortunately, no data exist to support these assertions, and no proof has been offered to suggest that a reduction of sexism would lead to increased intimacy. In our view, it is more likely that mutual respect, empathy, appreciation, admiration, and an understanding of the other's fears, achievements, and struggles are more likely to lead to intimacy than the insistence on removing all forms of politically defined inequality from marriage.

The Myth of Intimacy

There is a widespread belief that the goal of marriage is the achievement of *intimacy* in all its myriad forms: *emotional*, in which partners feel free and willing to bare their souls to one another; *psychological*, in which mates allow themselves to be totally vulnerable to their partners; and *sexual*, in which partners engage in a full range of sexual activities that provide mutual pleasure. A pretty tall order!

When therapists hold this myth and strive to convince all their clients that it is a necessary requirement for a successful relationship, they may fail to take into consideration that for many couples, this ideal is neither desirable nor attainable either at any one particular period of a couple's life or, possibly, over their lifetime. Indeed, for some couples, a relationship based on other more easily achievable goals, such as the raising of a family, and the comforts derived from belonging, safety, and security may be more desirable. In fact, intimacy, like the idea of romantic love, is neither universal nor required in many cultures.

How then should therapists respond when intimacy is restrained in a couple? Should we impose this ideal on the couple? Should we suggest to the couple that their relationship is deficient? Should we suggest that they find other partners with whom intimacy might be developed? If therapists make intimacy a necessary or singular goal for a relationship, they may overtly or covertly undermine the relationship. If, on the other hand, we consider the ideals of romantic love or intimacy as myths and view marriage from a broader perspective, other possibilities open up. Marriage can fulfill any one of a number of meaningful objectives other than intimacy and, by so doing, satisfy the couple's need for togetherness or partnership.

In a 1994 article in *The New Yorker*, entitled "The Home Front," Doris Kearns Goodwin described a famous marriage that was not based on intimacy, that of President Franklin D. and Eleanor Roosevelt. Their relationship was based on trust, respect, and a shared belief in the purpose of their lives: to alleviate the suffering of their fellow Americans. Emotional, psychological, and probably sexual intimacy were reserved for others outside of the marital bond. Franklin had Missy, his private secretary to whom he turned for his personal needs. In return, Eleanor had her independent life, with her friends occupying the role of affectionate partners. Was their marriage a failure? Not by any stretch of the imagination. They were partners, sharing a love and respect for one another that allowed them to make the necessary accommodations to their very divergent personality requirements.

Strong marriages need not be based on intimacy. Rather, they are based on shared beliefs and goals that require combined efforts; each partner has a role and function to play, the fulfillment of which ultimately strengthens the other partner.

The Myths About Conflict and Compatibility

Conflict is inherent in all human relationships since the needs, wants, and wishes of the participating parties will inevitably be discordant at times. Conflict and its resolution are particularly crucial problems among emotionally close and psychologically interdependent units.

In recognition that many couples flounder on the shoals of conflict, the myth that couples should strive for a marriage devoid of all conflict has arisen among couples therapists. Like the myth of intimacy, that of a conflict-free marriage may also be held by our clients. Nevertheless, when we hold and perpetuate this myth and impose it in an absolutist manner on our clients, we inevitably inhibit our efforts as couples therapists.

The myth of the conflict-free marriage often contains a subsidiary myth—that all conflicts should be resolved in an understanding, cooperative, rational, and emotionally neutral climate. While this form of conflict resolution may have become the ideal standard in Western thinking, it is by no means the only form of conflict resolution or the most desirable form for many couples.

Recent work by John Gottman suggests that satisfying marriages depend less on the emotional climate around conflicts and
their resolution than on the partners' ability to maintain an overall positive affective balance that minimizes such destructive
behaviors as criticism, defensiveness, contempt, and stonewalling
during angry exchanges. Even among partners with a volatile,
highly emotionally charged style of dealing with conflicts, their
marriage was rated as satisfying so long as they maintained a relatively positive balance of affective interactions. Likewise, couples who tend to avoid conflict or are sometimes said to be "in
denial" regarding their conflicts may also have highly satisfying
marriages.

Members of a troubled couple frequently have opposing styles
of conflict resolution. The resulting friction may prompt them
to dread all conflicts and yearn for the myth of a conflict-free
marriage. For example, a husband who had acquired the art of
verbal bantering and fencing from his highly articulate family
married a woman who was fearful of all types of confrontation.
She experienced him as aggressive, abusive, and demanding,
while he was dismayed by her accusations and avoidance. In
therapy they learned to accommodate by correctly identifying
the meaning of each other's styles and needs. As the more verbally facile partner, the husband took the initiative in finding a
mutually acceptable midpoint by disagreeing in a smoothing and
soothing tone as he went along. At no time was it suggested to
the couple that they could or should strive for a marriage devoid
of conflict.

MYTHS THERAPISTS HAVE
ABOUT COUPLES THERAPY

Theories, like statistical averages, are general statements or vague
maps of reality that often have little or no relevance to the specific individual(s) being treated. A theory is, at best, an intelligent
guess for explaining why, how, and what is actually occurring in

reality. As mental constructs, their value is mainly heuristic, as generators of hypotheses that guide our thinking about our clients and how best to help them.

Alan Jacobs has written much on the dangers inherent in the uncritical acceptance of theory or the elevation of theory into an absolute truth or ideology that transforms it into a myth—a myth with perils since all theories have fallacies. For example, in the 1930s, adherents of psychological behaviorism convinced pediatricians and parents that infants should be fed on a strict four-hour schedule, despite the howls and needs of individual babies. Today, that theory has been discredited, and children are fed on demand.

In this section we will discuss several elements of some current theories of couples therapy that are assuming mythic status. These beliefs have their origin in deconstructionistic thinking as applied to the psychotherapeutic situation. Most pernicious are the myths that individual normative standards are irrelevant and that clinicians have no special knowledge and authority.

Normative Standards

With respect to normative standards, Becvar and Becvar, espousing ecosystemic theory, a derivative of systems theory, recently stated, "Our focus shifted from pathology with the individual to the pathology of the system of which the individual is a part. Dysfunctional behavior in an individual came to be seen as *normal*, or *logical*, in the context of the family" (italics added).

Note how normal and logical are equated. This is erroneous, in our view, because logic refers to basic *principles of reasoning* applicable to any field of knowledge, whereas normality refers to a *standard* by which behavior is measured. They are distinctly different concepts. It may be logical for a patient to be clinically depressed, given her particular circumstances, but that doesn't make depression normal.

By subtly shifting the meaning of behavioral standards as being an integral part of the system, it is implied that individual normative standards are essentially irrelevant. From this base it follows that the clinical assessment of and the use of psycho-metric diagnostic tools to shed light on individual pathology are no longer necessary or no longer pertinent to our understand-ing of couples and families. It is not that the notion of pathol-ogy is absent in ecosystemic thinking; it is more that the therapeutic focus of pathology has been shifted from the indi-vidual to the system, particularly the much overworked "dys-functional family." Since the definition of the dysfunctional family is itself a vague concept, subjective, untested criteria of pathology are increasingly serving as substitutes for the more objective ones provided by clinical assessment and other diag-nostic tools. Assessment of individual abilities and personality may have become suspect and seen as potentially oppressive as a result of a misapplication and misunderstanding of the proper use of assessment methodologies.

Failing to employ normative standards may obscure the ther-apist's observation and identification of individual pathology when working within a couple or family. Serious consequences may follow. If, for example, a paranoid father is driving his wife and children to distraction, getting that father into individual treatment or identifying his effect on the family and helping oth-ers cope with his paranoia may be more efficacious then label-ing the family or couple as dysfunctional and insisting on only treating the unit as a whole.

Who Is in Charge?

By defining the therapist as having no special knowledge and therefore no legitimate source for special authority and position, some current theories have significantly compromised the ther-apist's unique role. The demotion of the therapist as expert is a fallout of the current political and philosophical zeitgeist that questions authority and often equates authority with authoritar-ianism and oppression.

Although many clients regard us as persons with authority by dint of our special knowledge, therapists who adopt this myth resist being so regarded. Some current theorists suggest that the only function of the therapist is to work together with the client to "co-evolve an alternative story" or script "that provides solutions that the client's original story did not." At best, such therapists function as facilitators, which, for a fairly well-functioning couple, may be minimally acceptable. With troubled couples, however, this stance and the therapy flowing from it may becomes chaotic, akin to a family in which the parents refuse to assume their leadership roles.

For example, a therapist, committed ideologically to a non-authority role, allowed couples therapy to disintegrate into weekly harangues in which the husband insisted that his wife was responsible for all his woes. Because he did not accept the notion of individual pathology, the therapist failed to notice that the husband had a cyclothymic personality and came into the sessions revved up and "ready to go." The therapist, by not taking charge and controlling the interactions in his office, allowed this couple to repeat their harmful and hurtful behavior uninterrupted. Because they viewed the therapist as an authority, the couple did not question his methods, until the wife, on the urging of a friend, decided to terminate treatment.

Accepting the mantle of authority defines us as the more knowing in the therapeutic situation, willing to direct the course of treatment. In one case, a couple came into therapy because they had trouble establishing a good working relationship, even though they liked each other. For one, the husband was not house-trained. He lived as if he still were a bachelor, leaving a messy trail behind him, forgetting to greet his wife appropriately when entering or leaving home, and so on.

The therapist decided to teach the husband about marriage and cooperation and how to be a good housemate. This was psychoeducational therapy. The wife was included intermittently in sessions in order to obtain her cooperation and to teach her to stop bugging him while he practiced new behaviors.

Whenever a theoretical formulation is elevated to an ideology and is adhered to unquestioningly by therapists in pursuit of the latest fad or by their need for certainty, our clients are in danger of being ill served. The myths discussed earlier are by no means the only ones abounding in current clinical practice. For example, some therapists may become so transfixed on intrapsychic functions that they may fail to note the impact of the individual on others. In one instance a young woman who was about to marry was understandably anxious about the correctness of her momentous decision. She had been in individual therapy for quite some time in which her behavior was viewed in isolation from her familial surround. This approach had unfortunate repercussions. Her father tended to respond to anxiety exhibited by one family member with corresponding anxiety. The effect was a rapid escalation of anxiety, which led to intolerable levels for everyone. In order to reduce the family's anxiety, the young lady thought that she should call off the wedding. She could no longer differentiate between *her* doubts and *their* anxiety. In turn, they told her that if she wanted to call off the wedding, they would support her. The message she heard was that indeed she was making a mistake and ought not to marry this most eligible man. In this case, slavishly adhering to intrapsychic phenomena failed to take into account the echoing effect of anxiety within a close-knit group.

KEEPING MYTHS OUT OF COUPLES THERAPY

Therapists can protect themselves from the nontherapeutic aspects of myths and prejudices by using two time-honored methods: diagnostic evaluation and consultation with experienced colleagues.

Evaluation has predictive features that are testable. Consultation with an appropriate colleague offers perspective and a confirmation or disconfirmation of the direction we are taking. It is a check on our blind spots. Both procedures introduce some degree of objectivity into our work and provide the distance and perspective we need to protect us and our clients from myths.

For example, one of us saw a woman in her fifties who was uncertain whether to remain with or divorce her second husband. She married him several years ago in the depths of loneliness soon after her first husband died. To help her answer her own question of whether this marriage could or should go forward, the therapist agreed to see both of them together.

It soon was apparent that the husband was strongly parasitic and planning to spend his wife's inheritance on his personal projects, not on mutual ones. Clinical evaluation of the husband revealed a long history of troubled personal and professional relationships. He constantly complained that others cheated him, yet his tales revealed that he took advantage of others. The wife knew something was wrong, but her fear of loneliness was blinding her to the facts. It was not the therapist's role to tell her to get a divorce but rather to help her make that decision on her own.

The purpose of the couple's therapy was to (1) bring his agenda out in the open, so that she could directly observe it, and (2) test out whether he was willing or able to alter his agenda.

The therapist feared that she was prejudiced against the husband and favoring the wife, and so she consulted with an experienced male therapist. After reviewing the case, he graphically summarized his overview: "He is pecking away at the dead husband's liver."

The therapist continued to work with the couple, asking pertinent questions, exploring the man's inconsistencies, and cutting through his many manipulative tactics. This calm exposure of the man's covert agenda through his own words and deeds allowed the wife to become aware that indeed, in her words, she had made a "terrible mistake" that was not only making her sick but also placing her children in jeopardy. The husband, on his own, terminated couples therapy. Shortly thereafter, the wife decided to end the marriage and file for divorce. As a further check (on the therapist's possible biases), the latter encouraged her to talk to her lawyers, friends, and family and get their perspectives. All were jubilant that she was strong enough to end what they, independently, felt had been a tragic situation.

❧

We are all vulnerable to the adoption of mythic beliefs of various kinds. They are commonplace in our cultural milieu but are especially prevalent during times of rapid cultural change. Such times seem to proliferate cultural gurus who are particularly adept in packaging mythic ideas and passing them off as the latest revelation of the *Truth*.

Myths exert a powerful effect and have a seductive appeal because they purport to provide simple answers to complex questions. Once incorporated into our thinking or attitudes, myths are perpetuated by our propensity to attend selectively to reinforcing messages.

In this chapter, we have attempted to elucidate some rather commonplace myths that we and our clients are likely to hold. In many instances, mythic beliefs may be perfectly harmless. But when they impede our clients' ability to resolve their relational conflicts or our ability to assist them in their struggles, then myths become truly dangerous.

Critical thinking—relying on substantive, factually derived proof and avoiding so-called "self-evident face validity"—can go a long way in helping us detect when and how we are being influenced by myths.

NOTES

P. 35, *A* myth *is a popular fable: Webster's unabridged dictionary.* (1979). New York: Simon & Schuster.

P. 36, *schizophrenogenic mothers:* Bateson, G., Jackson, D. D., Haley, J., & Weakland, J. (1956). Towards a theory of schizophrenia. *Behavioral Science, 1,* 251–264.

P. 36, *"let it all hang out":* Perls, F. S. (1969). *Gestalt therapy verbatim.* Lafayette, CA: Science and Behavior Books.

P. 36, *"therapeutic misadventures":* McHugh, P. (1992). Psychiatric misadventures. *The American Scholar, 61,* 497–510.

P. 47, *Therapists . . . use clinical authority:* Singer, M. T. (in press). Therapy, thought reform, and cults. *Transactional Analysis Journal, 26*(1); Singer, M. T. (1995). *Cults in our midst.* San Francisco: Jossey-Bass.

P. 49, *The myths involving gender are too numerous to specify:* Marecek, J. (1995). Gender, politics, and psychology's way of knowing. *American Psychologist, 50*(3), 162–163; Eagly, A. H. (1995). The science and politics of comparing women and men. *American Psychologist, 50*(3), 145–158.

P. 50, *sexism contributes . . . leading to a loss of intimacy:* Schnieder, P., & Schnieder, H. (1991). Mutuality in couples therapy: Addressing the effects of sexism in the marital relationship. *American Journal of Family Therapy, 19,* 119–128.

P. 51, *intimacy . . . is neither universal nor required in many cultures:* Dion, K. K., & Dion, K. L. (1993). Individualistic and collectivistic perspectives on gender and the cultural context of love and intimacy. *Journal of Social Issues, 49*(3), 53–69.

P. 51, *famous marriage . . . Eleanor Roosevelt:* Goodwin, D. K., (1994, August 15). The home front. *The New Yorker,* pp. 38–61.

P. 53, *conflicts and their resolution . . . angry exchanges:* Gottman, J. (1994). *Why marriages succeed or fail.* New York: Simon & Schuster.

P. 54, *uncritical acceptance of theory . . . all theories have fallacies:* Jacobs, A. (1994). Theory as ideology: Reparenting and thought reform. *Transactional Analysis Journal, 24,* 39–56.

P. 54, *origin in deconstructionistic thinking . . . psychotherapeutic situation:* Kuhlman, T. L. (1995). Identity politics and the tower of Babel. *American Psychologist, 50*(1), 48–49.

P. 54, *normative standards . . . context of the family:* Becvar, R. J., & Becvar, D. S. (1994). The ecosystemic story: A story about stories. *Journal of Mental Health Counseling, 16,* 22–32.

P. 55, *pathology is absent . . . diagnostic tools:* Hinkle, J. S. (1994). Ecosystems and mental health counseling: Reactions to Becvar and Becvar. *Journal of Mental Health Counseling, 16,* 33–36.

P. 55, *Assessment of individual abilities . . . as potentially oppressive:* Brown, D. C. (1994). Subgroup norming: Legitimate testing practice or reverse discrimination? *American Psychologist, 49,* 927–928.

3

INTERRACIAL, INTERETHNIC, AND INTERFAITH RELATIONSHIPS

Joel Crohn

A quiet revolution is sweeping the world as millions defy ancient taboos to form intimate relationships with partners from other ethnic, religious, and racial backgrounds. Nowhere has this social transformation been more dramatic than in American society. In the United States, many unions that were once nearly unthinkable have today become commonplace. The increasing frequency of intermarriage, though, has not erased the power of the past. The influence of different ethnic identities, interpersonal norms, and religious beliefs has powerful effects on relationship dynamics, even in the most cosmopolitan and secular of relationships. In order for therapists to successfully treat the ever-increasing number of mixed matches seeking counseling, they must develop the ability to understand the impact of cultural as well as psychological history in the creation of relationship conflict.

Intermarriage statistics suggest the magnitude and rapidity of these social changes that have resulted in tremendous familial,

Note: Parts of this chapter were adapted with permission from Crohn, J. (1995), *Mixed Matches: How to Create Successful Interracial, Interethnic, and Interfaith Relationships.* New York: Fawcett/Columbine. Copyright © 1995 by Joel Crohn, Ph.D. Adapted and reprinted by permission of Fawcett Books, published by Ballantine Books, a division of Random House, Inc., and the author.

cultural, and communal transformations and dislocations. As both an ethnic and a religious group, Jews were the white ethnics least likely to intermarry. As recently as 1960, less than 10 percent of Jews married out of the faith. Today, over 52 percent of weddings involving Jews are intermarriages. Other kinds of religious intermarriages are also increasingly common, and thirty-three million Americans live in interfaith households.

There are now more than a million Hispanic/non-Hispanic marriages in the United States, more than double the number in 1970. Intermarriage was very rare among Japanese Americans before World War II; only about 3 percent intermarried. But in a remarkable historical turnabout, since World War II the Japanese-American intermarriage rate has reached 65 percent. While the legacy of slavery and racism makes black/white marriage the most stigmatized, controversial, and least frequent kind of mixed match, census numbers demonstrate that even among blacks and whites, significant changes are occurring. The number of black/white married couples has tripled in two decades from 65,000 in 1970 to 231,000 in 1991, and over that same period of time the number of births to black/white couples quintupled.

These changing marital choices result from greater tolerance and expanded opportunities for people from different backgrounds to meet each other in schools and in the workplace. The breakdown of rigid intergroup boundaries results from changes that were set into motion by the Industrial Revolution and that affect all families. Ties to kin and culture were weakened and sometimes severed as families were transformed into commodities, like so many interchangeable parts of commerce, that could be quickly redistributed from place to place according to the laws of supply and demand. The flexible, autonomous, and isolated postmodern nuclear family represents a truly radical break with the past.

Throughout time family life had always been *supported* and *regulated* by kin, community, and religious faith. These traditional bulwarks created the context in which family life was lived, and without them the nuclear family has proven to be a rather unstable institution. The popularity of couples and family therapy has exploded as the traditional supports of the family have eroded.

In spite of the individualism of American society, humans remain social animals. When therapists fail to take into account the potential importance of community in supporting the family, they can contribute to the ills they seek to cure. Especially in working with cross-cultural couples, in which ties to tradition may be in conflict, it is crucial to be aware of each partner's relationship to a broader social, cultural, and religious context.

DEALING WITH CROSS-CULTURAL ISSUES

While some clients quickly identify their different backgrounds as contributing to their problems, others will avoid any mention of ethnic, religious, or racial contrasts unless the therapist focuses on the issues. In reality, there is no way for the therapist actually to know the importance of the cultural component in a particular couple's conflict without exploring their cultural histories. In an era of managed care, though, many therapists are uncomfortable focusing on issues other than the clients' presenting problems. Delving into cultural histories may seem like an unnecessary and extravagant expansion of the scope of a therapy.

One brief example, though, can illustrate how dealing with cultural history can be used to clarify and expedite the therapy process. One patient, the son of Holocaust survivors, reported that in his previous therapy the therapist had neglected even to question him about the impact on him of his parents' experiences during the war. The therapist knew that the patient was Jewish, that his parents had lived in Europe during World War II, and that he was terribly ambivalent about his relationship with his fiancée, who was not Jewish. But since the patient had told the therapist that he was not religious, both he and the therapist agreed that it was not really an interfaith relationship and that they should focus on "interpersonal" issues.

Two years later, he was still engaged, but the wedding had been postponed several times. When he reentered therapy and I asked him whether he thought there might be a connection between his parents' experience in the Holocaust and his never-ending and never-consummated engagement, a torrent of guilt and anger poured out. He felt that marrying a non-Jew would "kill" his parents who had suffered so much, but he was also enraged with the ways they had used their suffering to control him. Only after revealing these feelings was he able to begin a process of couples therapy with his fiancée and to deal openly with these painful issues in which personal and group history intersect.

Americans' ignorance of history and discomfort and anxiety around cultural, religious, and racial issues often make it very difficult for intermarried couples—and their therapists—to acknowledge and discuss how they are affected by the different backgrounds they bring to their relationships. There are no simple methods to separate them out, but when therapists are attuned to the possible ways that group differences affect couples, it is much easier to integrate a useful cultural perspective into the therapeutic process.

Cultural Countertransference

A form of "cultural countertransference" often impedes therapists' work with cross-cultural couples. As today's secular priests, psychotherapists are often blind to how their own attitudes about race, religion, and culture affect their treatment of others. Each religion throughout history has renounced the prior religion out of which it evolved. The strong links between *psychotherapy*, literally "the care of the soul," and religion are precisely why therapists often have such difficulty with religious and cultural issues in psychotherapy.

The ideology of psychotherapy has traditionally encouraged a pan-cultural thinking. We are taught to view the world in a "value-free" manner. At least until recently, psychotherapy con-

sidered itself a meta-framework that could understand the ultimate human concerns. Theorists such as Jung looked for man-
ifestations of the same drives and conflicts in all cultures.

But archetypal thinking can be dangerous when applied too
freely in trying to understand the dynamics of a cross-cultural
relationship. Real and important differences divide cultures, and
looking for a common denominator can obscure cultural contrasts that need to be acknowledged. Also, the impossibility of
the therapist's neutrality can lead to therapist confusion and the
distortion of information. Bending over backward to act like "all
people are the same" is ultimately as disrespectful as assuming
that every stereotype about a cultural, racial, or religious group
is true.

It's important to remember the obvious: none of us springs
from a culture-neutral family or social environment. And like
most people, we tend to take our own cultural frames of reference for granted and to use them to assess what is normal and
what is not. In order to work effectively with cultural differences
in couples therapy, therapists themselves must first work to
become more aware of their own relationships with their own
cultural and religious heritages. Therapists must also honestly
face their own preconceptions and biases about members of the
cultures they treat. Pretending to be bias-free and to see all people as essentially the same can give denied prejudices and stereo-
typed views of other groups a perverse power.

Also, we need to become aware of the cultural codes we ourselves are most comfortable with. Depending on the interpersonal norms of their own cultural backgrounds, two therapists
may reach starkly different conclusions about the nature of a particular couple's conflict. In a case conference about an Irish-
Italian couple who were fighting over how often to visit their
families, one therapist, who was from a New England, white
Protestant background, focused on what she thought was the
Italian woman's excessive need to remain attached to her family.
She cited the fact that the woman called her parents long-
distance every week as evidence of excessive "enmeshment." Her

colleague, who had immigrated to the United States from northern India when she was nineteen, focused on the Irish-American husband's "overly disengaged" family style as the center of the problem. She saw the husband as a cold person who constantly prevented his wife from expressing what she thought was a very normal attachment to her family.

The therapists' own life experiences created the cultural lenses through which they viewed the case. The WASP therapist grew up in a cultural milieu that stressed autonomy and individuality. She herself thought that visiting her own family three times a year was about right. Unaware of her own "cultural lenses," she was certain that the Italian woman's behavior resulted from unhealthy dependence and a "failure to adequately differentiate."

The Indian therapist lived with her husband in a house next to her own parents. Her young children were cared for daily by their grandparents, just as the therapist herself had been cared for by her grandparents when she was raised in India. Interdependence and daily contact with her parents seemed a natural part of life. But rather than seeing herself "enmeshed" with her parents, she considered herself quite liberated in relationship to Indian culture and her Indian family. She had chosen her husband and her career over her parents' objections and had decided on her own where to go to college.

The cultural assumptions about family cohesion and of the rights and obligations of Indian and WASP cultures are radically different, yet both therapists spoke about the family cohesion (or lack of it) of the patients they discussed as if the words *enmeshment* and *disengagement* were objective measures of family structure referenced against national norms that applied equally to all ethnic groups. Clearly they aren't, and without acknowledging how different their own cultural frames of reference were, they themselves had become a kind of conflicted mixed match, each mystified and annoyed by the other's failure to see the obvious.

To avoid the pitfalls of cultural countertransference, therapists must integrate the role of psychotherapist with that of a participant/observer anthropologist. The therapist's basic tasks in working with intermarried couples are no different than in all couples therapy. Partners in conflict have to be helped to acknowledge their differences, make choices, and face necessary losses in life before they can really have healthy relationships. But for mixed matches, the content of the struggles include cultural, religious, and identity issues as well as the usual male/female struggles. The therapist needs to be able to help partners in an intercultural relationship understand the different meanings and intensities of their cultural pasts and to deal with contrasts in their cultural codes.

None of us can be an expert on every culture, nor does one need to be in order to work successfully with partners from different cultural backgrounds. When therapists can approach partners from cultures they are unfamiliar with like a good anthropologist, curiosity and respect can be their most important tools. While exhibiting some knowledge of an individual's culture can be reassuring to a minority group member or immigrant who feels like an outsider, it is sometimes useful to reveal less about a culture than one actually knows.

One of the fathers of family therapy, Salvador Minuchin, an Argentinean, made a practice of not understanding people. Even though he has an excellent command of English (he has written a number of lucid books in English), he still speaks with an accent. In a demonstration interview he conducted with an American family, he explained to the family that he had difficulty understanding some "big English words" they were using and asked them to speak more slowly and use simpler words. He used this "dumb" ploy to encourage the family members to be clearer in their communications. If they assumed that he had trouble understanding them, they might spell out their feelings and thoughts more clearly. Similarly, the therapist working with cross-cultural couples can elicit more information by not overplaying or exaggerating his or her knowledge of a patient's culture.

My goal in this chapter is to help therapists incorporate an awareness of cultural and social issues into their existing modes of practice. There is no one way to work with mixed matches.

They are affected not only by their cultural differences but by the same issues as all other couples: the stress of modern life, failures in communication, and the effects of characterological problems as they are acted out in intimate relationships. So rather than creating a new form of therapy specifically designed for cross-cultural couples, this chapter is written to help therapists develop a greater sensitivity to the impact of the differences mixed matches bring to their relationships and integrate a cultural perspective into their current therapeutic style.

CONFLICTS RESULTING FROM DIFFERENT CULTURAL CODES

Just as children cannot identify the complex rules of grammar and syntax that they learn and use successfully long before they study them in school, people usually cannot describe clearly the rules of their culture. But complex and largely unconscious cultural codes permeate every aspect of belief and behavior. Primal in their power, they are programmed from birth by a mother's touch, the smells and sounds of the home, and the entire social world in which a person is raised. They have a profound influence on attitudes about money and work, what is considered "on time" or "late," eating habits, child rearing and discipline, flirting and sex, small talk and big talk, why and how anger is expressed, or how people apologize.

The norms of a culture are internalized at an early age and taken for granted. Therefore, when one partner gets angry with the other because of a behavior that violates cultural norms, the angry partner's first assumption is that the mate as an *individual* is behaving in an offensive manner, and not that the two of them are playing the game of intimacy using different cultural rulebooks.

One of the most important tasks for therapists working with mixed matches is to help them become more aware of invisible differences in the cultural codes they bring to their relationship.

Even if a clinician is not very familiar with a particular culture, the therapist's inquiry can be guided by focusing on the following six dimensions that are crucial in understanding the differences between cultures:

- Time
- The nature of the universe
- Cohesiveness of the family
- Emotional expressiveness
- Interpersonal relationships
- Gender roles

Every culture has a mix of attitudes about each of these dimensions with a most valued, secondary, and least valued form. The specific priorities a culture assigns to each of these dimensions influences the ways its members interpret all of the inevitable ambiguity of the human condition. In any given setting, these cultural value preferences serve as a personal compass that points people toward their definition of correct behavior, shaping inner experience as well as outer behavior. The sets of cultural rules that partners in mixed matches bring to their relationships may be comfortably similar in one or more of these dimensions and disturbingly different in others.

Time

Future: Always plan ahead for tomorrow.

Present: The enjoyment of today is most important.

Past: Remember and honor family and cultural history.

While no culture is purely present, past, or future oriented, each varies in the importance that they place on each of these temporal frames of reference. Agrarian cultures dependent on the vagaries of the weather tend to be present oriented. In many industrialized societies, the future is often the reference point.

But many Asian societies, even those that have industrialized, are careful to honor ancestors even while planning for the future. These different values about time may mean that partners in a mixed match have very different definitions of what constitutes being late, how important achievement and production are, and even when to eat or sleep.

The Nature of the Universe

Good: Life and people inherently good. There is a force that makes things turn out for the best.

Indifferent: Life is not inherently good or evil. We are responsible to try and make it good.

Evil: You must never put your guard down. Human life is difficult, and people can't be trusted to be good.

Does life have some intrinsic orderliness? Or do we live in a random and ultimately meaningless universe out of which we have to create any pleasure, satisfaction, or meaning? Are people naturally evil or good? Are children amoral creatures who have to be taught to distinguish between right and wrong?

The ways that people create answers to these questions are shaped not only by their religious heritages but by the history of their cultural group. Even the worldview of assimilated and secular grandchildren of immigrants is deeply affected by the historical experience of their ancestors. The history of slavery for African Americans, the Holocaust for Jews, the struggles for survival of Southeast Asian refugees, the Civil War for Southerners, Hiroshima for the Japanese, and the genocide of the Armenians early in the twentieth century are existential shocks that reverberate through the generations.

Cohesiveness of the Family

Enmeshed: To be separate from family is to be missing an essential part of yourself.

Mixed: The needs of the family and of the individual need to be balanced.

Disengaged: The individual and his or her needs are more important than those of the family.

The Northern European and white American Protestant culture that has traditionally been at the center of what until now has been known as "American culture" places a very high value on individualism and tends to produce more disengaged family structures. The concept of the separate, bounded, autonomous self that many Americans take for granted would be considered bizarre, if not downright evil, in many other more collective societies. In agrarian and less industrialized cultures where it is clear to everyone that the fate of the individual and the fate of the group are inseparable, the enmeshed family structure is the norm.

A culture's values regarding family connections, interdependence, and loyalty shape the nature of parents' and children's relationships, the frequency of interaction between members of the nuclear family as well as the extended family, and the process of separation and individuation that children go through as they develop.

Emotional Expressiveness

High Intensity: Feelings are meant to be expressed.

Mixed: It's only OK to show how you feel in particular situations.

High Formality: Emotional self-control is most important.

Cultures that stress a high level of emotional intensity are those that value emotional engagement more than calmness and order. High formality cultures, on the other hand, are more rule bound and structured, especially when it comes to social interaction. While we may associate high intensity with tight, enmeshed families, emotional expressiveness and family cohesiveness are independent characteristics. Both Latin and Japanese cultures tend to foster more enmeshed style family structures. Both value keeping child and parent tightly emotionally bound.

But the rules governing the expression of emotion in the two cultures are vastly different.

Interpersonal Relations

Hierarchical: Respecting authority and tradition is most important.

Cooperative: The needs of the group are more important than the needs of any one person.

Individualistic: Each person is ultimately responsible for self.

People in hierarchical societies like Japan tend to use status, age, power, or caste as the primary organizers of social life. In individualistic societies, like the United States, individual rights are protected, and the responsibility for success and failure falls on the individual. The fluidity of American society requires constant interaction with new people. Minimizing differences in authority and creating a quick sense of familiarity with strangers are essential in lubricating the social gears of a culture where the only constant is change.

Collective cultures put the interests and welfare of the group before the importance of authority or the rights of the individual. Collective cultures are typically agriculturally based societies or ethnic groups who are minorities in a hostile environment. For these people, the survival of the group is dependent on close cooperation.

Gender Roles

Overlapping: Men and women are equal. Each person should be able to be what he or she wishes irrespective of gender.

Partial Overlap: There should be some overlap in the roles of men and women, but it's also important to acknowledge differences between the sexes.

Differentiated: The world of men and of women are totally different. It is important to keep them separate.

Of all the differences that affect mixed matches, perhaps none has a greater effect on relationships than the cultural rules that define men's and women's roles. While Western European nations and the United States are far from gender-neutral societies, they tolerate and even legislate far more overlapping in the public and personal realms of life than most cultures. But the total separation of men and women's worlds that seems increasingly alien to Westerners is more the norm than the exception in cultures throughout the rest of the world. In many societies, the roles of men and women are clearly and often rigidly differentiated.

HELPING COUPLES RESOLVE CULTURAL CONFLICT

Jorge and Cindy's relationship clearly illustrates the effect that cultural differences can have on a relationship, even years after people leave the direct influence of their birth cultures. Jorge and Cindy lived in Tucson, Arizona, and were both twenty-eight years old when they met. Jorge was born and raised in an upper-middle-class family in Monterey, Mexico. When he was eighteen, he moved to Los Angeles to live with his aunt so that he could study structural engineering at UCLA. Cindy, who worked as an architect, had been raised by her middle-class Irish/WASP family in Los Angeles.

A year after they met, they moved in together and a short time later got engaged. On the way to mail the invitations for their wedding, they got into a big fight. Cindy was very upset about how seductively Jorge had behaved with another woman at a party the previous night. Jorge was hurt by Cindy's lack of trust, because he knew that he had been simply behaving in a friendly but nonsexual manner. He became very angry, grabbed the box of invitations, threw them in the back of his car, and said that it was clear that they weren't ready to get married. Since they were in love, they had incorrectly assumed that they understood the meaning of each other's behavior. They didn't.

Psychiatrist Carlos Sluzki has observed in "The Latin Lover Revisited" that all cultures have rules that define the meaning of placing one's body at close, intermediate, or distant positions relative to another person. These rules are crucial in the ways we define and negotiate our relationships. We use our bodies like the subtitles in a foreign movie. They tell us what's really going on.

We reserve the distant zone to communicate respect *or* dislike, the intermediate zone to convey an emotionally neutral social interaction, and the close zone to broadcast threat *or* sexual interest. In almost all cultures, standing in the close zone and smiling at someone of the opposite sex has connotations of intimacy or sexuality.

The definition of these zones is programmed into us by our experiences and observations of social interaction beginning in infancy. How and when our parents touch us; watching our family interact with kin, friends, and strangers; the responses of schoolmates to our awkward experiments in touch—all provide us with an intuitive and visceral sense of the appropriate use of our bodies. No one ever has to spell it out, but we all end up knowing the exact definition of each of the zones within a centimeter or two. But, as Sluzki points out, the distances are "relative rather than absolute." Latin American zones happen to specify shorter distances than Anglo-American zones. In each of the three zones, Latin Americans tend to position themselves closer to those they interact with than Anglo Americans do. These differences create the potential for misinterpretations; distances the Latin defines as neutral, the Anglo may interpret as threatening or sexual.

Social scientists have long observed that a combination of nonverbal and subverbal forms of communication—body language, silences, interruptions, and the tone, intensity, and tempo of our words—convey as much information as the actual content of what we say. Words themselves are like the notes of a musical score written down on paper. They are brought alive only by how they are performed. The way we use and interpret nonverbal cues determines the emotional significance we give to our own words and to those of others. And every aspect of how we use and interpret words is governed by our cultural conditioning.

These rules are very resistant to change, because they are mostly unconscious and learned early in life. Neither their love for one another nor one partner's successful adaptation to another culture can completely erase differences in cultural conditioning.

When Jorge and Cindy began counseling to deal with the emotional turmoil that had been set off by their fight, they were able to begin to talk about their differences for the first time. To facilitate the process, I had them each fill out two identical charts (see Table 3.1) and label one "My Family" and the other "My Partner's Family." I had them use each sheet to write down some adjectives or a sentence or two that described their feelings and perceptions about their own family and their partner's family in relation to each of these dimensions.

The goal of this exercise is to help clients better understand the contradictory feelings they have about the interpersonal norms of their own culture as well as their partner's. The exercise also reveals attitudes about cultural, religious, and racial identity. Ambivalence is central to the human condition, and helping clients acknowledge their mixed feelings about their own backgrounds, as well as their partner's, makes it much easier for them to depolarize their conflict. Tables 3.2 and 3.3 are Jorge's and Cindy's charts describing their own families of origin.

Completing this exercise helped Cindy and Jorge place their current crisis into a broader perspective. It provided each of them with important information about the roots of both their attraction as well as some of their misunderstandings in their relationship. By helping them talk about the very different emotional climates of each of their families and cultures of origin, I was able to remind them that the behaviors that now seemed so problematic were part of what attracted them in the first place. This helped them to de-escalate their conflict as they began to explore the connections between past passion and current conflict.

Table 3.1
My Family and My Partner's Family

	Positives	*Negatives*
Sex roles		
Family involvement		
Emotional expression		
Cultural identity		
Religion		

Sex roles: The division of roles of men and women in your (your partner's) family regarding work, power, money, housework, and so forth

Family involvement: Sense of concern, mutual involvement, and support in your (your partner's) family

Emotional expression: The intensity and nature of emotional expression in your (your partner's) family

Cultural identity: The manner and intensity with which your (your partner's) family expresses its cultural identity

Religion: The way your (your partner's) family expresses its religious beliefs

When they met, Cindy was attracted to Jorge's expressiveness. She felt he was much warmer and more emotionally expressive than the men in her family and felt drawn to him because of this difference. Jorge was attracted to what he thought was Cindy's self-control. As he had become Americanized, he had begun to see his Mexican-American family as too emotionally intense and demanding. In a sense, part of the dynamics in their relationship was a search for synthesis. But contained within this search was a paradox that is part of many cross-cultural relationship: they were each attracted to the very traits their partner was so ambivalent about themselves. Cindy

Table 3.2
My Mexican-American Family

	Positives	*Negatives*
Sex roles	No ambiguity. Women knew their roles and men knew theirs.	Rigid expectations. No chance for women or men to experiment.
Family involvement	Knew my family would always be there for me. No doubt about the strength of our connection	Felt suffocating at times. Guilty if I tried to be independent.
Emotional expression	I liked how warm and expressive everyone was.	Sometimes felt embarrassed by how boisterous my family was in public, especially after I moved to California.
Cultural identity	Felt proud of my traditions.	Felt ashamed that people looked down on us because we were Mexican. I used to trade my tortillas for white bread with friend before school.
Religion	Loved pageantry of church as I was growing up.	Turned off by rigid morality of church as I got older.

Table 3.3
My WASP/Irish-American Family

	Positives	*Negatives*
Sex roles	Women have more freedom because they ran the home	Men seem uninvolved in family life.
Family involvement	Everyone was free to do their own thing.	No one seemed very connected to one another.
Emotional expression	People are very "polite" in public.	Family seems very emotionally restrained, except when they got boisterous after drinking at parties.
Cultural identity	Being Irish American makes it easy to fit in. Seems just white to me.	Being half Irish doesn't really seem that important. Sometimes I feel like I'm a nothing.
Religion	We didn't take the Church too seriously. Made it easier to not get caught up in all the rules.	Our version of being Catholic seemed austere. Not much color or celebration.

was drawn to the expressive emotional style that Jorge was trying to moderate. He was drawn to the self-control that she felt trapped by. And as their fight demonstrated, as attractive as these differences were, they could also lead to misunderstandings and conflict. In working with couples, the job of the therapist is to act as a kind of simultaneous translator for two people who may think they understand one another but who are actually using different cultural "languages."

As we shall see in the following section, the complexities facing mixed matches go beyond the attraction and conflicts created by different cultural codes. In their relationship, Cindy was as intrigued with Jorge's Mexican roots as he was by her Anglo "Americanness." She had always been interested in Spanish and Latin cultures, and she felt that her own diluted Irish/WASP background was uninteresting. Jorge, though, was ambivalent about his Mexican identity and at one time had seriously considered changing his name to George. Just as they struggled with the different cultural communication styles they brought to their relationship, they were also drawn together and pushed apart by their mixed feelings about their own cultural identities.

Conflicts About Family Identity

One of the most commonly cited reasons for attraction across religious, ethnic, or racial lines is the fascination between people from individualistic and collectivistic cultures. Individualistic cultures stress personal autonomy, self-realization, and personal initiative and decision making. Collectivistic cultures, on the other hand, stress loyalty to the group and place a high value on the interconnectedness of family, community, and society. Many Americans of northern and western European descent who were raised with individualistic cultural values find themselves drawn to partners from more collective, communal cultures. They feel attracted to what seems to be the greater warmth and caring of their partners' more interdependent personal and family styles. Conversely, people from Latin American, southern European, and Asian backgrounds are sometimes drawn to the sense of autonomy and freedom that their cross-cultural partners seemed to embody.

In this age of mass migrations and easy travel across great distances, people from cultures that have had little to do with one another throughout history are suddenly thrown into close contact. Cultural assumptions that had been secure and stable for countless generations are suddenly challenged and, sometimes, uprooted. People living in communal cultures who are exposed to the freedom of the West suddenly find themselves feeling limited by traditions that had always seemed unquestionable. And westerners who have had the opportunity to experience the unity and support that more communal cultures offer suddenly find their self-sufficiency and individualism very lonely. It's no wonder that people from opposite sides of the earth could feel so attracted to one another. Idealization is the other side of the coin of prejudice, and it is just as easy to project our wishes as well as our fears onto people and cultures unlike our own.

On the surface, when mixed matches get into conflict over the identity of their family, it appears simply to result from a reemergence of different cultural or religious loyalties that had been minimized for the sake of new love. Often, though, the counseling process reveals that each partner's own confusion about his or her own identity greatly complicates and confuses the conflict about the cultural or religious identity of the family.

Although they traditionally overlap, culture and religion are not the same, and when partners mistake one for the other, they often find themselves unable to resolve their differences. It is important for therapists to be clear about the very important distinctions between the two if they are going to successfully assist couples.

Modern life has fused and confused cultural, family, religious, and national loyalties in ways that make it difficult for many partners in mixed matches to understand and deal with the different loyalties they bring to their relationships. When uprooted people reach back into their collective pasts in an attempt to create an identity, each person reclaims different components of an identity matrix. Instead of a balanced cultural/national/religious/family identity, some people emphasize religion, others their cultural or national roots, and some their family roots. Often they end up having difficulty distinguishing between the different meanings of the elements of their identity collage.

Religious faith offers a language for the soul and brings order out of the chaos of human life by creating moral codes that regulate the relationships between husbands and wives, parents and children, workers and employers, and even friends and enemies. Its rituals comfort people through times of loss, and sanctify and give meaning to the life cycle transitions of birth, marriage, and death. Culture is more particular. While each religion includes many cultures, cultural identity is an affirmation of a distinctive sense of peoplehood. Whether mythical or literal, cultural identity honors common ancestors and is reinforced by food, festivals, folkways, language, and ritual. It is rooted in the remembrances of a shared past and the expectation of a common fate in the years to come.

Recent statistics further clarify the distinctions between culture and religion. In bicultural homes in which one partner converts to the religion of the other, the divorce rate is significantly lower. While some couples for whom religion is not an important factor in their lives, the symbols of two religions can be combined and coexist, albeit on a relatively superficial level. But if either or both partners have deep religious convictions, it may be very counterproductive to attempt to help spouses "compromise" by encouraging them to merge their religious beliefs.

Exploring Religious Backgrounds

When couples can't find ways to deal with their religious differences, it can lead to what Paul and Rachel Cowan called spiritual gridlock. This gridlock usually takes the form of an agreement by both partners to minimize their connection to their religious heritages out of fear of the consequences of facing their differences. Their agreement is usually unspoken and takes the following form: "You give up whatever connection you have to your religion in exchange for my giving up mine."

The risk of not dealing with differences is that they may later reappear in spite of efforts to suppress them, especially around life cycle rituals such as marriage, birth, and death. Dealing with them now may be not be easy, but trying to resolve them in the midst of a crisis surrounding a wedding, birth, or death is usually even more difficult. *Now* is almost always the best time.

Some of the problems that interfaith couples experience in their attempts to reconcile their different faiths result not only from very real differences in theology but from partners who bring different degrees of religious literacy and different intensities of religious practice to their relationship. Many people end their formal religious training in early adolescence. Although they may be very sophisticated in most aspects of their lives, they often find that their vocabulary for talking about religion is very limited. Other partners in mixed matches have strong religious backgrounds, and some are still actively involved in their religious practice. Even many who have "fallen away" from a strong religious faith remain deeply affected by the values and thought patterns of their religious pasts.

Ask your clients to reflect on the meaning of their religious heritages and beliefs and to talk with their family members and each other about the evolution of their own religious and spiritual beliefs. The following questions may be useful:

- How important are your religious beliefs to you now?
- How do you put those religious beliefs into practice?
- Are religious practice and belief more of an individual spiritual path that you can pursue by yourself, or do you see your religion as inseparable from its practice in a community of others who share the same beliefs?
- Do you contribute money to religious institutions or causes?
- What feelings are you aware of when you consider exploring your partner's religion? How would you feel about your partner exploring your religion?

Exploring the Cultural History of Childhood

When partners in a mixed match are locked in conflict over the cultural identity of their family, it can help to explore the cultural history of each of their childhoods. Often the denial of the relevance of the past is striking in working with cross-cultural couples. While some couples overemphasize their differences, more seem to try to ignore them.

One of the advantages of couples therapy is that the therapist is free to ask questions and be curious about cultural and religious issues that may be too charged for the partners in a relationship to directly address. The therapist, who is interested in each person as well as the relationship, enables each partner to learn more about the other. Use the following questions as a way to guide a couple's exploration:

- How did each partner's family express their pride as well as their anxiety about their ethnic or racial roots?

- Did either partner have foreign-born relatives? What was their experience of immigration to a new land? Did either have relatives who were bilingual or who didn't speak English? What were each partner's feelings about these family members as they grew up?

- Did either partner or their family experience prejudice, discrimination, racism, or stereotyping as a member of his or her cultural group? Do either have relatives or ancestors who were persecuted or who persecuted others? How did their families deal with these kinds of painful events and memories? How has each partner?

- What were their families' attitudes toward "outsiders" who were of other ethnic, racial, and cultural groups?

- What was most important to each partner about belonging to their group as they grew up? How has each partner's identity changed over time?

- Has either partner ever visited their family's cultural "homeland"? What was that experience like? If they haven't ever gone, what are their feelings about visiting it?

LIFE CYCLE AS CATALYST TO CONFLICT

Intercultural couples are most likely to enter therapy during a crisis precipitated by a life cycle event. The rituals that are part of life passages like marriage, birth, and death are used to acknowledge and affirm bonds of community, blood, and belief. They reveal not only the warmth and connection in family relationships but the unresolved tensions and conflicts as well. Reaching across time and space, they bring together family and friends, often from long distances, and create a stage for families to act out their most passionate dramas. For partners in mixed matches, these times can be particularly stressful for two important reasons:

1. They bring into focus unsettled cultural or religious differences between partners or members of the extended family.
2. The presence of extended family vividly demonstrates the contrasting cultural communication codes governing emotional expression in each partner's culture.

Because the couple brings different traditions to their marriage, the wedding ceremony itself can be a particularly important and emotionally charged time for mixed matches. Weddings symbolically condense and display how a couple intends to live their life in relationship to family, culture, friends, spirituality, and success. The ceremony is an event that is designed to honor tradition. By their very nature, mixed matches are usually defying tradition. A couple can feel torn between their own different desires as well as those of their two families. But the wedding also presents an opportunity for the couple to start designing a blueprint and laying down the foundation for the future cultural and religious framework of their new family.

Nothing, though, is more powerful in revealing the interplay of religious and cultural differences in a relationship than children. The birth of children exposes denied religious or cultural loyalties. The process of helping children define their identities inevitably reveals the unacknowledged power of the parents' different pasts.

Children are the messengers to the future; they carry the individual beyond death. But most people realize that it's not enough for their children simply to carry their genes. In order to bestow a real sense of immortality, children need to carry something even more important: a parent's values, traditions, and identity. And one of the most important ways that people define and try to transmit those aspects of themselves is through some combination of religious and cultural identities. People do not often talk explicitly about these existential concerns, but they often drive the intensity of conflicts over children. It is important for the therapist to be able to recognize these issues and help the partners begin to address them more directly.

RON AND JULIE: THE BIRTH OF A CHILD AND THE DEATH OF DENIAL

Ron and Julie's story illustrates the potential for deepening relationships when a couple uses the crisis of birth to clarify their own cultural confusion. It also reveals how current conflicts can be intertwined with cultural as well as personal history.

Ron had called me from the hospital anxiously requesting a counseling session as soon as possible. One day after their son's birth, he and Julie found themselves locked in a bitter argument over what to name him. The next day they came for their appointment with their unnamed three-day-old son.

Ron was a forty-six-year-old Japanese-American biologist, and Julie was a thirty-six-year-old teacher and self-described "generic white Protestant American." After a few minutes of introductions, they plunged into the issue that had precipitated their crisis.

"It's very important to me," said Ron, "that we give our boy a name that honors my grandfather, Tomoji. I know I never made it clear during the pregnancy, but when I saw our son for the first time, I suddenly realized how important it is to me."

Julie had checked out of the hospital early that morning and her response had a tired, angry edge to it: "You agreed that we could name the baby Sam if it was a boy or Samantha if it was a girl. I respect your feelings about your family traditions, but I don't want a name that labels our child as being from any particular culture."

Until the birth of their child, Ron and Julie had always felt proud of their transcendence of the limiting identities of their birth cultures. They had often quoted John Lennon's song "Imagine," which looks forward to a better time when people have left behind the racial, cultural, and religious attachments that seemed to be the cause of so much conflict in the world. Even after Julie got pregnant, they never felt that it was necessary to talk about how they would shape the cultural identity of their biracial child.

When Julie went into preterm labor, she called Ron, who was at a conference in a nearby city. He quickly left the meeting to join her at the hospital, but their new son arrived before his father. As Ron ran into the delivery room, the first words that burst out of his mouth were, "What shape are his eyes?" Julie looked up at him in shock and confusion. Several hours after the baby's birth, Ron told Julie for the first time about his wish to name their child after his grandfather. In spite of their shared ideology emphasizing the universal, Ron found himself obsessed with the particular. Ron and Julie finally had to deal with old and deep cultural loyalties that do not simply disappear.

Talking openly about their cultural contrasts had always seemed dangerous rather than potentially enriching. They both feared that the past might highlight their differences and pull them apart. Underlying the bond of their common values, they each had very different feelings about their pasts. They both sensed that dealing directly with these issues might open old wounds from their own complicated and conflicted histories.

At this point, several of my questions led Ron and Julie to begin to share the experiences that had shaped their cultural identities in their families of origin. They focused on their family's celebrations of holidays, the experiences they had with members of other ethnic groups, and their families' own attitudes about their cultural identities. For the first time, Ron talked about his feelings about his parents' wartime incarceration for the crime of being of Japanese ancestry. Exploring these experiences helped them more clearly understand the cultural aspects of their childhoods that were painful as well as those that brought them a sense of meaning and belonging.

This process also helped de-escalate their conflict. When they were able to see that at least some of the roots of their conflict lay in a larger cultural and historical framework, they became less angry about each other's behavior and less confused and guilty about their own. As they took the risk of lowering their defenses and of trying to understand their conflict in this larger framework, they began working toward more compassionate solutions to their differences.

Like many couples, they found that the *idea* of talking about different cultural pasts was far more threatening than the reality of really exploring them. Relaxed curiosity is one of the most important tools the therapist has in dealing with cultural differences in a relationship. By showing interest in each partner's background, the therapist paves the way for partners to begin to explore the meaning of their own and each other's.

Helping Children Develop a Solid Identity

Often, cross-cultural couples will enter therapy around child-rearing conflicts. There are no simple formulas for raising the children of intermarriage, because the best path for any particular family depends on so many variables. Approaches that work well for some families spell disaster for others.

Children and families living in more tolerant environments face different issues than those living in areas plagued by pervasive racial and social tensions. Wealthy families may be able to afford a lifestyle that insulates them from harsher aspects of life that families of more modest means may not be able to avoid. Single parents have different concerns than parents with intact marriages. Stepparents and blended families may introduce even more complexity into a family situation, creating a rainbow array of cultures in one household. And while many children do better having a unified family faith, some children thrive without any organized religion or in families that practice a blend of religions.

But in all families, the better able partners are at deciding which aspects of their different cultural and religious backgrounds they want to bring into their family life, the more successful they will be in helping their children create a solid sense of belonging. Children are aware before they enter kindergarten that people are divided and categorized by race, language, and religion. They naturally turn to adults to help them figure out where they fit in the complex social matrix they struggle to understand. When parents are unable to wholeheartedly agree on how to define their family's religious and cultural identity, it's very difficult for them to provide their children with the guidance they need.

While the primary task of the therapist working with couples is to help them resolve their own conflicts, it is important to provide cross-cultural parents with information about effective child rearing. The following information can help in resolving and preventing relationship problems. The role of the therapist should include a component as educator: it can be useful to advise parents and give them information as part of the process of helping them resolve their conflicts.

Normalize Ambivalence.   Children, as well as adults, naturally like to be on the "winning" side. Biracial and religious and racial minority group children feel disturbed when they become aware of the disadvantages and vulnerabilities attached to either one of their parent's group status. They often go through periods of identity experimentation, rejecting and accentuating different parts of their identities. For example, research has shown that preschool biracial children will often initially only play with white dolls, even when offered dolls that more closely resemble them. During latency, many of these same children will choose exclusively dark-skinned dolls. It is important to allow children the freedom to engage in this process of experimentation, but it can be very difficult for parents, especially when they feel that their children's behavior is a result of something they have done wrong or of bias in the classroom.

Help Children Deal with Prejudice. Children need to learn about the nature of the world they live in. Encourage parents to help them begin to make sense of the senseless. Books, museums, the stories of grandparents, and carefully selected movies and television programs can be important sources of information about the never-ending battles that have always raged between good and evil.

Remind them, however, that as important as it is to prepare their children to deal with unpleasant realities, they should not overwhelm them with too much too soon. Like most things for children, learning about hatred in the world needs to be graduated. A five-year-old is not ready for overly graphic lectures on the history of racism and ethnic hatred. The four-foot walls around some of the most horrific exhibits at the Holocaust Museum in Washington, D.C., are designed to protect young children from being flooded with images they are not yet prepared to face. The museum's "Daniel's Story," a re-creation of the house a Jewish boy lived in during the Nazi onslaught, allows children to begin to develop an awareness of history without overwhelming them.

Every culture has rituals that allow parents and children to acknowledge painful parts of their group's history in ways that can help build a sense of community, connection, and meaning. Memorial Day pays homage to soldiers who have died in battle and is a ritual that allows Americans to create a feeling of commonality based on shared sacrifice. For African Americans, the celebration of Juneteenth Day acknowledges their history of slavery and celebrates its end. Yom Hashoah is a day that Jews use to commemorate and remember the Holocaust. Each of these kinds of days uses a sense of collective loss as one of the building blocks of identity.

Confront Problems. Because children spend so much of their time in school, all of parents' efforts to help their children develop a positive identity can be either reinforced or undermined by schools. One of the most important ways to prepare your children to deal with bigotry and bias in the world is to be able to observe parents who effectively confront bias when it affects their children's education or social environment. This not only can help a child through a current difficulty but also models the importance of dealing with troubling situations.

Provide Children with Positive Experiences. It is important that parents provide their children with positive experiences about both sides of their cultural heritage so that they can find ways to be proud of all of who they are. Even when parents decide to practice a single religion, they still can find ways to incorporate aspects of both parents' cultures into the life of the family.

Dealing with Family and Social Rejection

While lack of family acceptance can destabilize a cross-cultural relationship, it can also have the opposite effect. Cut off from the usual sources of support, the couple who feels exiled is figuratively pushed into one another's arms. Resenting the judgments of others, they focus their anger on their families and may fail to experience normal ambivalence about their new relationship. Like a nation threatened by enemies from without, they close ranks and temporarily forget their own differences. It is our task to help couples acknowledge and deal with the differences that they bring to their relationships. Couples need to be helped in assessing the nature of family opposition to their relationships. If they don't understand why their family opposes their relationship, it makes it very difficult to respond effectively.

A family's cultural history can have a major effect on how it responds to an "outsider." If they have been victims of tyranny, they may fear and mistrust outsiders. If they are recent immigrants or refugees, they may be concerned about protecting what feels like the threatened solidarity of their own cultural or religious traditions in a new land where they are now part of a minority group. Also, some families may simply not be comfortable with people who are culturally different than they are, especially when it comes to marrying one of their own. The negative reaction of a family member who has "never met one of them" may have more to do with anxiety or discomfort than with unbending intolerance.

Perhaps the greatest difficulties are faced by "Romeo and Juliet" couples who come from cultures that are historically hostile to one another. I spoke with a Turkish woman and an Armenian man who were engaged to be married. They were both painfully aware that their families would oppose their relationship based on events that had occurred long before they were born. Likewise, relationships between Germans and Jews or Chinese and Japanese may carry heavy historical baggage. And while an interethnic, interreligious marriage of an Irish-American Catholic and a white Methodist in Iowa doesn't raise many eyebrows these days, the marriage of an Irish Protestant to an Irish Catholic in Northern Ireland certainly raises more than eyebrows. A couple in love may believe that they have transcended the hatreds and pain of the past. But their families often have not.

When one partner is from a widely scapegoated group, such as blacks, Latinos, or Jews, at least part of the reaction of family, friends, and society to the relationship may result from the violation of a basic social taboo. One way or another, others communicate their disapproval. Of all the contrasts that partners in a mixed match may bring to their relationship, race is the most visible and inescapable. It's the most likely to target a couple for others' intolerance. While Caucasian interethnic and interreligious couples can choose how and when they will reveal their differences to strangers, interracial couples don't have a choice. Their differences are written on their faces. More than any other kind of mixed match, interracial couples must find ways to deal with social as well as family reactions to their relationships. Even when couples share similar religious, cultural, class, and educational backgrounds, racial differences can lead to family and social opposition to a relationship.

Class Differences. The Brazilian saying "A rich Negro is a white and a poor white is a Negro" is a reflection of the fact that in some cultures, class and educational attainment are more important than race in determining family and social reactions to intermarriage. To varying degrees in different countries, wealth, and sometimes the lack of it, can erase other social distinctions. In many societies, there is more intermixing of cultures and races at the top and, sometimes, at the bottom of the social ladder. Money lubricates social interactions in many groups, and the wealthy have been among the first to marry out. Similarly, the shared burden of poverty and social stigma can sometimes minimize other social distinctions. Frequent intermarriage between blacks and Native Americans in the years before and after the Civil War is one example of two low-status groups intermarrying.

Every family has its own unique set of priorities and values, but it's often difficult to discern exactly what they are, even for members of the family. Help your clients reflect about how their families have reacted to others, and it should become clearer whether it is race, religion, class, or education that is most important to them.

I spoke to one young woman from a white Protestant background whose parents were extremely upset when she began to date a Chinese-American man who worked as a landscaper.

> My parents worked hard to talk me out of my relationship. They never talked about his income, which wasn't great, but kept on focusing on the problems they claimed that most interracial couples had. They cited some statistics they had read somewhere about the incredibly high divorce rates of interracial couples. Two years later, after Bob and I broke up, I started going out with Alan, who happens to be Japanese American and who also happens to be a physician. Suddenly, my parents' racial concerns were forgotten. I never confronted them about their change of heart. It was weird. I always assumed that they were kind of racist, but now I realize that what they really are is *classist*.

Smoke Screen. Sometimes the content of family objections is really a smoke screen used to conceal family and psychological conflict. While parents in these families may use religion, class, race, or culture as the focus of their opposition to a relationship, what they are really opposed to is their child growing up.

Clearly, this sort of problem can seldom be resolved by trying to address the cultural or religious content of their parents' objections. As soon as they respond to the supposed issues, they evaporate and new ones appear. The constantly changing issues create a smoke screen that prevents the more fundamental problems from being addressed. In these situations, it is important to help the couple confront inconsistencies in their families' behavior, and to set limits. Ultimately, the unspoken rule prohibiting separation will become clear, at least to you.

Some family theorists have focused on how intermarriage is motivated by attempts to emotionally separate from dysfunctional families of origin. Therapist Edwin Friedman, in an article entitled "The Myth of the Shiksa," claimed that in the great majority of the Jewish/gentile couples he worked with, Jewish partners were motivated to marry out in an attempt to separate and individuate from Jewish parents they saw as intrusive and controlling. He went on to say that almost all were either first children who felt an undue amount of parental pressure by virtue of being the eldest or the children "most triangulated" in their parents' marriage, acting as emotional go-betweens for unhappy spouses. In either case, Friedman argued, the children who are stuck in propping up their parents' marriages use intermarriage as a way to escape. He overstates his case by implying that the dynamics he described are nearly universal in intermarriage, but he does make an important point. Some people, by choosing a partner from another race or religion unacceptable to their parents, use their relationships as a way to distance themselves emotionally or literally from complicated and painful family situations.

Religious Beliefs. Religion and the name of God are often invoked for ends that are hardly spiritual. Soldiers of two warring nations may share a common religion, and yet both invoke the same God to pray for victory over one another. Just as nations sometimes use religion for narrow and nationalistic ends, families and institutions may use religion as a way to mask racist, classist, or ethnocentric objections to your relationship. God's will is always a popular tool for those seeking to justify their biases.

Some families' objections to intermarriage, though, are genuinely religious. For the truly religious, race, class, ethnicity, and nationality are not the important issues. What they do seek is to have their children carry on what they believe is God's truth. Genuinely religious families and clergy are often more than willing to accept intermarriage of people from different races or cultures as long as they share the same religion.

The great religions, at their cores, transcend national, racial, and class lines. In mosques, churches, and synagogues around the world, one can see rich and poor, black and white, and people born in different lands using the same words to worship a common god.

Even if your clients don't share their parents' beliefs, it's important to help them not stereotype religious devotion as simply just another form of intolerance. If they do so, they may be confusing belief with bigotry. They aren't the same, and it's important to be able to distinguish between them when deciding how to deal with objections to your relationship that are framed in religious terms.

There are several ways to diagnose the sincerity of family objections to your client's relationship that are based on religious differences. The following questions can be helpful for the couple in addressing this issue:

1. Are the family members who are objecting to the relationship religiously observant in a meaningful way?
2. Do family members who are concerned by your interreligious relationship accept converts as true members of the religion?

If you have been successful in helping your clients understand others' reactions, it can help them deal more creatively with them. It demands a lot of maturity for them to take the time and emotional energy to try to diagnose the underlying causes of the hostility, anger, or rejection of family members, friends, or others. If their family senses that your clients are trying to understand their concerns, it can sometimes go a long way toward helping build bridges.

CULTURAL GENERALIZATIONS: HANDLE WITH CARE

Couples therapy is a challenging enterprise, and working with cross-cultural couples adds new layers of complexity to the process. It is important for therapists working with mixed matches to be attuned to the powerful effects of culture, race, and religion in intimate relationships. But even as the therapist seeks to understand differences between cultural groups, it is equally important to hold generalizations about group contrasts lightly.

The variations in attitudes, behaviors, and beliefs *within* a cultural or religious group are at least as great as the variation *between* groups. Saying that someone is African American or Chinese American, or Jewish, or WASP can only be a starting point in trying to understand individuals and their interactions. Generalizing about cultural differences is a tool we must handle with care when working with couples who bring different pasts to the job of creating a shared future.

NOTES

P. 62, *Other kinds of religious intermarriages:* Kosmin, B. A., & Lachman, S. P. (1993). *One nation under God: Religion in contemporary American society* (p. 242). New York: Harmony Books.

P. 62, *The number of black/white:* Author unknown. (1992, December). *Population Today, 20*(12).

P. 74, *Psychiatrist Carlos Sluzki has observed:* Sluzki, C. E. (1982). The Latin lover revisited. In M. McGoldrick, S. K. Pearce, & J. Giordano (Eds.), *Ethnicity and family therapy.* New York: Guilford.

P. 81, *Recent statistics further clarify:* Author unknown. (1993, August). *Demography.*

P. 81, *When couples can't find ways:* Cowan, P., & Cowan, R. (1987). *Mixed blessings: Marriages between Jews and Christians.* New York: Doubleday.

P. 88, *For example, research has shown:* Jacobs, J. H. (1992). Identity development in biracial children. In M. Root (Ed.), *Racially mixed people in America.* Newbury Park, CA: Sage.

P. 92, *Frequent intermarriage between blacks and Native:* Wilson, T. P. (1992). Blood quantum: Native American mixed bloods. In M. Root (Ed.), *Racially mixed people in America.* Newbury Park, CA: Sage.

P. 93, *Edwin Friedman, in an article entitled:* Friedman, E. (1982). The myth of the shiksa. In M. McGoldrick, S. K. Pearce, & J. Giordano (Eds.), *Ethnicity and family therapy.* New York: Guilford.

4

THE HOMOSEXUAL COUPLE

Jack Schiemann and Wendy L. Smith

Couples—be they gay, lesbian, or heterosexual—face many similar challenges as they try to make a life together. What does it mean to be in a relationship? What roles do we assume, and what roles do we expect of the other? How might these roles change over time? What are the "rules" of being a couple, and which ones will work best for us? What principles and values will we live by? How might we handle conflict and the many disappointments that come with any intimate relationship?

While couples often share much in common, regardless of sexual orientation, there are significant differences that therapists need to understand in order to work effectively with a gay population. For instance, therapists treating lesbian and gay couples need to be familiar with how antihomosexual bias in society affects their clients. Because many lesbian and gay couples tend to internalize antigay bias, they may view their relationship as somewhat less suitable or viable than their heterosexual counterparts. This is not the only contributing factor to difficulties in gay and lesbian relationships, but nonetheless it does account for some of the problems these couples face.

Heterosexual bias based on social enculturation may also shape the way both homosexual and heterosexual therapists view lesbian and gay couples—namely, that these couples are not as "natural" as heterosexual couples. Awareness of the social approbation that society has against lesbians and gays is not just something to be used in helping clients but something to examine in ourselves as therapists, whether we're homosexual or heterosexual. One of the challenges of the psychotherapist is to respect the lesbian and gay couple as a viable and suitable family unit. This is often a curative and crucial stance for the therapist to model.

This chapter will look at a few of the major concerns lesbian and gay couples present to therapists and some ways to help clients deal with these problems. As gay therapists, we have been working with individuals and couples for many years now. We have come to appreciate the positive therapeutic value of approaching our clients from a gay-affirming stance, one that envisions homosexuality as part of the rich diversity in human experience. From this perspective we find our work with heterosexual and homosexual couples to be mutually enhancing.

Wendy has been working with gay, lesbian, bisexual, and heterosexual individuals and couples for the past ten years in a variety of contexts. She relies on several theoretical viewpoints in her work, among them the control-mastery framework for psychodynamic understandings, family systems theory to encourage the individuals to see interlocking dynamics, and a cognitive/behavioral approach when more problem solving would serve them best. Wendy feels that it's important to convey to the couple that she is an ally to each partner as they struggle to elucidate the difficulties interfering with their growth as a couple.

Jack pays close attention to the developmental "season" a couple finds themselves in, focusing on the challenges of each period in a relationship's lifespan. "I find that couples tend to be unaware of the typical patterns and problems they share with other couples who are in a similar developmental period," he says. "For instance, the problems of a beginning couple are often quite different from those of longer-term partnerships. Often couples fail to recognize that problems in their relationship may have less to do with their personal dynamics than with the larger challenges of their current developmental period. Consequently, they may tend to personalize their difficulties either by assigning blame to their partner or by feeling personally inadequate."

Many gay men who attempt to forge a relationship feel isolated and uncertain of what to do since there are few role models to rely on. Consequently, much of Jack's work is educative as he helps clients deal with their particular concerns.

"My style is to be open about my own experience as a gay man in a relationship and to use this in the therapy," Jack says. "I find that self-disclosure, when used judiciously, not only creates an alliance with the couple I'm treating but serves as a way to depersonalize the larger challenges all couples must face. One of my goals is to help clients appreciate the typical difficulties faced by all couples. Many couples operate under the myth of the perfect relationship and hence come to therapy with overblown expectations and low tolerance for the messes we all bring to our partnerships by virtue of being human."

Jack is influenced by the adult developmental theory of Daniel Levinson and the archetypal psychology of James Hillman, both of whom appreciate how patterns in society and in our psyches shape human development in both destructive and creative ways. He works actively with a couple's life structure, paying close attention to how they live day to day, what their living environments look like, how they spend their time together and apart, their individual and collective fantasies about the relationship. Jack has also conducted psychobiographical research in the coming-out process of gay men who have careers in the military, the church, and academia—occupations where the public disclosure of being gay could jeopardize job security.

CREATING A BOND

Lesbian and gay couples frequently run into difficulties in the beginning period of their relationship. We have found that a considerable portion of our caseload is made up of these clients and that many of the difficulties they face have a familiar ring to them: finding a balance between differentiation and attachment, discovering and accepting various roles in the partnership, working out living arrangements, defining the boundaries of the relationship in terms of monogamy or nonmonogamy, and how much to be in or out of the closet.

Many gay men bring to their relationships a hidden belief that they are in some way inherently defective, a belief often formed in response to childhood traumatic experiences of being different. As a consequence, these men tend to feel excessively responsible for the behavior of others, even when that behavior clearly has nothing to do with them. These hidden beliefs may influence gay men to act in ways that sabotage their well-being and promote the idea that they deserve to be mistreated.

Hidden beliefs form in many ways. For instance, the parents of some gay men may unconsciously distance themselves from their son because of their discomfort with the perception that their son acts or otherwise seems different from other boys; this withdrawal contributes to the son's belief that his difference is dangerous and that he, by virtue of being different, drives significant others away.

Because he comes to believe that he is responsible for and deserves this withdrawal, he may enter into relationships later in life that duplicate the one he had with his primary caregivers. In an effort to heal old wounds, he may choose partners who treat him the way he was treated as a child and act toward others the way he behaved in the presence of his parents. Or he may act toward his partner like his parents acted toward him, wishing that his partner would respond in better ways than he responded to his parents. In the following case vignette, Jack demonstrates how underlying beliefs of inferiority can contribute to a beginning couple's difficulties and offers some strategies for helping the new couple appreciate the destructive power of these beliefs as well as some ways to mitigate their influence on the relationship.

OLIVER AND BRUCE

"This is so hard, and I'm afraid we're not doing a very good job of it." Barely able to contain his frustration, Oliver opened the first couples therapy session with Bruce, his partner of eleven months. While committed to working on the relationship, both men were feeling discouraged and were beset by what Bruce called "our ghosts of relationships past." And what a conglomeration of ghosts they were! Oliver's father died when he was four. His mother soon remarried, but Oliver grew to detest his stepfather. "He wanted to 'make a man' out of me, whatever that meant. He pushed competitive sports, and I resisted. I enjoyed track and field but had no interest in football or baseball. I loved to read and was kind of shy; he labeled that 'being a sissy.'" As their relationship grew distant, Oliver's stepfather verbally attacked his masculinity while accusing Oliver's mother of babying him.

At about the age of six, Oliver began to feel that he was different in some way but didn't have a name for the experience. He associated this sense of difference with his stepfather's disapproval. Worse yet, he was teased frequently at school for being a "fairy" and a "queer," though he wasn't quite sure what these slurs meant. Oliver came to believe that being different signified a defect in his character. When he finally identified himself as homosexual, he associated this word with feelings of shame and guilt triggered by the hidden pathogenic belief that being different caused others to dislike him.

Although Oliver accepted his homosexuality intellectually when he began dating men in his early twenties, he tended to pick partners who either accused him of not being masculine enough or who withdrew after the first few months of intimacy. He blamed himself for his partner's behavior. Oliver tended to shun men who were warm and loving toward him, thereby sabotaging potentially healthy relationships.

Bruce treated Oliver well, but Oliver often undermined this by behaving toward Bruce the way his father behaved toward him, using sarcasm and other forms of verbal hostility. They were helped to recognize the meaning and function of their reenactments and to imagine new ways of being together.

The partners were encouraged to talk about old wounds. At times a whole session was spent having one partner talk about his past while the other simply listened. Hearing about one another's experiences enabled them to have compassion and not take their partner's problems so personally. Oliver spent a whole session talking about the shame he felt growing up in a household that pathologized being different. In turn, Bruce reported several similarities in his background. Jack pointed out that because many of their destructive beliefs sounded familiar to both of them, perhaps their new relationship might provide an opportunity to lessen the tyranny of these beliefs.

Bruce learned to let Oliver know how hurt he was whenever Oliver used cutting sarcasm to make a complaint. By slowing down interchanges in the session and microanalyzing these together, they were able to pinpoint specific offending phrases and gestures.

For instance, when Oliver addressed Bruce in a sarcastic manner during the session, the interchange was stopped and Bruce was asked to tell Oliver what he was thinking or feeling at that moment. Often, Oliver was unaware of the impact he had on Bruce or the particular words or gestures that gave offense. Bruce was then encouraged to coach Oliver in how to better express discontent. The retort "I'm not your father" became part of Bruce's repertoire in cuing Oliver that a ghost was present in their interactions.

For Bruce, who came from a family in which conflict was poorly tolerated, this was new behavior. His alcoholic parents often exploded in terrifying fits of rage. Bruce tried to make light of it by putting the best construction on such frightening situations. During intense fights, he would retreat to his room or withdraw into silence. When Oliver behaved toward Bruce in ways reminiscent of his father's attacks on him, Bruce simply collapsed in an anxious silence much as he had done in his own family. Oliver interpreted this as hostile withdrawal, which infuriated him even more. And so their dance spiraled into ugly fights.

Oliver unconsciously wanted Bruce to disconfirm the belief that he deserved to be rejected, a powerful schema that haunted him much of his life. By identifying and naming destructive hidden beliefs and the behaviors they sponsor, couples are able to recognize when and how the ghosts of past relationships haunt their current situation. When the opportunity arose, Jack pointed out to Oliver that the hidden belief that he deserved to be rejected often played a crucial role in the words he chose or the gestures he used when talking to Bruce. Oliver became more proficient over time in recognizing how he invited rejection. And Bruce became more aware of how the unconscious belief that conflict spells disaster inhibited his freedom to voice disagreements with Oliver, behavior the latter experienced as aggressive withdrawal. Learning to recognize their hidden beliefs and the behaviors they aroused in the relationship helped the two of them turn ghosts into ancestors.

DEALING WITH CONFLICT

A major task for the beginning couple is to deal with conflict in such a way that it becomes an opportunity for increased intimacy. Beginning couples soon discover the uncomfortable reality that differences are both attractive and repellant. As the newness of a relationship wears off, the very qualities that seemed attractive in a partner may become a major irritation. For instance, Bruce was attracted initially to Oliver's outgoing nature, his ability to express himself directly. Bruce was less direct with his feelings. Within a few months of the relationship, Oliver's "directness" became the Achilles' heel of the relationship.

Jack worked with Bruce and Oliver to appreciate that conflict evoked by differences in temperament and personality style is often a means for achieving intimacy. For instance, when Bruce complained about Oliver's "in-your-face hostility," he was asked to paint a specific picture. What did this hostility look like? By creating an image of the offending behavior, they were able to deal with it more objectively, to depersonalize it a bit. What might Oliver do differently to modify the image, to make it less threatening and more aesthetically pleasing? With this approach, each partner coached the other in specific ways of behaving that allowed for communication while avoiding physical and verbal behaviors that pushed one another's buttons. Jack will stop couples when they paint an ugly picture of relating, much as a director might stop a filming session. At times he might actively direct a new scene or help them write a new script. Once he said to a couple, "We've all seen this picture before, and I think you'll agree, it's not very pretty. Let's do something different with this scene. Let's make it more aesthetically pleasing than the one you've just performed."

Bruce and Oliver learned the specific verbal and physical cues that set the other off and found new ways to express disagreements. Oliver learned to scrap his use of sarcasm as a way of expressing disappointment or frustration with Bruce. Jack helped him write a new script for getting his feelings across. Instead of being sarcastic, he was able to say, "I am frustrated with you when you fail to call me if you're going to be late" or "I am disappointed when you retreat into silence because then I feel shut out."

Additionally, Jack told them that many couples find it helpful to shelve an argument until a later date when hot affects have cooled. He taught them to "strike while the iron is cold"—that is, to let the affects generated by conflict cool down before engaging in the kind of dialogue meant for healing. When things cooled down, he had them listen to each other without offering an interpretation. After voicing their complaints fully, they learned to identify specifically what it was about the other's behavior that triggered the painful feeling.

When troublesome behavior is identified, Jack has both partners brainstorm ways of performing a request or a complaint that is less apt to trigger old schemas and to acknowledge when the other is successful in doing that. This couple was able to do an effective "postmortem" examination of their fights that helped them to be more tolerant of conflict. They made significant progress in how to give feedback and how to coach each other in more effective ways of communication. With practice and a few follow-up sessions, they turned the noisy ghosts into quiet ancestors.

RENEGOTIATING RELATIONS WITH PREVIOUS PARTNERS

Those ghosts can materialize all too vividly for couples in therapy when one of the partners wants to continue in a relationship with an ex-lover. Wendy has seen numerous couples in therapy who were no longer involved in a romantic relationship but came to her wanting to work through old unresolved conflicts so they could remain active friends. On the other hand, when a lesbian decides to sever most ties with an ex-lover, therapists can teach practical negotiation skills for the expected and unexpected meetings at social events or community activities. Wendy's work with Laura and Sue provides a common presenting dilemma for many lesbian couples.

LAURA AND SUE

Laura and Sue's entry into therapy was triggered by Laura's ongoing friendship with Lois, her former lover over the past six years. Sue, who had only recently begun to explore her lesbian feelings, was unsure of making a commitment to Laura because she sensed Laura's attachment to Lois as potential trouble, given what she perceived as their "excessive" contact. Lois and Laura saw each other a few times a week and phoned daily. Laura could not appreciate Sue's fears and felt that her nonsexual friendship with Lois was "just fine" since, from her perspective, it didn't impact her relationship with Sue.

To provide a greater context for understanding their conflict, each woman was asked to talk about her family of origin, its structure, emotional climate and connections beyond the immediate family. Their current and past patterns of relationship were compared.

Laura equated her friendship with Lois with her wish for ongoing emotional familial connections, in contrast to the relationship in her family of origin, which tended to be superficial and dissatisfying. Her parents had little emotional energy for Laura or her siblings, leaving

Laura starved for emotional input. She had been expected to care for her younger siblings and was unconsciously echoing a learned pattern of exaggerated responsibility for others whom she viewed as needy. Her frequent contact with Lois, who had remained single since their break-up, was motivated in part by guilt for having left her and worry about her welfare. Laura was helped to make this association and differentiate between her current concerns for Lois and her responsibility for her sibs.

Sue had initially been so surprised by her powerful attraction to Laura that she soon began to dream about a storybook romance unfolding between them. As she became more and more suspicious of Laura's ties to her ex-lover, her dreams eroded and she felt stunned by the ensuing disappointment.

Sue's family structure and relationships resembled her current triangulated situation. She was an only child in a very close and verbal family. Her discomfort with the level of contact between Laura and Lois paralleled her mother's discomfort with Sue's closeness to her father. At the same time, Sue was trying to classify her relationship with Laura as special and distinguish it from Laura's friendship with Lois, a distinction that evaded her in her family of origin.

Sue's desire to protect the sanctity and primacy of her relationship with Laura was validated, whereas her idea that meaningful ties with others outside the primary couple were necessarily suspect was challenged. Wendy encouraged her to articulate specifically how she perceived Laura's contact with Lois to be damaging. She had a difficult time coming up with concrete reasons for her upset. The issues of loyalty and disloyalty were confusing and upsetting for Sue. She experienced her mother's negative reactions to her relationship with her father as an act of disloyalty, or was it the other way around— had she been disloyal to her mother? Sue began to understand that she was attempting to comprehend old limiting fears in order to be able to expand her repertoire of loving responses.

In discussing the differences between her own values and those of her parents, Sue realized that her relationship with Laura meant acknowledging her separation from her family of origin. This meant moving away from them psychologically, and thus potentially experiencing loss.

After they both came to appreciate the myriad meanings of their respective viewpoints, it became clear that by making slight shifts, they could accommodate each other's needs. Laura began to set limits and establish appropriate boundaries around her contact with Lois and handled the guilt that evoked more effectively. Sue came to recognize that her distrust of Laura was in part a reflection of old maternally derived and reenacted beliefs.

They also had to recognize and deal with the differences between Laura's and Sue's lesbian identities. Sue was a novice grieving the loss of what had been her familiar world, while Laura's inclusion in the lesbian community a decade earlier didn't entail the loss of close family ties. It was useful to provide Sue with an understanding of the gay and lesbian community and to encourage Laura to be tolerant of Sue's reasonable conflicts. At the same time, Sue learned to appreciate that since homosexuals often lose the traditional support of their families of origin, their connections with friends and lovers (including ex-lovers) become necessarily more cherished. Therapy facilitated their respective attempts to work through old patterns of interpersonal ties and master new ones. It enabled them to empathize with the other's struggle and to see beyond their own historically derived interpretations.

This vignette typifies a common process often found in the early stage of a relationship—a first step that Judith Wallerstein calls consolidating separation and building connectedness. These two women utilized the therapy sessions on many levels—a structured weekly time to fully acknowledge their emerging union, the acquisition of practical negotiation skills, and an appreciation of the psychological complexity of both themselves and their partner, resulting in a newfound respect for one another.

RESISTING GENDER-ROLE STEREOTYPES

Another way therapists can facilitate self-awareness for their gay and lesbian clients is to question assumptions based on gender roles. The therapist can provide a useful service by questioning the idea that a person's appearance, which may seem gendered (masculine or feminine), necessarily indicates that they are better suited for particular tasks or that they have personality characteristics that have culturally become associated with either men or women.

In the initial stages of a relationship, these buried assumptions can create confusion and conflict when one person assumes the other is purposely withholding love by not adhering to the behavior patterns that are stereotypical of their gendered appearance. If these assumptions are not questioned by the therapist, the acceptance of constraining roles can prevent the relationship from moving forward.

For instance, a woman who has grown up in a society that insists that women are necessarily the nurturers can feel unloving or unloved if her nurturing style is different from her partner's. Additionally, the expectation of perfect nurturance from one's woman lover can become a burden for both. It often is liberating if the therapist can encourage the couple to respect and sometimes find the humor in their human inconsistencies and eccentricities. Wendy points out the tyranny of expecting perfection from a partner so that clients can begin to loosen the grip of this concept on themselves and their partners.

Gay men often struggle with the roles they have learned from significant men in their lives and enact patterns of adaptation that affect current relationships. For instance, sex-role conflicts frequently arise from the experience of living with another person who has been socialized for similar roles. This is especially true around the issue of competitiveness or the need to be vulnerable and transparent in the relationship. During the course of their treatment, Bruce and Oliver experimented with new roles in the relationship. Bruce learned to cook (something he believed he had no aptitude for), and Oliver tended the maintenance of their vehicles—"If only my stepfather could see me now!" Both entertained the idea that it was fine to experiment with a number of ways of being in the relationship and realized that rigid role expectations only served to shrink their life together, not expand it. Additionally, even "seasoned" gay men may need to be reminded about the subtle ways internalized antigay bias works to erode self-worth.

Jack has clients pay attention to the language they use in reference to their gayness. What might appear to be mild "jokes" about being gay (for example, "she's such a queen") often mask a deeper internalized shame, even hatred of being gay. For example, when Oliver described his childhood and the ridicule he received at school, he more than once stated, "I was such a nellie thing!" Jack wondered aloud whether Oliver noticed the way in which he described himself as a child. What might that say about how he viewed himself then and now? This proved to be a rich opportunity to explore internalized antigay bias for both Bruce and Oliver (and Jack as their therapist).

STAYING IN OR COMING OUT
OF THE CLOSET

The choice of whether to stay in or come out of the closet (publicly disclose one's gayness) can be a point of contention for homosexual couples who are creating a bond. For instance, one partner by virtue of his career may choose to remain discrete about his homosexuality, while the other, able to be fully out, may grow impatient with his mate's choice not to disclose his homosexuality to family, co-workers, and friends. Couples may need help to differentiate issues of personal integrity from choices to stay in or come out of the closet.

A current myth in the gay community may be part of the problem. This myth avers that in order to be whole, one must come out of the closet fully. Much of our work with couples is to debunk the myth that coming out is *always* the best choice and that staying in is *always* antithetical to mental health and well-being. Indeed, current studies show that coming out of the closet prematurely may not be the best choice to make. Such choices are complex, and each person's timetable must be respected.

We find it helpful to explore what the choice to stay in or come out really means to each partner. In his work with couples, Jack often finds hidden thoughts like, "If you really loved me, you would prove it by coming out along with me" or "Your insistence that I come out is yet another example of the way in which you invalidate my choice of career, the things important to my life." For example, Craig and John came to couples therapy because of a conflict centering on Craig's decision to remain in the closet and John's frustration with that choice.

CRAIG AND JOHN

Together barely a year, Craig and John's conflict had escalated to a point of separation. John had the opinion that any choice to stay in the closet was a sign of "internalized homophobia." As a college professor, he was fully "out" in the workplace and taught a gay studies course. Craig, a minister in a church that barred homosexuals from the clergy, chose the closet for good reason: he had invested many years preparing to be a pastor. While he was angered by the church's position on homosexuality, Craig nevertheless loved being a minister and was willing to pay the price of silence.

John, on the other hand, did not like having to play the role of "pastor's roommate." He felt that he was placed in an untenable position: if he were to make a slip up, it could cost Craig his job. The stress of secrecy was taking its toll on John, who felt that Craig underestimated its impact on him. Craig, for his part, viewed John as not respecting his profession since he had little tolerance for the church. Both felt unheard and stalemated in the relationship.

Jack's approach to couples is to be equally unfair to all, taking the side of the relationship itself. He wondered out loud what fantasies and dreams they entertained for their relationship. He asked them to bring their images of the relationship into the room by having them paint a picture of what it might look like five, ten, fifteen years from now. They began to talk about sharing a home together and traveling as a couple. They had thoughts of adopting a child or two and felt that they would make excellent parents. As John quipped, "I think mothering and fathering are gender-free activities."

During the weeks that followed, a flood of very specific images and ideas about the relationship flowed into the room for us to entertain. Jack had them imagine possible futures without foreclosing on any one idea prematurely. He wanted them to hear each other's ideas and to live with them for a time, take their ideas out to lunch, wine and dine them. By bringing imagination to their relationship, John and Craig began to see their partnership as a living, developing "entity" requiring their nurturance and intelligence. With a number of ideas about the relationship on the table, we were able to focus on the ones that resonated most with them and to amplify them further. Out of this process, they decided to hire a lawyer and initiate legal instruments to protect their relationship; they set up a joint savings account and drafted a will. Above all, they made substantial progress in seeing the relationship as an organism with its own distinctive needs.

In time, Craig decided to choose another career that would make use of the skills he honed as a pastor while affording him the freedom to be openly gay. What surfaced in the therapy was his own exhaustion trying to maintain a facade in a church hostile to his very being. Jack had him describe at length the pain of trying to do a job he truly loved while living in fear of being "found out." Jack's hope was that John would also recognize this pain and develop deeper empathy for Craig's dilemma.

Jack pointed out that it seemed that Craig wanted out of the closet too but resisted John's pressure because it reminded him of his parents' continual harangue that he be a physician. Becoming a minister was, in part, a protest against their wishes. He discovered that what attracted him to the ministry was the act of helping others. He decided to leave it and chose a career that satisfied his wish to help others while allowing him the freedom to be open about being gay.

In therapy John was able to acknowledge his partner's integrity as a minister and that his work was deeply appreciated by the many he served in his congregation. John's acknowledgment, in turn, helped free Craig to acknowledge the difficulties John had to face as a spouse of a public figure whose career depended on being closeted. John described in detail the frustration he felt trying to maintain secrecy about their relationship for fear of jeopardizing Craig's career.

In working with this couple, Jack often had one partner remain silent for the duration of a session while the other told his version of what he experienced in the relationship. It was not uncommon for the silent one to learn something new about his partner and for both to discover that they knew far less about each other than they thought they did.

Other coming-out issues may center around family-of-origin problems. One or both partners may choose to be closeted with some or all members of their family of origin. This can create difficulties during holidays if the tradition is to spend them with the family of origin.

GREG AND ADAM

Greg, a twenty-year-old college student newly partnered with Adam, came out to his parents as a freshman. In retrospect, he felt that he made the decision in order to conform to the gay myth that coming out to family and friends as soon as possible is always a good decision. He also experienced peer pressure from gay friends to do so. When Greg told his parents that he was gay, they withdrew their financial and emotional support at a time when he needed them most. The ensuing crisis affected his performance at school and put stress on his relationship with Adam, who was not out to his parents and did not want them to know about Greg. In therapy Jack focused on the strengths of their budding relationship, especially the way in which they demonstrated loyalty to one another in the face of conflicts over how to deal with their respective families; they were able to detach somewhat from family of origin conflicts.

Jack helped Greg slowly mend his relationship with his confused and angry parents by encouraging him to let them in on his experience of being gay. He began by writing them about his feelings of being different as a child and how much he appreciated their parenting. In his letters he let them know that they need not feel guilty about his sexuality. By helping him approach his parents patiently, Jack helped Greg open channels of communication with them. He encouraged him to read his letters aloud in their therapy sessions and to share his parents' responses if he felt comfortable doing so.

By hearing this, Adam gained a greater appreciation of his partner's sensitivity and also received modeling for how he might come out to his own parents. Both learned to choose to come out or stay in the closet based on their needs and desires rather than on peer expectations. Eventually Greg's parents took a great leap of faith and attended a Parents and Friends of Lesbians and Gays group, which offered them an opportunity to express their feelings and learn more about the unique issues parents of gays face. A milestone occurred when Greg's parents invited both him and Adam for a holiday celebration.

Having been helped to view themselves as a legitimate couple, Greg and Adam began to act as if they were about to embark on a life project together.

In working with gay couples, Jack often initiates sessions by bringing up such topics as finances, living arrangements, expectations and roles, open or closed relationships. By doing so he hopes to have the couple imagine their relationship's future and to see that it has needs and requirements. He wants them to realize that a relationship has a life of its own, goes through developmental periods, and needs specific things to keep it alive and well. With very young gay men who have few role models, Jack finds this kind of practical, educative therapy most effective. He's not adverse to spending one or two sessions with a couple making a budget or, as in the preceding example, writing an important letter.

BALANCING CLOSENESS AND DISTANCE

A good part of our work is to help couples recognize, accept, and even welcome the differences between them. In her work with lesbians, Wendy pays attention in the first few sessions to how each partner formulates the couples' problems and if they tend to obscure or minimize their different styles, beliefs, and backgrounds. The ways that they differ may not be the root of the problem, but, if they can't talk openly about their differences, then future problems can certainly be expected. Wendy asks them how they've discussed the ways they are very different from one another outside the therapy office. Has there been something about that process that feels destructive to the relationship?

When lesbians come for couples therapy, they often complain about "overmerger." By their use of this terminology, they reveal their acceptance of the widespread myth that pathologizes a process that many couples—heterosexual and gay—undergo. The real issue for these couples is how to move more easily between closeness and distance. Wendy offers reassuring ideas by educating clients about the nature of love when it manifests in such seemingly contradictory ways: one moment feeling so close as to be one with the partner (as if the other is an extension of oneself), yet in the next moment being brought up short by the real mystery of the other (who is she, anyway?).

Wendy encourages clients to entertain subtlety and paradox and to cultivate ideas of themselves as co-creators of the relationship. By speaking about the art of relationships, she fosters an appreciation for the sometimes delicate interplay between familiarity and mystery and for the tension (or the released energy) created as they traverse back and forth between those two poles. This becomes a reframing of the tension between the two individuals, which might be reconceptualized as the thrill of adventure, as they set out on the path to mutual discovery. By highlighting the more mythic aspects of this path to togetherness, likening it to prototypes found in myths and folktales from across the ages and around the world, Wendy places their struggles on a more universal, and therefore more valued, plane.

When we work with lesbian and gay couples, we consciously and explicitly acknowledge to the couple our respect for the unique privilege of acting as a historian of the newly created relationship by offering support and acceptance in a societal vacuum and, additionally, of acting as champion of its future. While friends can and do serve as a support system, therapy as an institution often represents the larger society to the couple. For that reason, acceptance and respect from the therapist can feel very empowering for the couple as they become accustomed to viewing themselves in a committed partnership.

We normalize the difficulties inherent in creating a family together with few role models, rules, or established societal sanctions and norms. In this way, we reframe the couple's relationship as that of a family in need of support and nurturance. With this awareness, the couple can more actively engage their network of friends to also act as binding agents when they go through the inevitable rough times that come with any long-term relationship. For example, couples may decide to hold a bonding ceremony in front of friends, family, and acquaintances, with an implicit or explicit request for support in the maintenance of the relationship.

SUSTAINING A COMMITMENT

Typical concerns of couples who have been together two or more years include sexual issues, blending finances as a symbol of trust and investment in the relationship's future, complaints about loss of excitement in the relationship, and problems with isolation.

Sexual Issues

Since many women have experienced some form of sexual abuse, it is useful to explore that possibility in therapy as soon as feasible.

Wendy usually asks for a brief sexual history, including their first sexual experiences, and also specifically whether they've been in sexual situations that they found abusive. If both women in the couple have been sexually abused or exploited, each partner may be at a different stage in working through these experiences.

While sexual abandon is antithetical to self-control, in facilitating recovery from sexual abuse it is imperative to provide the abuse survivor with ways of experiencing control before she can move on to greater levels of trust and relaxation. This necessary groundwork became particularly evident in Wendy's work with Joyce and Audrey.

JOYCE AND AUDREY

Joyce and Audrey walked into the therapy office at a funereal pace, their faces full of tension and despair. They began to describe a four-year relationship that had begun in an atmosphere of sexual vitality only to deteriorate over the years into one of sexual mistrust, emotional wariness, and sadness over the loss of what had once been a sexually satisfying relationship. They remained committed to each other and felt their years together in a loving relationship had created enough security to finally take a clear look at their sexual situation.

Wendy began by asking each of them to describe what typically happens between them sexually. Who initiates? How is each woman aware of her own sexual desire or needs? How does a sexual encounter progress? What are their typical sexual activities? How do they communicate about preferences? What feels unsatisfying about the encounter? How does their current behavior reflect or contradict how they began as sexual partners in the relationship? How is it similar or different from how they've been sexually with previous partners? At this stage Wendy wanted to create a lighter atmosphere in which to explore sexual matters. Therefore, her questions were as matter-of-fact as possible.

Joyce was the more talkative partner and already had a fairly detailed explanation for their problems. She attributed most of the difficulties to Audrey's childhood experience of being sexually abused by an uncle. Consequently, as an adult Audrey had problems identifying her own sexual desires and being fully present during sexual interactions. For instance, she would rely on Joyce to initiate lovemaking and would focus on satisfying Joyce's sexual wishes.

Joyce felt abandoned by Audrey during sexual intimacy. When they tried to discuss the problem, Audrey would fall silent and Joyce became angry. Both felt desperately stuck.

Wendy's first task was to provide them with a measure of safety with each other. Initially, she encouraged them not to focus on orgasm-driven experiences but to develop a language and system of communication that provided them with a means of addressing what felt good and what did not. She suggested various sensual experiences for them that emphasized touch and the sensations of being physically close without progressing to genital sex. In this atmosphere of mutual cooperation, the couple moved to greater levels of comfort with one another and into more explicitly sexual behaviors.

Lesbian and gay couples often succumb to the prevailing myth that peak sexual experience signals a healthy relationship. We have found that sexual difficulties in couples have more to do with overblown expectations of what sex "should" be like for partners than with particular technical problems in bed. Much of our work is to help couples simply reconnect in ways that foster better communication.

For instance, when Jack works with gay couples experiencing sexual difficulties, he begins the therapy by helping them get reacquainted with each other in nonsexual ways. He suggests that they carve out time during the week to talk about their day, their hopes for the future, even world events. "I am often surprised at how little couples really talk with each other," Jack says. Progressing slowly, he has the couple begin to share sensual experiences like taking a shower together or giving slow, nonsexual body massages. They are encouraged to verbalize their feelings during these encounters, thereby guiding each other as to what feels good.

Jack will meet with each partner individually to take a fairly complete sexual history. He asks about family composition and lifestyle, religious upbringing if relevant, early messages received about sex from the family of origin, early memories of sexual feelings and experimentation, the experience of puberty, the first sexual experience with another person, current sexual practices, preferences, sexual fantasies, changes in sexual activities because of AIDS, body likes and dislikes. He conducts this rather informally and if possible asks clients to write responses down (which can prove to be quite revealing to clients). Many clients do not feel comfortable talking about their sexual history in front of their partners, and unless the therapist asks, clients tend not to volunteer this information. Hence, the importance of conducting a sexual history interview. He has found that once both clients have done this (it usually takes more than one session), they are more comfortable talking about their current sexual problems together in couples therapy.

Additionally, the sex history gives Jack an idea of the level of sexual information a couple possesses. Where there may be gaps in information, he uses the therapy as a time to educate by offering new information to dispel myths. One couple, for instance, thought that it was the norm to have sex at least five times a week. When Jack suggested that twice a month is about the norm, they were surprised and relieved! Another partner thought he had a problem with premature ejaculation because he ejaculated after "only twenty minutes of intercourse."

Much of the work is to help couples enjoy being physical together without the expectation that every encounter must lead to genital sex. Jack has found that many couples feel that their relationship is deficient because it doesn't conform to the myth that orgasm is the cornerstone of loving and being together. "Over the years I have found that gay male couples feel relieved to hear that mature couples develop multiple ways of sharing intimacy," Jack says, "and that sexual intimacy for a large portion of the population is not the keystone to the relationship but only a part of it." For many homosexual couples, companionship and the deep intimacy that develops through traversing the peaks and vales of life together is of far-lasting value.

FINANCIAL DIFFICULTIES

Established couples often bump up against financial disagreements two to three years into the relationship. Jack worked with a couple having difficulties making a decision to purchase a house together.

Many couples entering therapy have not entertained the idea that their relationship is an entity all to itself, that it has a developmental history and a future that needs to be provided for. Jack talks about the relationship as if it was a fourth being in the room. He and the couple together ponder the various ways they might take better care of this "being." For example, during the first few sessions of therapy, Jack encourages the couple to tell the story of their relationship, how they met, what attracted them to each other, what hopes and dreams they entertained for their life together. He finds it especially useful to ask them to discuss the relationship's strengths when they are in crisis.

Couples often forget their successes together. Having them tell the story of their relationship with a particular focus on their strengths has a way of mitigating the tyranny of the current problem. Looking at the relationship as a whole helps the couple ask, "What did we do in the past to handle a problem like this one? How will our choices to solve this problem impact on our shared hopes for the future? Might there be alternative ways of imagining our current difficulty?"

STEVE AND PHILLIP

Steve and Phillip wanted to blend their finances to buy a house. Their relationship of five years had matured and they no longer enjoyed living in separate apartments. Like most gay couples, they faced this task with few guiding role models. As Steve put it, "I feel like we're inventing all of the rules as we go along; I guess its kind of new territory for us."

The myth that gay male relationships are evanescent bothered them. McWhirter and Mattison claim, in their study of gay male couples, that the two most misleading beliefs that contribute to a premature split-up at the end of one year or so are that the quieting of limerance signals the end of love and that male couples do not last long anyway.

Steve wanted to purchase a house with Phillip, but as the time drew near to make a commitment, he hesitated. Phillip interpreted this as ambivalence toward the relationship and expressed his anger by declaring that the idea of buying a home was a bad one anyway and that he would have no part of it. As their estrangement grew, they decided to enter couples therapy.

Steve had been hurt badly by a former lover who left him after seven years for another man. While he loved Phillip, who was not at all like his former lover, Steve was afraid of having his trust betrayed again.

Jack helped this couple clarify the nature and origin of some of their fears. Phillip came to realize that Steve's reticence to make a financial commitment to the house had little to do with their relationship. He worked with Phillip to hear and understand Steve's concerns without jumping to a conclusion about them as a couple. Steve felt tremendous relief in at least being heard and understood. In turn, he was able to hear Phillip's disappointment when his expectation for making a home together was stalled by Steve's ambivalence.

Jack will often spend a number of sessions having each partner describe as fully as possible his concerns. If someone attempts to interrupt or interpret, Jack will gently but firmly direct the session back to the one speaking. He finds that this allows room for concerns to be aired and creates a feeling of safety in the room.

Couples often need to retell the story of their relationship, to focus on the relationship's strengths and how they have nurtured and have been nurtured by it. Steve and Phillip came to appreciate the solid foundation already in place and, from what Jack could gather, well maintained. This couple needed to hear and see that they were in pretty good shape and that they would probably weather this new challenge fairly well.

After many of the issues that brought them to therapy were clarified and worked through, Jack helped them create a ritual that symbolized their growing commitment to each other and also helped Steve achieve some closure on his previous relationship. Rituals can be very important for gay couples. Since many are childless, they have few visible markers to signify the passage of time. Steve and Phillip imagined ways in which they might build a home together, creating a sense of family for themselves. On their anniversary, they placed their written hopes for creating a home in a box to be opened and shared at the moment they began looking for a house. This proved to be a tangible, powerful reminder of their future together. Like many couples, they had not imagined their relationship had a specific future. The few goals they did have were vague.

Without benefit of a marriage contract and the societally sanctioned rituals around it, many gay men find that sharing finances and joining to buy a house together serve as a symbol of the couple's seriousness. It's difficult to end a relationship in which the partners have a considerable financial as well as emotional investment. Shared financial commitments are barriers to premature separation.

It is no surprise, then, that money is a key concern for many couples. By approaching the couple as a family in the making, Jack finds that many of the problems of financial planning and priorities take on a different tone. Mutual financial planning for the relationship tends to strengthen the notion that the partnership is important, that it has a future worth investing in, and that part of its future includes good stewardship of its resources. Opening joint bank accounts, buying a house together, writing a will, planning for retirement are more than merely family responsibilities—for the gay couple they take on enormous symbolic value. Money has to do with worth, value, and hope. By financing their partnership gay men proclaim the value of their relationship.

Phillip and Steve experienced a significant deepening of their commitment to one another when they hired a lawyer to set up durable and business powers of attorney along with writing a will. By viewing their relationship as a budding family rather than two individuals who happened to be "lovers," they were able to discuss their fears of "getting in deeper" as well as their yearning for more stability and security in their partnership. The visit to the lawyer not only symbolized the seriousness of their commitment but confronted them with the idea that their life together was finite and that perhaps they ought to engage it seriously and joyfully.

Writing the will became a turning point in their life together, what Daniel Levinson terms a marker event. They realized that their relationship had a life that far exceeded the boundaries of their individual commitments to each other.

For gay men in particular, the fear of losing a sense of security in the world gets coded into the need to have a stable income. The anxiety of setting up mutual finances has less to do with "What if our relationship fails—I'll lose my money" than it has to do with the fear of engaging in a project that requires great courage in the face of cultural stigma. A therapist, by focusing on the mundane and practical aspects of the couple's life together, does them a great service by sending the message that this relationship is worthy of all the legal and emotional support currently available.

ACTIVE PROBLEM SOLVING

By placing problems in a context, couples are able to "strike while the iron is cold" and learn to talk differences and problems through, to respond rather than react to them. With Steve and Phillip, for example, Jack taught them to shelve an argument hot with emotion until a later time when tempers had calmed so that the problem solving phase of a disagreement might be separated from the emotional arousal phase. By teaching couples to engage in problem solving at appropriate times, Jack hopes to show them that conflicts do not have to be "resolved" immediately, that good solutions often emerge long after the embers of anger extinguish. He reminds couples that negotiating and working their way through inevitable problems in a relationship is the best way of strengthening their partnership; it gives them some success trophies to look back on when future trouble strikes.

By framing the relationship as an entity with a life of its own, a history and a future, the idea of providing for the relationship in the present took on new meaning for Steve and Phillip. They renewed their commitment to each other and to the relationship using a ritual of Holy Union conducted by their minister. After the ceremony, they invited their friends to celebrate this new juncture in their life.

MONOGAMY AND OPEN RELATIONSHIPS

Homosexual couples in the beginning and middle stages of a relationship often struggle with the question of whether to have an "open" relationship. In our work with couples, the idea of an open relationship, while it may sound like a reasonable proposition ("no one can possibly satisfy all of my sexual needs"), crumbles when one or both partners act on their impulse to have sex outside of the relationship. This often leads to jealousy, deep hurt, and a feeling of betrayal; many of these feelings are left unexpressed because of the "reasonable" agreement made beforehand. These resentments find oblique expressions and, if left untreated, may do serious damage to the integrity of the relationship.

This can be a delicate subject for many gay men. The wish to be free of heterosexual beliefs and values has led some gay couples to mutually agree to experiment with the boundaries of their relationship, an experiment that often serves them poorly.

Jack finds that fidelity in any relationship, be it homosexual or heterosexual, is as important a principle as loyalty to one's partner. He has noticed that gay male couples who have created a viable and enduring family together and who initially adopted the open relationship approach abandoned this model as their partnership gained priority.

Therapists need to help gay couples acknowledge that it is all right to swim against the many legends associated with gay experience and that a relationship based on the principles of fidelity and loyalty is neither a heterosexual principle nor a homosexual one; it just seems to make good psychological sense. We want our partners to be faithful and loyal to us. And in this time of upheaval and confusion among couples of all stripes, affirming these principles is something we clinicians can offer to our clients. Therapists make a mistake approaching their work as if it were "value-free." Part of our responsibility is to share with couples what we have observed over the years works for others.

We all share a need for structure, predictability, safety, and a sense of creating something greater than the sum of its parts. Aaron Beck offers seven principles that seem to be part of a healthy couple: cooperation, commitment, basic trust, assuming goodwill, giving the other the benefit of the doubt, loyalty, and fidelity. It is helpful to talk about these principles with couples, and doing so bolsters their faith in the partnership. An open discussion of the principles of a sound relationship goes a long way toward helping couples value what they intuitively experience as right for them. Jack often asks couples, "Is this what *you* want or what you've been told gay relationships are about?" He will ask each partner to list specifically what they want from a relationship and what principles they value.

HIV ISSUES

Many gay men and lesbians have been affected by the AIDS epidemic, incurring innumerable losses of lovers and friends. AIDS poses special problems for gay couples. For example, one partner may be HIV-positive while the other partner is HIV-negative; this triggers a host of challenges. When the HIV-positive partner becomes seriously incapacitated, how will the HIV-negative partner cope? Will he be able to offer his mate physical and emotional support? How well has he coped in the past with serious illness and loss? How helpful will the HIV-positive partner's family of origin be? What kind of legal arrangements have been made, such as power of attorney, financial arrangements, wills, trusts, and insurance prepayment? How will the couple cope with the financial burden of the disease? What couples issues might be exacerbated by the progression of the disease? How will they deal with reordering their priorities in the face of AIDS? How will they deal with issues of sexual intimacy? What are their thoughts about death?

The HIV-negative partner is often overlooked by helping professionals because most services are geared toward those infected with the virus. Often the HIV-negative partner has no place to talk about his feelings. He may feel unworthy to receive emotional support because his spouse is ill, or he may suffer survivor guilt as he sees not only his partner but also his friends become ill while he remains healthy.

In treating couples in which one or both partners is HIV-positive, it is important to help them sort out these issues and talk about each of them openly. This reduces the feeling of being overwhelmed and gives room for issues to be discussed thoroughly. For example, Jack will make sure to focus on the HIV-negative partner's concerns and experiences in the course of couples work. At times, he will meet with this partner alone to address his survivor guilt and how it can lead to unsafe behavior (for instance, putting oneself at risk for the disease out of loyalty to the positive partner or out of guilt for being negative).

HIV-negative partners appreciate these individual sessions where they can express their feelings of fear, sadness, and guilt. Often the HIV-negative partner will not express these feelings in the presence of his mate. Jack also uses these individual sessions to talk about ways that the HIV-negative partner can care for himself while caring for his mate. They discuss the limits of caregiving and when to seek outside assistance. Gay men often have a difficult time asking for what they need because they fear that being needy means being vulnerable, which triggers fears of disappointment or, worse, outright hostility. Jack tries to mitigate the HIV-negative partner's temptation to be heroic by pointing out that his mate will benefit greatly from outside assistance. A burned-out caregiver is not helpful. Learning to ask for help is a powerful way of disconfirming the fear that expressing needs will always end in disappointment and shame.

Many gay couples dealing with HIV issues may not have openly discussed their feelings about sexual intimacy. Jack initiates a review of safe and unsafe sex. They talk about the use of condoms in a positive way. He encourages the couple to try new ways of lovemaking that are both fun and safe. Talking explicitly about safe sex practice may also become an opportunity to deal with other sexual concerns of the couple.

Jack will meet with the HIV-positive partner alone to address his concerns. Often HIV-positive partners feel guilty that they are overburdening their mates. They may wish to talk about dying from the disease but feel reluctant to bring this up with their partner for fear of upsetting him even more. Like their negative partner, they may feel anticipatory grief over the prospect of saying goodbye but have no place to talk about this grief. While hope is important, there may be the need for both partners to talk about death and loss. Because many gay men are often alienated from their religious backgrounds, they may have few places to talk about death. The therapist can provide a way of having that conversation.

With couples in which one partner or both partners are HIV affected, the background noise of HIV/AIDS is always there. Patients wonder, "How serious is it? When will new symptoms occur? What will they look like?" Each new stage of the disease is a crisis for the HIV-positive client and his partner. And each step of diminished health is a new grief with attendant anxiety and sadness. But new problems can be an opportunity for growth, self-discovery, and personal awareness.

Many couples living with HIV/AIDS feel uncomfortable asking for help for fear of overburdening their family and friends. Working with clients living with AIDS requires a very active, inquiring stance. You cannot assume the client will raise concerns. You, the therapist, must bring them up. For instance, newly HIV-positive clients may shut down sexually, unable to let anyone in. "Coming out" as HIV-positive is a new step. And the

HIV-negative partner may wonder, "Am I going to be safe?" but feel guilty asking about this or talking about it.

In dealing with couples living with AIDS, a few commonsense guidelines help. First of all, be present with your clients. Don't try to "fix" the pain. Don't placate with simplistic platitudes of hope. Just be with the truth. Most of all, acknowledge your own grief. Jack has found that the following countertransference issues need to be acknowledged and contained:

- Fear of contagion
- Fear of death and dying
- Fear of the unknown
- Denial of helplessness
- Fear of homosexuality
- Overidentification
- Anger
- Need for professional omnipotence

These countertransference issues can be successfully dealt with by identifying your own issues, educating and sensitizing yourself to the lifestyle and concerns of persons living with HIV/AIDS and their partners, knowing when to ask for consultation, and constructing a peer support system with other practitioners who work with persons living with HIV/AIDS. Finally, Jack has found it humbling and empowering to acknowledge that his clients know more about living with HIV/AIDS than he does and that they are his teachers.

RENEWING AND REVITALIZING THE RELATIONSHIP

When long-term couples come into therapy complaining of a lack of vitality in the relationship, it may be that one or both partners may be inhibiting personal growth for fear of disrupting the harmony they've established over many years. The inevitable result of blocked individual development is a complacent and stale relationship. The couple may need to be encouraged to pursue their personal goals while simultaneously attending to the needs of the relationship.

When a couple becomes socially isolated, the relationship is likely to become dull and claustrophobic. Partners are likely to rely on one another to satisfy all of their needs as well as expect the other to generate excitement. We can help clarify the sources of their frustration by facilitating discussions about their own personal paths and how they may have gone astray. This actually helps the individuals feel more in control of the situation because they can do something about their own plans. It also inhibits the tendency to attribute the couple's problems to a partner who seems unamenable to change.

Couples who are in a rut may be worried that it presages the future end of the relationship. We encourage the couple to try new behaviors, and we try to instill an appreciation for experimentation as a method for revitalizing the relationship. If appropriate, we encourage them to generate excitement for play—sexual or otherwise. For example, adult board games that are not gender-specific ("An Enchanted Evening," and so on) are helpful and stimulating because they provide a structure for revealing parts of the self in the aim of greater intimacy. Taking time out in therapy sessions to recall what first attracted one partner to the other can diminish the tendency for long-term partners to take one another for granted. It also reminds them of their partner's positive qualities. Each partner needs the capacity and the willingness to see the other as both the early ideal and the present reality.

Remodeling the Relationship

Therapists can help older couples write new, emboldening scripts to infuse vitality into an otherwise lackluster relationship, and the changes do not have to be dramatic. Jack often tells couples that small changes in a relationship can have, over time, very positive results.

Jack uses the image of a ship sailing across the Atlantic; one degree of change can mean the difference between landing in France or bumping against the coast of Africa. If the relationship has built up enough equity of trust over the years, these changes can be made over time without too much angst. Early in the treatment, he assesses the relationship's foundational integrity by listening for the degree of loyalty, trust, and pleasure they have gained from being together over the years. Can they remember good times and what made them that way? What initially attracted them? While they may hate each other now, can they remember times of closeness, shared interests, hopes? Can they remember when the bond between them began to deteriorate? What was going on in their individual lives at that time? Couples often underestimate the impact of external contingencies on their lives.

GEORGE AND SIL

Jack worked with George and Sil to change their perceptions of their relationship in order to enliven it. When they came to him, they had recently celebrated their twentieth anniversary. They enjoyed a stable relationship, owned their own home, and had good incomes. They came to couples therapy to work on a growing sense of staleness in the relationship.

"We have such a predictable schedule. Sil and I work long hours and often don't get home until nine or later. And it's the usual routine. We make a late dinner, turn on the tube, and zone out." Their sex life had dwindled to once, maybe twice in three months. On the weekends, they tended household chores and visited the same friends from their church.

Jack worked with them to renovate their week as if they were remodeling a house. What did they like about their current life structure, and what would they care to change? What would the new week look like? The work was very explicit. At first, they complained that the exercise felt tedious, but once they began to look at their life structure more carefully, making minor adjustments here and there, they soon grew enthusiastic about the process.

They focused on their sex life, what worked and what didn't. George tended to feel comfortable with a narrow repertoire of sexual expressions, while Sil enjoyed exploring different ways of pleasuring himself and his partner. At times this difference in taste and comfort produced conflicts. To lighten matters up a bit, Jack suggested that they develop a sexual menu of a variety of sexual positions, expressions, and fantasies. They were to tell each other what did or did not feel comfortable, what they might be willing to try just once, and what, for now, was off limits. Because this couple already had a solid foundation of trust, fidelity, and loyalty, these exercises promoted excitement and fun. In less stable relationships, Jack tends to proceed with more caution by inviting the couple to begin with very small steps toward feeling comfortable just being with each other physically. As their comfort levels increase, they graduate to giving each other finger massages or foot rubs. If the relationship has been seriously eroded by years of resentment and distrust, the couple may need to learn to be friends again without focusing on sexual expression. Jack does not believe that good sexual intimacy necessarily reflects relational health. Couples can have great sex and a lousy foundation for the partnership.

George and Sil had built a lot of trust and loyalty in their relationship and could afford to try new things without much risk to the partnership. They used the sexual menu exercise to good advantage, including making sex dates at different times of the day instead of waiting until the evening when they were exhausted from work. They tried new ways of sexual expression heretofore unexplored either because they assumed the other would be scandalized or because they thought they might not enjoy it.

Sil and George had lost well over fifty close friends to AIDS, many of whom were in relationships like theirs. When Jack heard them tell how they stopped attending funerals because they could not bear the pain of yet another loss, he felt a heaviness in his body. The shear burden of their grief and loss was palpable in the room; they just sat in the silence of despair beyond language. In time they explored how that loss affected their relationship. They stopped attending annual ski trips because too many of the old gang were no longer alive. As George and Sil watched their social world shrink, the relationship became weighted down and burdened with the role of fulfilling community functions. With fewer trusted friends, especially in partnerships, they experienced a dwindling of the network of support they once enjoyed.

Older couples with well-established friendships over the years may have a more difficult time gaining entrance into other well-established gay male circles. Jack has found, anecdotally at least, that older gay couples who have lived through the ravages of AIDS report feeling somewhat alone and less grounded in the community; they may feel reluctant to make new friends for fear of losing them too.

Depending more on each other for company, with a smaller circle of support, many couples experience a heightening of strain when problems arise between them. Just by addressing the impact of external circumstances as the loss of friends to AIDS or discrimination against homosexuals in our culture, couples come to appreciate the real stresses and strains they must deal with as a gay couple in today's world. Through this appreciation, they often learn to be more generous with each other and appreciative of how far they have come as a couple. Jack talks with them about the courage it takes to sustain a gay relationship in even the friendliest of communities. Creating a partnership without benefit of societal support, while difficult at times, has the payoff of building into the relationship an enduring experience of success. Many older gay couples have developed strong friendships with heterosexual couples over the years. Jack encourages gay couples to do more with their heterosexual friends, thereby broadening their social network.

GAY AND LESBIAN PARENTS

Increasingly, lesbians and gay men are deciding to have children either through adoption, artificial insemination, or pursuing custody of children from a former marriage. A summary of current research of gay and lesbian families reveals the following important findings:

- Lesbian and gay parents look remarkably like their heterosexual counterparts.

- Homosexuals make very good parents, thereby disputing the myth that they will make poor parents.

- Most gay men and lesbians attempt to provide opposite-sex role models for their children.

- Most children of gay fathers find out about their parents' gayness from their own fathers, while others are informed by their mother, overhear their parents discussing it, or figure it out for themselves. Children's reactions range from positive to angry and confused. Younger children have fewer difficulties than older ones.

- Parents' homosexuality seems to create few long-term problems for children who seem to accept it better than their parents anticipated.

- Most homosexual parents have positive relationships with their children; parental sexual orientation is of little importance in the overall parent-child relationship.

- Lesbian and heterosexual mothers did not differ significantly in maternal attitude or self-concept.

- Gay or lesbian parenting does not correlate with the sexual identity development of the children. Quality of parenthood, not sexual orientation, was the most salient factor in the children's development.

- Children of gay fathers were concerned that they not be thought of as gay. They used various strategies to determine when and where they would be seen with their fathers.

- Children of lesbian and gay couples have few gender identity problems. There was little evidence of gender-identity conflict or poor peer relationships.

- Most children do not feel stigmatized by having a lesbian or gay parent, although some problems do occur (which we will address in this section).

Given these findings, there seems to be little difference in the quality of parenting between homosexual and heterosexual couples. A few problems do crop up for lesbian and gay parents that may need to be addressed in couples therapy. The most common of these has to do with the prejudice some children may experience because their parents belong to a stigmatized minority in the culture.

We find it helpful to share the research findings listed here with homosexual couples because while they may feel good about their parenting skills, the prevailing attitude in our society does not favor homosexuals' parenting children. Simply by reviewing current research with couples, we find that their self-esteem as parents is raised and that they know that we believe in them as competent parents.

When couples ask us how to address their children's problems with peer prejudice and stigmatization by friends (and in some cases, teachers, clergy, physicians), we listen carefully to the given circumstances surrounding the upsetting event. Gay and lesbian parents may need to intervene with prejudiced teachers, for instance, by firmly insisting that their child not be singled out or embarrassed. If the offending behavior does not stop, parents should be encouraged to take necessary steps to ensure their child's safety.

However, we have found that the single most effective way of helping lesbian and gay parents prevent these kind of difficulties is to encourage them to explain to their children why, with their friends and some adults, it may be best to refer to the parent's lover as aunt or uncle or as a "housemate." While this approach may sound like a step back, it relieves the children from having to deal with a powerful stigma at a time when they may not be ready to do so. As the children gain a trusting group of friends with whom they feel safe to share more of themselves, then they can be in charge of how much to disclose based on their own comfort levels.

We encourage gay and lesbian parents to help their children deal with these difficult situations as they arise. The research shows that children are often proud of their parents' standing up for themselves and that doing so may give support to their own efforts to speak up.

We have found that heterosexual and homosexual couples share more in common than one might assume. Being sensitive to the particular stressors homosexual couples face can greatly assist therapists in their work with this population. We have much to learn from each other. We hope that clinicians will welcome the opportunity to work with lesbian and gay couples and so help erase the barriers that have long divided heterosexuals and homosexuals from experiencing mutual understanding and respect for each other.

NOTES

P. 99, *developmental theory of Daniel Levinson:* Levinson, D., Darrow, C., Klein, E., Levinson, M., and McKee, B. (1978). *The seasons of a man's life.* New York: Knopf.

P. 99, *archetypal psychology of James Hillman:* Hillman, J. (1975). *Re-visioning psychology.* New York: Harper & Row.

P. 107, *This vignette typifies a common process:* Wallerstein, J. S. (1994). The early psychological tasks of marriage: Part I. *American Journal of Orthopsychiatry, 64*(4), 640–650.

P. 107, *question assumptions based on gender roles:* Smith, W. (1994). *Self-styled gender: Its relationship to gender stereotyping in person perception.* Unpublished doctoral dissertation, The Wright Institute, Berkeley.

P. 109, *current studies show that coming out of the closet:* Schiemann, J. S. (1994). *Staying in or coming out: A biographical study of early adulthood among gay men.* Unpublished doctoral dissertation, The Wright Institute, Berkeley.

P. 111, *take their ideas out to lunch:* Hillman, J. (1975). *Re-visioning psychology* (pp. 115–161). New York: Harper & Row.

P. 115, *many women have experienced . . . sexual abuse:* Browning, C., & Reynolds, A. L. (1991). Affirmative psychotherapy for lesbian women. *Counseling Psychologist, 19*(2), 177–196.

P. 120, *McWhirter and Mattison claim:* McWhirter, D. P., & Mattison, A. M. (1984). *The male couple.* Englewood Cliffs, NJ: Prentice-Hall.

P. 122, *what Daniel Levinson terms a marker event:* Levinson, D., Darrow, C., Klein, E., Levinson, M., & McKee, B. (1978). *The seasons of a man's life.* New York: Knopf.

P. 124, *seven principles that seem to be part of a healthy couple:* Beck, A. (1988). *Love is never enough.* New York: Harper & Row.

P. 132, *A summary of current research of gay and lesbian families:* Gonsiorek, J. C., & Weinrich, J. D. (1991). *Homosexuality: Research implications for public policy* (pp. 197–214). Newbury Park, CA: Sage.

P. 133, *Most children do not feel stigmatized:* Gonsiorek, J. C., & Weinrich, J. D. (1991). *ibid.*

FOR FURTHER READING

Beck, A. (1998). *Love is never enough.* New York: Harper & Row.

Blumstein, P., & Schwarz, P. (1983). *American couples.* New York: Morrow.

Bradford, J., Caitlin, R., & Rothblum, E. D. (1994). National lesbian health care survey: Implications for mental health care. *Journal of Consulting and Clinical Psychology, 62*(2), 228–242.

Browning, C., & Reynolds, A. L. (1991). Affirmative psychotherapy for lesbian women. *The Counseling Psychologist, 19*(2), 177–196.

Clunis, D. M., & Green, G. D. (1988). *Lesbian couples.* Seattle: Seal Press.

Eldridge, N. S., & Gilbert, L. A. (1990). Correlates of relationship satisfaction in lesbian couples. *Psychology of Women Quarterly, 14*, 43–62.

Goodrich, T. J., Rampage, C., Ellman, B., & Halstead, K. (1988). *Feminist family therapy: A casebook.* New York: W.W. Norton.

Gonsiorek, J., & Weinrich, J. (1991). *Homosexuality: Research implications for public policy.* New York: Sage.

Hillman, J. (1975). *Re-visioning psychology.* New York: Harper & Row.

Isay, R. A. (1989). *Being homosexual.* New York: Farrar, Straus, Giroux.

Kurdek, L. A. (1994). The mature and correlates of relationship quality in gay, lesbian, and heterosexual cohabiting couples: A test of the individual difference, interdependence, and discrepancy models. *Lesbian and Gay Psychology: Theory, Research, and Clinical Applications, 1,* 133–155.

Levinson, D., Darrow, C., Klein, E., Levinson, M., & McKee, B. (1978). *The seasons of a man's life.* New York: Knopf.

Loulan, J. (1987). *Lesbian passion: Loving ourselves and each other.* San Francisco: Spinsters/Aunt Lute.

Loulan, J. (1984). *Lesbian sex.* San Francisco: Spinsters/Aunt Lute.

McWhirter, D. P., & Mattison, A. M. (1984). *The male couple.* Englewood Cliffs, NJ: Prentice-Hall.

Morgan, K. S., & Eliason, M. J. (1992). The role of psychotherapy in Caucasian lesbians' lives. *Women & Therapy, 13*(4), 27–52.

Nichols, M. (1987). Lesbian sexuality: Issues in developing theory. In Boston Lesbian Psychologies Collective (Ed.), *Lesbian psychology: Explorations and challenges.* Urbana: University of Illinois Press.

Pies, C. (1988). *Considering parenthood.* San Francisco: Spinsters/Aunt Lute.

Porat, N. (1986). Support groups for battered lesbians. In K. Lobel (Ed.), *Naming the violence: Speaking out about lesbian battering.* Seattle: Seal Press.

Rohrbaugh, J. B. (1992). Lesbian families: Clinical issues and theoretical implications. *Professional Psychology: Research and Practice, 23*(6), 467–473.

Schiemann, J. S. (1994). *Staying in or coming out: A biographical study of early adulthood among gay men.* Unpublished doctoral dissertation, The Wright Institute, Berkeley.

Slater, S., & Mencher, J. (1991). The lesbian family life cycle: A contextual approach. *American Journal of Orthopsychiatry, 61*(3), 372–382.

Smith, W. L. (1994). *Self-styled gender: Its relationship to gender stereotyping in person perception.* Unpublished doctoral dissertation, The Wright Institute, Berkeley.

Wallerstein, J. S. (1994). The early psychological tasks of marriage: Part I. *American Journal of Orthopsychiatry, 64*(4), 640–650.

5

HEALTH ISSUES IN COUPLES THERAPY

Seymour Kessler

Health issues frequently provide the context or focus for many of the problems couples bring to therapy. Some of these issues are brought by the individual into the relationship, whereas others only become apparent later on after the individuals have become a couple. Among the former are the family myths and the real and imagined hereditary disorders with which the individual is burdened. All of these may exert a dominant role in shaping the person's thinking and, in turn, affecting a couple's relationship. Among the latter are the unanticipated illnesses and traumas with which a couple may have to deal during the course of their life together as well as the expected changes that occur naturally over time.

Because of a long-standing professional interest in the interface of psychology and biology, I have been sensitive to the role health issues play in human behavior. When couples come into therapy with health problems, all too often therapists neglect these problems as an underlying source of or a major contributing factor in interpersonal difficulties. But since health and illness invariably involve such psychosocial fundamentals as survival, dependency, and the giving or receiving of care and love, therapists, unwittingly, may come to play a role not dissimilar to that of a significant other, in the life of one or both partners.

In my work I have found that at least three factors need to be taken into account when working with couples around health issues: (1) the role health issues play in the couple's dynamics; (2) the meaning the couple assigns to these issues, specifically, the meaning given to illness and being ill; and (3) the schema each person has regarding their body and that of their mate—in short, body image.

ROLE OF HEALTH ISSUES

Health issues play multiple roles in interpersonal relationships. At the simplest level, illness is frequently used to elicit attention and special caring. As children, most of us learn that being sick has its rewards as well as its liabilities, since we tend to receive extra attention and solicitous care when we fall ill. Once children realize the rewarding aspects of illness, it facilitates the use of illness (or feigned illness) to avoid going to school, evade family pressures, and elude or postpone dealing with other unpleasantries or anxieties. This latter strategy is frequently brought into adulthood and adult relationships.

Illnesses, actual or fabricated, may also be used as a rationale to avoiding dealing with one's fears and anxieties. Persons with social and other phobias, for example, tend to use illnesses as a way of avoiding situations likely to raise their anxiety (a convenient headache frequently serves this purpose). Using illness this way has the additional advantage that others won't usually censure the ill person in such circumstances. On the contrary, the illness may often elicit sympathy from friends and professionals. When the use of illness begins to become habitual to the point where it interferes with our ability to function effectively in various aspects of life or in relationships, it becomes problematic.

Illness may become an organizing principle for interpersonal behavior. For example, a man, on the verge of retirement, looked forward to taking care of his wife, who he believed had a neurological disorder that would eventually make her an invalid. However, after further examinations and tests, it became clear that she had been misdiagnosed and that the medical problems she experienced would clear up. As a reaction to the good news, he became clinically depressed.

Health issues may also be used in complex ways as part of individual and couples dynamics. Persons who may feel guilt over past acts of omission or commission may use health issues as a means of self-punishment or the expiation of guilt. The partner of such an individual may be affected profoundly by the mate's self-punitive behavior and may come to feel that *they* are the one being punished or deprived. In other instances, the mate of a self-punishing partner may support the latter's behavior out of their own defensive needs (see the case history presented later).

Lastly, illness may be used in an attempt to influence the behavior of others, especially when the person feels helpless (for instance, "You'll give me a heart attack if you go out with that girl"). Used this way, illness tends to instill guilt in the other.

THE MEANING OF ILLNESS

Perhaps the most salient meaning given to illness in couples dynamics is as a means to obtain emotional nurturance. Illness in childhood frequently elicits attention and parental caretaking. However, when caretaking is inadequate, inconsistent, or given with reluctance or resentment, the child may learn to up the ante in an effort to elicit the caregiving he or she desires. By the time the person becomes a partner in an adult relationship, using health issues as an expression of the wish for nurturance may be a life habit or a well-entrenched strategy.

Health Anxiety

Inconsistent parental caregiving also may produce considerable anxiety in the child, especially when he or she becomes ill and the need for caretaking is at its height; a child may never be certain that caregiving will be provided. Brought into adulthood, this anxiety may affect a couple's relationship. For example, by anticipating that one's needs will not be met, the ill partner may react prematurely with disappointment, irritation, resentment, and so forth, thus interfering with the mate's ability to give succor and nurturance.

Some mates become "infected" with the ill person's anxiety and may overreact to the partner, exaggerating minor incidences of ill health as if they were major crises, or fail to react by withdrawing from the sick person as a means of dealing with their own anxiety.

When neglect has occurred in childhood, abandonment fears may become a dominant response in the face of illness. Fears of anticipated abandonment may also unleash intense emotions of anger or rage at the anticipated abandoner, the mate. In turn, these emotions may "push" the mate away or otherwise interfere with the latter's ability to give comfort and succor, even if he or she wanted to. This would tend to reinforce the partner's sense of being abandoned.

Family Styles of Dealing with Illness

The meaning given to illness is often related to the quality of care the individual received in childhood. Some families appear to be overinvested in illness, giving enormous emotional weight to even the most trivial of health events (say, temporary constipation), whereas others may be underinvested and ignore or be slow to respond to major health problems when they arise. Children frequently acquire their individual family's perceptions about health issues and learn emotional and behavioral responses to illness that they take with them into adulthood.

When there is a mismatch in the meaning given to health problems in a couple's relationship, disappointments and miscommunications are likely to occur. The mate of an individual coming from an "overinvested" family may become dismissive of his or her partner when the latter attempts to obtain sympathy or nurturance because of the overuse of the strategy; the partner may be seen as crying "wolf" once too often. In the face of a major health event, the mate may not react appropriately or quickly enough.

On the other hand, the mate of a person from an "underinvested" family may become confused when the partner underreacts to a health problem that, in his or her opinion, requires greater or more urgent attention. The mate may feel unsure whether or not to be more insistent that the partner seek medical attention if, in general, the latter tends to minimize health problems. This lack of certainty may lead to inconsistent responses and promotes considerable anxiety, disappointment, and, at times, ill health in the partner.

For example, a man who developed precancerous growths on his vocal cords dismissed his wife's urging to see a physician and accused her of overreacting. Between the period of his first noticing the growths and obtaining a definitive diagnosis, three months elapsed during which time she had multiple flu infections, skin eruptions, and other illnesses.

BODY IMAGE

As we shall see later when discussing unexpected traumas and illnesses, one of the important factors the therapist needs to keep in mind when working with couples around health issues is their body image constellation.

Schemas about the body develop early in life; the child already seems to have a picture of what an adult's body (of both genders) "should" look like. As we mature, body images of the self and others become consolidated. By adolescence, we frequently have an inner picture of the kind of mate that attracts and sexually excites us, his or her size, shape, body type, and so forth.

Once a couple forms a relationship, however, the bodies of one or both partners frequently undergoes significant changes. Weight is often gained. Pregnancies may leave their mark.

Illnesses may occur. And, of course, there is the aging process itself. All of these changes may conflict with the inner body image and may promote responses of disappointment, distancing, withdrawal, and, at times, repugnance and revulsion, which have significant meaning for the couple's relationship and may interfere with their sexuality and the achievement of intimacy.

FAMILY ATTRIBUTIONS CONCERNING HEALTH

Family attributions about health are an example of the beliefs brought into a relationship that sometimes interfere with the couple's ability to make successful adaptations to one another and to the life issues every couple faces.

Some children are singled out early in life on the basis of physical resemblance, gender, or some other, sometimes trivial characteristic to follow in a specific relative's footsteps in their behavior or health. Thus, they come to be labeled as constitutionally or morally "weak" or "strong," a label believed by almost everyone in the family and often having a self-fulfilling quality. Such attributions serve to give family members the illusion of control over a realistically unknown future and to bind their personal health anxieties. In the case of some hereditary disorders, in which being or not being affected is due to chance, preselecting one family member to become "affected" with the disorder later in life helps others in the family contain their anxieties. In some cancer-prone families, for instance, some family members distance themselves from the possibility of developing cancer by telling themselves that "Only females in the family will get it," even though no evidence to that effect may exist.

SKELETONS IN THE CLOSET

When the presence of hereditary disorders in one's family is kept secret from one's spouse, it may have major consequences for the couple.

In one such instance, a newly married man failed to inform his wife that he had two severely retarded brothers in a state institution. When she stumbled on the truth, he confessed and she promptly had the marriage annulled.

In another case, a man kept from his wife the fact that he had a family history of Huntington's disease, an inherited neurodegenerative disorder. As he became symptomatic, his personality gradually changed, and he had continual difficulty maintaining employment. He would rationalize the motoric difficulties that resulted from the disorder as stemming from nervousness about work-related problems. His wife began to suspect that more was involved in the changes she was observing and approached other members of his family, who finally told her the truth. By that time they had been married twenty years and had one child. After researching the nature and prognosis of the disease, she decided to divorce her husband, something she was able to do with minimal guilt since she felt that he had betrayed her by keeping the secret.

HEALTH ISSUES IN ESTABLISHED RELATIONSHIPS

Health problems in the established couple's relationship inevitably occur in one or both of the partners or in their offspring or other close relatives (for example, an aging parent). In each case, they tend to have a profound impact on the relationship.

Adult Health Problems

Chronic illness in one partner in a relationship occurs all too frequently in the life of couples. Couples in which *both* partners manifest health problems are rarer, but they are among the more fascinating to treat.

One such couple, Phil and June, came into therapy for a non-health-related "communication problem," but it quickly became apparent that the question of health dominated their relationship. They were in their late thirties, childless, and married about fifteen years. The first thing I noted was that June had difficulty walking. As they took their seats, I also noticed that both wore Medic-Alert bracelets.

June was a thin, frail-looking woman who said she had a progressive disorder, diagnosed as multiple sclerosis (MS). She had not been able to work since early on in their marriage and was completely dependant on her husband for financial support. She was brought up in a home in which alcoholism and physical and mental abuse were prominent. She complained that although she was doing a lot "to get her life together" (attending support groups, eating a sparse diet, reading Twelve-Step literature, and so forth), her husband was not interested in self-development, and, as a result, they were drawing apart.

Phil wore the Medic-Alert bracelet because he had mitral valve prolapse (a faulty valve in the heart), which, in his case, neither required treatment nor had major clinical implications. He came from a home in which his father was authoritarian, intrusive, excessively complaining, and narcissistically self-absorbed. As a child he learned to cope with the home situation by keeping his feelings to himself and withdrawing from interaction as a means of controlling his emotions. As an adult, he was still browbeaten by his father and had considerable antagonism toward him. When I asked about his work life, Phil said he hated his job and felt trapped in it.

Apparently, he repeated the same behaviors he used to cope with his father in his relationship with his superiors. Thus, when he came home from work he was irritable and spouting venom about his bosses and co-workers. His wife was disturbed by this behavior, since it was too evocative of her own childhood experiences, and so she gave him little or no sympathy.

Problems with health had come to dominate their relationship, and the couple became competitive as to who would be the most needy. As his tendency to withdraw and his depressive style became prominent, her health invariably deteriorated. This led to his feeling increasingly helpless and to her becoming increasingly an invalid. They seemed stuck in a downward spiral in which their past needs for nurturance remained unsatisfied and frustrated, just as they had been in their families of origin. The Medic-Alert bracelets were symbolic of their needs to be taken care of by the other.

Although Phil was somewhat depressed when couples work began, he was nonetheless able to work and, relative to June, had a greater capacity to maintain his health. Thus, I concluded that there might be more possibility of therapeutic movement for this particular couple if I concentrated on him.

After a few couples sessions, I began to spend ten to fifteen minutes of each session working with each partner separately. These "intense" mini-sessions focused on explaining the responses of the mate and educating them as to alternative ways of dealing with the other. I gave each one suggestions of things to do and say at the appropriate time so that each started to become more empathic to the other. Because the mate did not hear me give the suggestion, the partner received "full credit" for the empathy he or she expressed. This approach began to defuse the tension between them.

Meanwhile, I gathered more details about their individual family histories, particularly about Phil's negative history concerning his father. In one session with him, I raised the issue of the Medic-Alert bracelet and in discussing it learned, not surprisingly, that he had a distorted understanding of his medical condition. I encouraged him to speak to his physician and to go to his public library and do some research about the condition to ascertain how truly serious it might be. I suggested to him that he might discover that it was relatively harmless, in which case he might try an experiment for one week to see how he might feel without wearing the bracelet.

"If you continue to wear the bracelet," I pointed out to him, "you're likely to think of yourself as an invalid, and others might see you that way too, especially your father. If you want to retain credibility with him as being in charge of your life, it might be important for him not to think of you as being an invalid. The only way that can happen is for you not to present yourself as one."

A week later, he came with his wife for a session and was beaming. He no longer wore the bracelet and reported having had a spirited conversation with his father from which he emerged with enormous self-satisfaction. He was sparkling with energy and so was his wife, who was seeing him afresh, as a vital, energetic man. Subsequently, he went on to make important career moves, and the relations as well as the communication between the couple improved dramatically.

Birth Defects and Other Health Problems in Children

Like other crises, the unexpected birth of a child with a physical or mental problem invariably tests the integrity of the family's constitution. If strong, the couple will tend to pull together and cope effectively with the crisis. If underlying problems exist, the couple is likely to fragment into bitterness, blaming one another. When this occurs, the couple is often referred for therapy. Such couples generally need active crisis management before they make better use of therapeutic time.

If blaming breaks out in a session, I find a firm statement to cut it out often helps to quiet things down so that therapy time can be used more effectively to mobilize the cooperative behaviors the couple needs in order to deal with the child's problems. Therapy continues to focus on helping the couple separate their personal, possibly long-standing conflicts from their need to cooperate around the child. I usually emphasize that their individual reactions are due largely to the pain they experience around the child's problems. Once the latter situation stabilizes, it becomes possible to deal with the couple's interpersonal difficulties.

Unresolved issues from the past and the shame and guilt of having produced a "defective" child frequently shape the couple's responses to one another and to the broader world. Family members and friends, out of their own feelings of anxiety or shame, do not often provide the support the couple needs at this point. At times, moreover, the couple rejects the support offered. Frequently, ambiguities about the etiology and prognosis of the child's condition interfere with coping efforts and make it difficult for the couple to resolve their interpersonal uncertainties.

Sudden infant death syndrome (SIDS) or the death of an infant from accident, infection, birth defect, or unknown causes often leaves parents bereft and filled with feelings of regret and guilt. "If only I had . . ." is a common refrain and the tendency to blame oneself or one's mate is equally as common. Self-blame may have an impact on the couple's relationship, especially when self-punishment is "required" by depriving oneself of usual pleasures (such as sex, vacations). Blaming the mate has a similar impact as the individual punishes him- or herself by punishing the mate.

As therapists, we should consider the fact that couples who have lost a child are often dazed, confused, and vulnerable to professional advice regarding mourning rituals, support groups, and so on. This is a time for us to provide maximum respect for the couple's needs rather than impose our own beliefs and assumptions regarding loss and grieving, the efficacy of which remains to be demonstrated.

HEALTH ISSUES AND PSYCHOLOGICAL DEFENSES

When health issues are intertwined with defensive needs, couples therapy becomes challenging since, as pointed out earlier, the expression of psychological defenses through the body (somatization) tends to elicit sympathy. Clients appear totally convincing in explaining their "problem," and many physicians and therapists are thus likely to focus attention on helping the client cope with the symptoms and miss the underlying dynamics. The couple tends to have an investment in protecting the defense, making therapeutic advance difficult to achieve.

FRED AND MARY

Fred, a recently retired salesman with a classic Type A personality, was referred for stress management work to help him reduce his high blood pressure. After an initial meeting, it became apparent that he had a marital problem, and soon thereafter we started couples therapy. He was on medication to lower his hypertension that had the unfortunate side effect of making it difficult for him to achieve and sustain an erection. Fred saw his marital problems and stress as stemming from the fact that his virility was undermined. His wife, Mary, said that she would like more tenderness from him, but, on the whole, she was satisfied with their sex life.

During the course of the therapy, Mary reported that he was more attentive to her, but because she had begun menopause her sexual needs were minimal. Fred, on the other hand, repeatedly complained that talking was not helping and, despite my best efforts to help him cope with stress, saw no change in the situation. He was beginning to explore the possibility of a penile implant as a solution to his impotency problem.

I found the lack of therapeutic movement puzzling and decided to see each partner separately for a few sessions. (When I begin therapy with couples, I invariably prepare them for this possibility.) In one such session with Mary, I asked, "How do you account for the fact that although you seem satisfied with what's going on, Fred is still complaining?" She replied, "That's just the way he is. He's been that way ever since. That's him." In exploring what she meant to say, it became clear that some important information was being withheld, namely that several years earlier at a Thanksgiving family gathering, one of the husband's sons from a previous marriage had fallen to his death, rock climbing. Mary saw the beginnings of Fred's loss of libido following this tragic event. She said, "They never talk about it."

I realized that what I had missed in my work to that point was that the impotency may have played a role in providing "punishment" for failing to protect his child, and such punishment was necessary to relieve Fred's guilt. Because she no longer wanted his sexual attention, Mary was somewhat complicit in maintaining the sexual status quo, but his threat of obtaining a penile implant operation may have encouraged her to "spill the beans."

I resumed couples work in which most of my attention now focused on the husband in the almost silent presence of the wife. (Mary had informed Fred of our previous conversation). I had him go back to his perceived origin of the impotency problem: a slow, careful, frame-by-frame analysis of events from just before the son's death, through that period, and finally, to his initial inklings of the impotency. The goal of our work was to help him reduce his guilt and subsequent need for self-punishment, which had the result of reducing the tensions between the two of them.

Illness as a Weapon

Health issues were a dominant aspect in the relationship of another couple, Carol and Jack, referred to me for marriage therapy. In this instance, illness was the proprietary focus of one partner and was used as an unsuccessful strategy to obtain understanding, closeness, and emotional support from the other.

Carol's health was a cudgel in their relationship. On more than one occasion she said that she expected recompense for the suffering she had endured in her life. The marriage became an arena in which the abuse to which she was subjected in childhood was repeatedly reenacted. Jack was expected to compensate for all the earlier pain, something he could not do, even if he wanted. The exact nature of such compensation was unclear, but it seemed to entitle Carol to be the one with a right to make demands and to reject any demand made by her spouse.

CAROL AND JACK

Carol was the oldest child, brought up in a lower-middle-class family in which she was pressed into a caregiving role at an early age. She had been sexually molested by her father and was subsequently confused about the motives of men and how to manage her simultaneous need for closeness and her enormous fear of it. These issues were being dealt with in her individual therapy with another therapist.

Jack was also the oldest child of a lower-middle-class family and strongly driven to succeed from an early age. He described his childhood as a happy one but, on the other hand, never had the feeling that his efforts were acknowledged. This was a common theme in his relationship with Carol. By dint of hard work, he became a regional sales manager for a large software company.

They married young (she saw marriage as a way of escaping from the intolerable situation at home), and both had successful careers. After the birth of the third child, Carol fell ill and underwent a series of surgeries including a hysterectomy and back surgery, which led to other disabling pains and medical problems. Doctors' appointments and hospitalizations became a way of life as difficulties compounded on difficulties. Pains gave way to a drug addiction, which, when resolved, led in turn to hormonal problems that could not be stabilized, which in turn led to memory problems. She had difficulty managing her medications, and under stress, her judgment seemed to become increasingly impaired. No organic basis for these problems was ever established, however.

The early years of their marriage were marked by a tendency to degenerate into ugliness, bordering on the physical. Over time, this style of conflict diminished, replaced mostly with insults, invective, and mutual denigration and fueled by alcohol consumption on both their parts. When I first saw them, their stories were mirror images of one another, and the truth was impossible to determine. Neither seemed to have anything positive to say about the other's functioning or parenting. They both threatened each other with divorce, but neither made a move in that direction. When asked why they continued to live together if things were as bad as they said they invariably found some rationale why long-term separation would not work, generally having to do with the deficiencies or vindictiveness of the partner. Also, they both said that underneath it all they loved each other, although on the surface, evidence for this seemed meager.

In working with this couple, I would frequently combine, or alternate between, individual and couples work. At one point, following another surgery, I visited the couple in their home and continued therapy there. In dealing with health issues, home visits sometimes become necessary when a person is bedridden, as, for example, after surgery, or can't for other reasons come to your office.

One learns a great deal about clients by making such visits. For example, some couples want you to see their dirty linen, as a metaphor of the disorganization in their inner lives, whereas others are scrupulously careful to let you see only their organized, "clean" side. The therapeutic material that emerges in such circumstances is often rewarding. Also, home visits give the therapist an opportunity to experience the therapeutic encounter on the clients' rather than their own turf, which often provides a fresh perspective on ostensibly familiar problems.

Some of the therapeutic interventions that seemed to help this couple consisted of the following:

1. Providing each with time to ventilate about the partner, a strategy that often brought short-term relief and improved the situation at home.

2. Interpreting the wife's use of health as a means of obtaining control over her environment. Repeatedly, I would point out how her fantasy of obtaining compensation for suffering was frustrated, leaving her angry and hateful toward her spouse. With repetition, using available instances as evidence, the frequency with which she asked for recompense declined noticeably. Simultaneously, any steps she took to improve her health were encouraged and rewarded.

3. Encouraging each to develop regular independent interests (for instance, regular golf for him, visits to relatives for her) to provide respite from the usual inclement climate in the home and to foster the development of sources of satisfaction not dependent on the partner.

4. Teaching the husband how to be more empathic to his wife, to distance himself from her occasional outbursts and invective, and to move physically closer to her in order to provide comforting.

5. Re-creating their reality by emphasizing, in the couples work, that underneath all the shouting and fighting was a desperate need to care about the other and to receive caring in return. It became important that as their joint ally they saw me as unperturbed by their "ugly" actions and able to see what was underneath it all: their need to be comforted and accepted. Also, whenever I used this strategy, it allowed their feelings of shame about their individual behavior to emerge and be verbalized.

UNEXPECTED TRAUMAS AND ILLNESSES

Into each relationship, rain must fall. For some it can be an overwhelming cloudburst: sudden heart attack, the diagnosis of cancer, or the need to have major surgery often shakes a couple's relationship to its foundation. The mate's confidence in the patient's physical integrity is often thrown into doubt. There is also a forceful reminder of the mate's mortality that could have manifold consequences for the family.

After major surgery or a serious illness, the patient tends to be perceived by the mate and others as being more fragile and vulnerable even if the former feels vigorous and strong. In many instances, mates suffer a great deal and may have few outlets to express their feelings given that it's the patient who has a health crisis to face. After surgery, angry feelings may be expressed for putting the mate through such pain or for not having taken better care of oneself so that the health crisis would not have occurred in the first place. If the patient is left debilitated by the illness or surgery, the mate may feel resentful that things turned out the way it did. One woman whose husband had a sudden incapacitating stroke put it this way: "It wasn't supposed to be this way. He was supposed to take care of me."

Trauma, too, may lead to behaviors that challenge the couple's coping ability. For example, a man was involved in a head-on collision that, among other things, damaged one of his arms. He experienced this as a narcissistic injury. He felt that because of his injuries he had become repugnant not only to himself but to others. Gradually this belief led to overeating and drinking and, consequently, he gained considerable weight. His wife found the weight gain a sexual turn-off, and between the two of them, sex came to a halt.

When several health-related events occur in a relatively short span of time, the couple's ability to cope successfully may be undermined. One couple, married nearly twenty-five years, had to deal with the husband's coronary bypass surgery and subsequent surgery for prostatic cancer within the short space of six months. From the onset, this marriage had been stormy. However, the wife's high dependency needs and lack of work skills led, after predictable periods of *Sturm und Drang*, to repeated reconciliations so that the marriage lasted, at least so long as the husband was seen as an economic provider. The surgeries, however, changed the picture. Her confidence in her husband's health and his ability to take care of her needs were shaken to such an extent that she divorced him in a fantasized attempt to find a more reliable provider.

The diagnosis of cancer often triggers massive confusion and terror in the face of which some couples become passive, leaving all decision making in the hands of "experts," whereas others mobilize themselves for the acquisition of information and the preparation for treatment. Couples work at this point is largely supportive crisis management aimed toward helping the couple contain emotions so that rational decision making might proceed.

When cancer is diagnosed in a person who is in individual therapy, a shift to couples work may help deal with the medical crisis. The mate may be confused as to how to support, console, and encourage the partner in whom the cancer has been found. The initial period of diagnosis generally is anxiety-laden for both partners, and the nonaffected mate may need active guidance to control his or her own anxiety and to respond appropriately to the partner.

As the person proceeds through treatment or surgery, other crises tend to develop, and the couple may become overwhelmed by the need for making life-and-death decisions; handling children, other family members, and friends; and dealing with the medical system. Periods of crisis tend to alternate with those of relative quiescence, providing opportunities to fine-tune therapy and therapeutic interventions to focus either on couples dynamics, the crisis, or both.

As pointed out earlier in the section on body image, bodily changes resulting from illnesses and their medical treatment may have profound effects on a couple's relationship. For example, mastectomy and chemotherapy, among other things, require major adjustments to the bodily changes that occur. Patients may experience themselves with repugnance and say to themselves, "How can my mate possibly find me attractive when I am so disfigured?" And indeed mates are sometimes repelled. These responses may lead to a withdrawal from one another and the experience of a loss of intimacy. Similar problems might be encountered among persons who had coronary bypass surgery or other disfiguring illnesses and traumas. In working with couples dealing with such body image issues, I often try to:

- Help them differentiate between the "disfigurement" and the overall person, so that the injured portion of the image is localized and contained rather than taking on a life of its own.

- Encourage each partner to talk about their feelings to the other, especially about what the "injury" represents to them, which helps defuse the emotionality of their responses.

- Help the mate understand the meaning of his or her partner's responses more clearly, as, for example, the response of post–coronary bypass individuals who tend to recoil when approached as if to protect themselves from further injury and pain to the chest region.

- Teach them new responses and effective ways of coping, as, for example, desensitizing procedures, such as massage, to help the spouse adapt to and incorporate the new bodily reality of the mate. Such procedures help contain emotional responses and also tend to reduce the latter's feelings of shame about their altered body image.

PROBLEMS FACED BY THE MATURING COUPLE

Perhaps the most challenging of health issues in couples therapy are those expected, normal changes that occur over time in the way our bodies look and function. All of us, therapists and clients alike, need, at some point in our lives, to adjust to the greying of our hair, the wrinkles, the weight gains, the loss or diminishing energy, the changes in libido, and so forth. When these changes come into conflict with our own or our partner's inner body image, disappointments and, at times, major friction erupt.

The fact that therapists share these problems with clients often lead them to overlook, deny, or misread the impact of body changes on their clients' functioning. By dealing with their clients' feelings, they are simultaneously exposing their own vulnerabilities regarding aging and mortality.

In the courtship period, potential mates generally attempt to present themselves in the most attractive light possible. After the relationship has been established, however, there is a tendency to relax the rigorous routines that keep the individual trim and in good shape. Weight gains often occur, especially after a pregnancy. These changes generally occur relatively early on in the couple's relationship and require adaptations on the part of both the individual and the mate. As the couple matures, further adaptations are required to accommodate to the changes that normally occur in the maturing body. Fat distribution patterns change, bellies protrude, skin tone diminishes, breasts begin to sag, and so forth. Some couples experience the changes in themselves or their mates with rejecting ("This person in the mirror is not me"), sometimes repugnant, loathsome feelings ("This person I'm living with is FAT!"). These feelings frequently interfere with the degree of intimacy a couple may achieve.

When partners engage in activities designed to maintain bodily functioning (for example, exercise, dietary control), it facilitates the acceptance of the changes that occur. Conversely, when a mate is seen as not caring for (generally, his) body, the partner sometimes withdraws emotionally, as if to prepare themselves for premature widowhood. In one instance, a woman saw her husband's inadequate health maintenance behavior as a sign of lost virility and as an indication that she needed to prepare herself for imminent long-term caretaking of an impaired spouse. This aroused considerable anger since that prospect was unpalatable.

How couples deal with body changes exposes the strengths and limitations of the relationship. Couples with a psychological sophistication or maturity often deal with these bodily changes in a way that allows the retention of attractive feelings toward the mate and the continued desire for intimacy, as well as empathy and understanding (for instance, "He's aging, but so am I"). Less mature couples tend to have difficulty differentiating between the part and the whole and are more rejecting of their partner when bodily changes occur. In my experience, men seem to have greater difficulty in accepting the body changes of their mates than women do.

Couples in midlife often experience major changes in their body and self-images underscored or in response to many personal, interpersonal, and cultural factors. Cultural factors are generally expressed in terms of mostly impossible "ideals" against which individuals evaluate themselves and generally come up deficient. The aging individual is less valued than the younger person in American culture. In fact, we equate youth with desirability as an overcompensation for our fears of disability and death.

Although cultural ideals for men are less stringent than those for women, many men and women experience aging as a narcissistic injury and as a reminder of one's mortality. This sometimes leads to behavior designed to undo the injury and to prove that one is still attractive, sexually desirable, and potent, behavior often directed outside the relationship and, generally, with major ramifications within the relationship. In some instances, both partners may simultaneously have extrarelational affairs. As one's career reaches its zenith or as one's energy flags in middle age, men's hearts and eyes may begin to roam to younger pastures. The involvement of men with younger women is a way of saying to oneself that one is still virile and young. It acts as a defense against the reality that one is aging.

When affairs are exposed, couples may enter therapy in an attempt to salvage their relationship. Some come in order to reduce the guilt they might feel terminating a relatively long-standing relationship with their partner so as to establish or continue another relationship with someone else. How the therapist manages the disappointments, hurt, and anger emerging in the early stages of couples therapy in such situations may have a determining impact on whether the original relationship can be saved. I almost invariably inform couples that I have a pro-marriage bias, and, if they continue to work with me in a cooperative way, I generally interpret it as their desire to reconcile.

In my experience, many therapists working with mature couples often fail to realize the extent to which difficulties in adjusting to body image changes and fears of death fuel the communication difficulties, frustrated or inadequate sexuality, insufficient intimacy, and the other complaints and discontents that bring such couples into therapy. By encouraging the couple to separate and divorce or to strive for self-fulfillment at this point in their lives, some therapists collude with the couple to avoid dealing with their underlying difficulties and fears. Therapy in such circumstances should help the couple focus their attention on the more basic difficulties regarding the meaning body changes has for each partner. Such therapy work consists largely of providing perspective on their life together and their present struggle.

For example, a couple was referred to me for marital therapy by their family physician. The husband, Ralph, was fifty-eight, and the wife, Joan, fifty-four. They were married thirty-one years and had three children, one grandchild, and another on the way. The marriage was rather traditional, with Joan having spent most of her married life as a homemaker. Just before the first grandchild was born, Ralph began an affair with a thirty-five-year-old woman he met on a business trip. They met periodically over the course of several years. One day Ralph came home and told Joan that he wanted a divorce. Joan was devastated, and the broader family went into turmoil. The couple entered brief marital counseling with a young therapist who advised them to separate. Joan continued therapy with the counselor, and Ralph moved out and attempted to create a new life with his "lady friend." In due time, Joan, on the urging of the counselor, sued for divorce and soon thereafter quit therapy. Ralph's relationship with his lady friend also fell apart, and he began to develop a cardiac arrhythmia that sent him to a family physician, who referred both of them to me.

The breakup of the husband's affair offered an opportunity for the couple to begin to see each other once more, tentatively and with enormous caution, each continuing to live in their separate residences. Besides brief sporadic telephone conversations, the meetings in my office became important contact points for the couple, which I encouraged them to extend by going out to dinner afterward so that they might continue to discuss the issues that came up in the session.

By meeting with each one individually as part of our weekly meetings, it was possible to take the temperature of the relationship in an ongoing way and identify "red-flag" or charged issues. I also found these meetings invaluable in assessing the strength of the couple's (often) unspoken wishes to come back together. In addition, it was possible to deal more intensely with the meaning of their behavior regarding aging and bodily changes. These behaviors were often shame-laden and difficult for them to share with much empathy and without discussions breaking down into defensive recriminations. By helping each one verbalize in "private" what was eventually said to one another, the shame and defensive aspects of these interactions were minimized.

Invariably, long-held discontents and resentments surfaced in the couple's sessions, giving the appearance that there was nothing left to save in their relationship. This left them in a hopelessly despairing place. I found that it became important, at such moments, to create the illusion that the couple's feelings of defeat were transient and that my extensive life experiences would be available to help them weather the storm.

Some of the issues or questions raised in their sessions were ones designed to help them find some perspective:

- Had they considered the positive aspects of their history together? In their life together they had achieved a great deal by working together. Had they lost sight of these achievements?

- Had they weighed the consequences of throwing away a relationship with a history, replete with shared experiences of pain and joy, one providing a context for tomorrow, for one without history and the need to develop context?

- Had they considered the possibilities of the loneliness, regret, and isolation they might likely experience if they cast away their familiar relationship, with all its trials and possible rewards, for untried and untested relationships they fantasized developing?

Eventually, after more than a year of couples therapy, during which each attempted to date others, Ralph moved back to (now) Joan's home. This transition did not work out well since both of them had grown somewhat accustomed to greater leg room and living alone. However, with my assistance, they worked out new ground rules for their interactions, and a second attempt of cohabitation succeeded. They moved to another neighborhood and purchased a new home as a symbol of a new beginning.

Ralph subsequently had surgery to install a pacemaker, and with his recuperation at their new home, their relationship stabilized. Last Christmas, I received a card from them informing me they had renewed their marriage vows and thanking me for "saving their marriage."

AGING COUPLES

As couples continue to age, more mental and physical problems emerge. For example, in the United States almost two million senior citizens a year are diagnosed with depression. This is reflected in the relatively higher suicide rate among persons sixty-five years and older. In addition, such diseases as Parkinsonism, Alzheimer's, and other disorders increase in frequency, requiring greater and greater contacts with the medical system and increasing the tendency to despondency and despair. Couples become aware of the fact that they are less energetic, more frail, and liable to disability and loneliness as friends die off or they themselves become disabled. The thought that one may have to care for a debilitated partner is an especially troubling one and may encourage one partner in a relationship to withdraw emotionally or physically in order to "save" themselves.

Therapy in cases of this kind often consists in helping the couple to problem-solve practical issues and find resources to assist them, and in providing a sense of encouragement by accentuating the positive. Also, it's important to ascertain the degree to which the couple is prepared practically for long-term care, chronic illness, and so forth, since when insurance, social support networks, and other practical matters are in place, it helps the couple deal with psychological issues more effectively.

Susan Sontag once wrote, "Illness is the night-side of life" and "sooner or later each of us is obliged . . . to identify ourselves as citizens of . . . [the realm of the sick]." The ubiquitous nature of

illness infiltrates the human condition and illuminates our vulnerabilities and dreads.

Morbidity portends mortality. Thus, when illness strikes, it
touches on fundamental human responses, from which therapists
are no more immune than clients. This makes health issues
among the more challenging for therapists to deal with in both
individual and couples therapy.

In working with couples around issues of health and illness,
you need to consider the:

- Psychological maturity of the couple
- Stage of the life cycle in which illness occurs (that is, the life
  tasks that need to be accomplished at that stage)
- Meaning given to illness by each partner
- Individual style of dealing with illness
- Individual body image

When dealing with health issues, don't close your eyes to their
presence in couples dynamics. Learn to master your own feelings of discomfort, anxiety, and fear about illness and death. This
is an ongoing, life-long learning. Get consultation or advice from
other professionals when you feel you are dealing with issues
beyond your ken. Also, stay informed about health issues and
recent advances in research. I recommend *Science News* as well
as the weekly science page and Jane Brody's weekly "Personal
Health" column in the *New York Times* as a way of staying on top
of current ideas in the field of biomedicine.

NOTES

P. 138, *Health issues play multiple roles in interpersonal relationships:* Shontz, F. C.
(1975). *The psychological aspects of physical illness and disability.* New York:
Macmillan.

P. 139, *Persons who may feel guilt . . . of self-punishment:* Shontz, F. C. (1975).
ibid. p. 165.

P. 141, *Schemas about the body develop early in life:* Shontz, F. C. (1975). *ibid.* pp. 64–70; Shontz, F. C. (1990). Body image and physical disability. In T. F. Cash & T. Pruzinsky (Eds.), *Body images: Deviance and change* (pp. 149–169). New York: Guilford.

P. 142, *Some children are singled out early in life:* Kessler, S. (1988). Psychological aspects of genetic counseling. V. Preselection: A family coping strategy in Huntington disease. *American Journal of Medical Genetics, 31,* 617–621.

P. 142, *preselecting . . . helps others . . . contain their anxieties:* Kessler, S. (1988). *ibid.*

P. 142, *When . . . hereditary disorders . . . kept secret:* Kessler, S. (1993). The spouse in the Huntington disease family. *Family Systems Medicine, 11,* 191–199.

P. 143, *Huntington's disease, an inherited . . . disorder:* Kessler, S. (1993). *ibid.*

P. 144, *multiple sclerosis (MS): Dorland's Illustrated Medical Dictionary* (1965, 24th ed., p. 1354). Philadelphia: Saunders; Silverberg, D. H. (1992). The demyelinating diseases. In J. B. Wyngaarden, L. H. Smith, Jr., & J. C. Bennett (Eds.), *Cecil's textbook of medicine* (19th ed., pp. 2196–2200). Philadelphia: Saunders.

P. 144, *mitral valve prolapse:* Rackley, C. E. (1992). Valvular heart disease. In J. B. Wyngaarden, L. H. Smith, Jr., & J. C. Bennett (Eds.), *Cecil's textbook of medicine* (19th ed., pp. 330–331). Philadelphia: Saunders.

P. 146, *shame and guilt of having . . . a "defective" child:* Kessler, S., Kessler, H., & Ward, P. (1984). Psychological aspects of genetic counseling. III. Management of guilt and shame. *American Journal of Medical Genetics, 17,* 673–697.

P. 148, *Type A personality:* Friedman, M., & Rosenman, R. H. (1974). *Type A behavior and your heart.* New York: Knopf.

P. 148, *failing to protect his child . . . guilt:* Lipowski, Z. J. (1970). Physical illness, the individual, and the coping process. *Psychiatry in Medicine, 1,* 91–102.

P. 152, *tends to be perceived . . . as being more fragile:* Kessler, S. (1995). *Heart bypass: How to prepare your mind, your emotions, and your self for a successful outcome.* New York: St. Martins.

P. 153, *The diagnosis of cancer:* McDaniel, S. H., Hepworth, J., & Doherty, W. (1993). A new prescription for family health care. *Networker, 17,* 18–29, 62–63.

P. 153, *The mate may be confused:* Locke, L. (1994). Breast cancer: Caring for the whole woman. *Stanford Alumni Association Magazine, 22,* 31–33.

P. 154, *mastectomy and chemotherapy:* Locke, L. (1994). *ibid.*

P. 154, *"How can my mate . . . find me attractive:* Locke, L. (1994). *ibid.*; Brody, J. (1994, November 30). After cancer and its treatment, planning can make a major difference in a patient's sex life. *New York Times*, p. B6.

P. 154, *response of post–coronary bypass individuals:* Kessler, S. (1995). *op. cit.*

P. 155, *the way our bodies look and function:* Scarf, M. (1992). The middle of the journey. *Networker, 16,* 51–55.

P. 156, *Couples in midlife . . . cultural factors:* Scarf, M. (1992). *ibid.*

P. 156, *The aging individual is less valued:* Scarf, M. (1992). *ibid.*

P. 160, *two million senior citizens . . . diagnosed with depression:* Author unknown. (1994, Fall). Battling the blues in the golden years. *Psych Update*, pp. 1–2; American Psychiatric Association. (1992). *Mental health of the elderly.* Washington, DC: Author.

P. 160, *Susan Sontag:* Sontag, S. (1978). Illness as metaphor. *New York Review of Books, 24,* pp. 10–16.

CHAPTER

6

THE DIFFICULT COUPLE

Steven A. Foreman

What makes the difficult couple difficult? As therapists, we describe couples as "difficult" based on the troubled feelings we are left with—uninspired, bored, mournful, or horrified—when treating or even thinking about them afterward. Our countertransference is the first identifying signal.

What experience triggers such an internal reaction? Usually it's when the couple refuses to get better. The partners fail to solve the problems with which they came into therapy. They suffer and struggle terribly but seem to drag each other down like drowning victims with their arms locked around each others' necks. The therapist feels he or she is watching or participating in the tragedy, like a third member pulled into the morass.

Therapists can feel victimized and unfairly attacked when difficult patients blame, criticize, or yell. Or we can feel responsible and guilty for failing to alleviate the suffering of one or both partners. With difficult couples, we invariably get drawn into the drama, facing the pain, despair, and sense of no way out that grips the couple.

This chapter will highlight some of the reasons that these couples are so difficult to treat; their identifying characteristics shed light on strategies we can use to extricate ourselves and our clients from these apparently impossible messes. Difficult couples seem to weave "spells" that paralyze and torment each other and the therapist. I'll outline the origins and mechanisms of these spells by illustrating how couples reenact pathological relationships from their past and how they engage each other and the therapist in dramas that reflect how little satisfaction they feel they deserve in their lives. Understanding the nature of their distorted beliefs and resisting the pernicious power of their spells can help the therapist forge an inspired treatment plan.

IDENTIFYING DIFFICULT COUPLES

In addition to using the barometer of our own countertransference, we can identify difficult couples by several factors:

1. Their interpersonal behaviors are more disturbed both inside and outside the therapy, characterized by abuse and self-destructiveness.

2. Their childhood experiences are more disturbed, and their histories are often marked by severe psychological trauma such as parental loss, abuse, or neglect.

3. There is often concomitant psychiatric illness such as major depression, serious substance abuse, or even psychosis.

The couple's disturbed current behavior and disturbed childhood experiences are directly related. Each partner reenacts pathological relationship patterns from the family of origin. The partners play different roles, including how each acted as a child, how the parents acted toward them, and how the parents treated each other. Reenactments in relationships are fairly universal and are often healthy since they're one of the ways people face and reexamine the normally painful experiences and parental mistakes they endured growing up. These reenactments are part of the growing process that relationships offer in life.

But sometimes people get stuck in their reenactments. Instead of breaking out of old patterns with a new relationship, a person can drag the new one into old patterns. This happens when the psychological issues of each partner intersect in ways that make it impossible to help each other and actually intensify or aggravate each person's pathological behaviors. Even though there are two dramas being reenacted (one from each family of origin), each person is only aware of the one in which he or she is consumed. In these intractable conflicts, two people are usually under the illusion they are fighting about the same thing. In reality, each partner is working on an individual issue, which is different from the partner's issue, even though both issues are occurring simultaneously.

So, difficult couples are stuck in unhappy repetitions of past family relationships. They are usually unaware that their current problems have any relation to the unresolved conflicts of their families of origin. They are also completely absorbed in their current despair and desperation. Almost all couples who seek therapy feel somewhat stuck. But difficult couples are more stuck. Their pathological families of origin resulted in more pathological reenactments in their adult relationship.

Such difficult couples often have an underlying belief that they have no hope and no right to solve their mess. This hopeless feeling is driven by lifelong experiences of interpersonal failure first as children and then as adults. The despair is also driven by an often unconscious, overwhelming feeling of guilt and self-blame.

As children in dysfunctional families they felt responsible, however irrationally, for their parents' failures and family suffering. Subsequently, they often feel very guilty trying to solve their relationship problems (which they desperately want to do) because they believe that if they get their needs met, they'll damage the other person in the relationship, just as they believed as children. Their exaggerated worries are reinforced, moreover, by watching their partners suffer following their repetitive painful interactions. This guilt about damaging others becomes more intense because they choose partners who, like their parents and siblings, are relatively psychologically fragile.

Partners in difficult couples feel guilty doing better than their parents and siblings, which is why they tend to repeat such

pathological relationships so faithfully, unconsciously, and tenaciously. They actively undermine themselves and each other in
their efforts to solve their problems. In therapy, they don't get
better, or else they get better then slip backward.

As these couples falter, the therapist feels anxious, deflated,
and helpless. The couple repeats their parents' pathologic behavior, and they unconsciously place the therapist in the same position they were in as children. The therapist ends up watching
the couple flail and flounder, feeling the same helplessness and
guilt each partner felt watching their parents.

In the treatment of almost all couples, blame plays a central
role. Most partners in conflict feel blamed and then blame one
another. But difficult couples have a more exquisite sensitivity to
blame. This is because they feel intolerably guilty and external-
ize blame more than most. They also have grown up with more
blame so they feel it and sling it back more readily.

Many people in relationships have a hard time asserting their
needs, which leads to unhappiness and problems in communication. Partners in difficult couples have even less ability to assert
their needs. There are many reasons for this inability including
cognitive and emotional deficits that inhibit awareness or expression of feelings. Much of this inability to express needs comes
from the partners' profound lack of a sense of appropriate entitlement based on their childhood histories of abuse or neglect.
Unconsciously, these unhappy people feel greedy for wanting
too much and guilty if they get what they need.

SAM AND JODY

I'd like to illustrate some of these general principles with a clinical
case description of a very difficult couple, Sam and Jody, who were
in their late forties. This couple came for treatment following a
recurrent incident in which Sam abusively humiliated Jody.

It was the second marriage for each. They both drank alcohol,
although Jody's dependence was more severe. Sam was a corporate

executive who was domineering and controlling. Jody retreated and withdrew when he got angry, which only provoked him to be more aggressively intrusive. Her alcohol use and cigarette smoking worried Sam. Then she would lie to him, hide bottles, and pretend she wasn't smoking, which worried and infuriated him more. He would chase her down and force her to listen to him. He became physically violent three or four times in the marriage, slapping her.

Sam's father died of an alcohol-related illness when Sam was twenty-one years old. Sam described his mother as intrusive and abusive. She would chase him around the house, yelling at him, complaining, and invading his privacy.

Jody's family had attended a fundamentalist church that required strict adherence to its edicts. Nonconformity was punished by banishment from the congregation and from the family. Though not alcoholic, her parents were physically out of control and verbally abusive to her as a child.

The current relationship of this couple repeated several pathological aspects of their families of origin. Sam was "sensitive" about his wife's alcohol use because it reminded him of his father's alcohol-related death. When he worried about her, he acted just like his mother treated him: intrusive, aggressive, and abusive. He didn't realize at first that his behavior was a reenactment of his mother's style but thought he needed to be "in control all the time." In his first session, he reported, "I inflict emotional pain. The more I do, the less I get. I'm not smart enough to control that." Later he said, "I've worn her down, broken her spirit. It's the opposite of what I want. . . . The last thing I want is to hurt her."

Jody was also repeating several patterns from her childhood. She was acting like a "bad" child by smoking and drinking, just as she did in her family of origin. They were always threatening to reject or punish her because of her rebellious behavior. She reenacted this relationship with her husband, whom she invited to punish or reject her. And just as she did with her parents, Jody felt responsible for her husband getting wildly out of control when provoked. In addition, her drinking was a form of acting out of control, a way of identifying with her parents. Sam, likewise, identified with his parents, particularly his mother, by acting out of control. Neither could stop their behavior or influence the other's behavior. Indeed, each only seemed to make the other worse.

This case illustrates how Jody's and Sam's individual issues were simultaneously operating without either one of them being aware of it. Jody wanted to be accepted and treated with respect in order to overcome her childhood belief that she had no right to expect that. Just as she provoked her parents in the unconscious hope of obtaining help and not rejection, she tested Sam with her "bad" behavior. In doing so, she inadvertently collided with Sam's issue of worry, which triggered his excessive controlling and abusive behavior.

Sam's behavior provoked Jody to continue her pattern, and her behavior provoked him to continue his. His behavior confirmed her belief that she deserved to live her life acting and being treated like a despicable creature.

Both saw the other's behavior through the lens of their individual experiences. For Sam, Jody's behavior was irresponsible and only served to torture him. For Jody, Sam was just another person abusing her because she was such a bad person. She could not see how truly worried he was about her, because his abusive behavior seemed inconsistent with such feelings.

TREATMENT

The treatment of the difficult couple begins like the treatment of any couple, by supporting both partners, by finding out where each person wants to go, and by stopping the cycle of blame. The therapist can wade into the fight and try to solve it. In so doing, the therapist can "translate" for each partner what the other is saying and then interpret how each misunderstands the other and inadvertently pushes each other's buttons. The therapist can encourage each partner to elucidate more clearly their needs as part of practical problem solving as well as part of a campaign to disabuse each partner of mistaken ideas about what the other really wants. In the course of trying to solve the couple's problem, the therapist can note what is getting in the way of the solution when initial problem solving doesn't work.

But it's usually the case with difficult couples that clarification of issues and rational problem solving will not be enough to resolve the couple's problems. The difficult couple does not get better in the same way as "other" couples. This chapter will outline a step-by-step process for effective treatment. It will discuss developing an appropriate attitude or therapeutic stance in which the therapist masters his or her own countertransference feelings and simultaneously helps break the spell that binds the couple.

Taking Both Sides

In any treatment, it is crucial for the therapist to approach the couple in the role of a resource and an ally to both members. This position cannot be sustained if the therapist takes one side against the other or falls into the invitation to blame either of them. The therapist has to be alert to the couple's sensitivity and avoid tactless communications that might be misperceived as blame. By mastering this, the therapist also serves as a model for the couple of the art of clear and straightforward communication. Difficult couples' hypersensitivity to blame becomes evident early in the treatment.

For example, in the first session of another case, when Julie yelled and snarled at her husband Bob for having an affair, he became inarticulate and confused. Bob was so paralyzed, he couldn't think clearly or present his side. Julie was so hurt and angry, she did little more than yell and blame. This pattern of communication was ineffective and exemplified long-standing problems in their relationship. Julie tended to suffer, blame, and not listen to Bob, while Bob tended to get confused, quietly withdraw, and avoid Julie.

As the therapist, I felt frustrated and a little irritated by each partner's obvious self-centeredness and insensitivity to the other. Julie's relentless complaining was grating, while Bob's passivity and marital betrayal was disappointing. Neither seemed motivated to change their repetitive interactional style even though it was damaging. If I was looking for an excuse to blame someone, both partners presented themselves as inviting candidates.

Any couples therapist knows that once you take sides with one partner against the other, the therapy will fail. I could have sided with Bob agreeing that Julie was miserable to live with, or I could have sided with Julie as the rightfully angry victim of a deceitful and psychologically paralyzed husband. Some therapists try to remedy this dilemma by blaming both partners equally, attempting to appear at least evenhanded. My experience has been that when therapists tell patients how awful they are, this does not lead to new insights and growth but instead confirms the patients' underlying beliefs that they are bad and undeserving, which intensifies their maladaptive behaviors.

Difficult patients, like other patients, test the therapist from the first session onward to see whether the therapist will be judgmental or rejecting. But the tests are more exaggerated and more compelling. The therapist feels intensely drawn to believe the patients' portrayal of themselves as blameworthy and rejectable. This is the "spell" difficult patients weave, convincing the people in their lives—the partner, the therapist, and others—of the veracity of their distorted beliefs about themselves and provoking them to respond negatively.

The therapist's strategy should be to avoid falling for the invitation to judge and blame. This may sound easy, but the therapist may often feel like Odysseus bound to the mast, trying to resist the Siren call. Even though we are intellectually committed to being nonjudgmental, sometimes therapists underestimate the patients' power to convince us of their monstrous self-image and to provoke us to judge or dismiss them based on that.

Not only should the therapist avoid blame, but it is helpful to be positive and supportive of both partners' wished-for personal goals. For example, Jody tried to overcome her belief that she was bad and deserving of punishment, while Sam tried to overcome his conviction that he was responsible for other people's pathology. They both wanted to overcome their compulsions to be out of control like their parents. Consequently, I allied myself with each one's strivings, and, at the same time, examined whether there was anything essentially incompatible about their needs in the relationship.

Determining Each Partner's Direction

Helping each person identify and achieve personal goals requires taking each person seriously. This is problematic with difficult patients because they invite you not to take them seriously. They look like they enjoy their hellish relationships and seem to have no interest in healthy goals. My strong assumption is that this is an illusion, another "spell" that the therapist should resist. Rather, we should actively reframe the difficult patients' behavior in a way that challenges their distorted beliefs about themselves and also helps shed light on what is adaptive about what they're trying to do.

For example, in the case of Sam and Jody, some therapists might have said that Sam sadistically enjoyed tormenting Jody and that Jody really wanted to suffer masochistically as a passive aggressive way to torment Sam. This formulation seems consistent with their behavior. However, I didn't believe that suffering and tormenting each other truly reflected what they wanted. I aligned myself with the part of Sam who said he didn't want to hurt Jody and the part of Jody who said she didn't want to be treated badly by Sam.

Early in therapy, I asked both of them about their individual goals to see whether there were any areas of common ground. It turned out there was considerable overlap—including their commitment to the marriage, their respect for each other, and their sexual interests—which instilled some hope. Then I encouraged both partners to spell out their side of the intense provocative cycle, enabling them to hear each other more clearly. It was at this point that Jody for the first time heard how worried Sam was about her, and, in turn, Sam heard how Jody really feared rejection. This allowed them to experience one another as real people rather than as ghosts from the past. Once it was clear to me what dramas each was reenacting, I could elucidate them, facilitating their disengagement from each other's repetitions. Even though people are compulsively drawn to repeat their troubled pasts, my assumption is that they actually want to be free not to repeat but to achieve some degree of intimacy and mutuality in their relationship.

Eventually, I told them that Jody repeated with Sam what she did with her parents: she acted like a "bad" kid and provoked Sam to be punitive like her parents. Similarly, I told them that Sam was repeating his mother's behavior by acting overbearing and abusive toward Jody, not because he liked it or wanted to but out of unconscious loyalty to his mother. I told him that he really wanted a different relationship with Jody than his mother had with him, which is why they were entering therapy to change these repetitive patterns.

Stopping the Cycle of Blame

Supporting both members and reframing the conflict psychologically are instrumental in stopping the partners from blaming each other. It is helpful for the therapist to address the cycle of blame directly: "No wonder you don't trust each other. You're in the middle of a battle. Blame is in the air. You can't really hear each other because you're both very sensitive to being blamed. When one of you rightfully defends yourself, the other one feels blamed and blames back. There is an illusion that what you both want is incompatible, but I don't think that's true based on what I hear you saying."

An example that illustrates stopping the blame cycle was the case of Betty, a forty-year-old woman who complained of recurrent health concerns, and her husband, Jack, who regularly dismissed and criticized her for being a "hypochondriac." Betty had a breast lump and wanted to be able to talk about her fears about breast cancer while the couple was waiting for the results of the biopsy. Jack didn't want to entertain speculations about cancer before the results of the biopsy were in. He encouraged her to take one step at a time and not to worry unnecessarily until they actually had a confirmed diagnosis. Betty felt dismissed and rejected by Jack's refusal to talk.

This interchange was upsetting to both of them. There had been other health scares, including an episode of rectal bleeding and recurrent abdominal pains. During each episode, Betty wanted support from Jack but was bitterly disappointed and angry when she felt shut out. Jack was fearful of getting swallowed up in Betty's "hysteria." He thought she enjoyed being in crisis and felt she perversely wanted to drag him down with her. He became resentful and avoided her when she was having her health crisis "of the week," as he called them. He derided and blamed her for creating problems unnecessarily.

Betty was quite hurt by Jack's anger and apparent indifference. She was convinced Jack didn't care about her since he was so hurtful when she felt vulnerable. She felt her needs to be cared for, loved, and heard were a burden to him. In her anger she fought back by blaming her husband for being insensitive and uncaring.

On his side, Jack felt overwhelmed by what he saw as Betty's endless physical problems and emotional needs. He felt responsible to solve her problems and suffered enormous guilt because he was unable to relieve her anxiety and physical discomfort. His guilt led him to blame Betty.

Their individual childhood experiences fanned their marital difficulties. Betty's mother was very depressed, needy, self-centered, and an inadequate caregiver. Betty came to believe that her own needs were burdensome to her mother and to everyone else, including Jack.

Jack's mother died of cancer when he was six years old, and his heightened sense of responsibility and failure to help Betty presumably derived from that experience. Betty's possible illness and emotional distress made him feel so threatened and helpless that he was unable to respond or even listen to her.

Betty's assumption that her fundamental needs for love and attention tormented her husband was reinforced by Jack's exaggerated painful responses to her. In fact, Jack was tormented, not by her needs but by his guilt that he was not able to help her more. His suffering only increased her guilt so that both came to believe that they were responsible for the other's suffering. Jack blamed Betty for being too needy, and she blamed him for not helping her enough, which confirmed each of their worst fears.

To stop the cycle of blame, I pointed out that Jack was really very worried about Betty's physical complaints and felt to blame for not being more effective in helping her. I noted that since Jack felt so much self-blame, he felt compelled to blame her for being too needy. I also pointed out that Betty felt very much to blame for having so many problems and burdening her husband. To counter her self-blame, she blamed him for being insensitive.

In order for Jack to stop blaming Betty, I told them he needed to relax his expectations to solve all her problems. I basically gave him permission to do much less than he thought he needed to. Instead of solving all her problems, he just had to listen and not attack her.

In order for Betty to stop blaming Jack for being too insensitive, I bolstered her sense of appropriate entitlement and said she should get more emotional support from him. Instead of retreating in shame from the accusations that she was too needy, I encouraged her to ask clearly for the time and attention she needed.

I was very concrete in facilitating negotiations to solve this problem. After ascertaining that Jack thought Betty needed twenty-four hours a day of hand holding, I asked Betty whether anything less than that would be sufficient for her needs. She said she needed some time from Jack she could count on because he always put her off and ended up giving her nothing. I asked her if fifteen or twenty minutes of time to talk would be enough.

He sneered that that would never be enough for her. She said that would actually be fine if he really did it, but she was sure he'd have no interest in giving her that much time.

Betty was suspicious when he said that was acceptable because she was sure he would let her down and not follow through. We agreed if it was inconvenient for him to talk at a particular time, he would suggest a specific later time. I helped them negotiate a plan that included fifteen to twenty minutes of time daily for Betty to talk about her physical complaints and for Jack to listen without trying to help too much and without being critical.

They were surprised to find out their worst fears did not come true: she was not a bottomless pit, and he was not completely uncaring. By encouraging both to articulate concretely what they wanted, their misconceptions were relieved. He discovered that he could help her a lot by doing much less work, and she discovered that he actually cared about her and was willing to give her time and attention. It slowly dawned on Jack that he was not omnipotently responsible for his wife, while Betty learned that her needs were not as excessive and toxic as she had thought.

WHEN SOLVING THE FIGHT DOESN'T WORK

In the therapy with Sam and Jody, I tried to help solve their conflicts as described earlier, by (1) identifying what each person was fighting about, (2) identifying hot buttons, and (3) identifying misunderstandings. Early on, we attempted to solve conflicts concretely by devising plans that addressed both of their needs.

For example, I worked with the couple about rules for arguing. They seemed to argue at any time about any subject. Jody complained that she was constantly criticized, so I suggested a fifteen-minute moratorium on criticism about any subject when Sam first came home from work. I worked with them to keep their arguments simple and to limit the duration.

Even though Sam and Jody seemed articulate, motivated, and capable of addressing the issues, they would go home and repeat the cycle with renewed vehemence. In the third session, they made an agreement to stop their intense fighting. In the fourth session, Jody reported, "Things aren't going well. He said I should be slapped around for lying."

I interpreted that both Sam and Jody were taking too much responsibility for the other's behavior. I suggested that when Jody drinks, Sam should not stop caring, but he should stop harassing her. I suggested that when Sam worries about her, Jody should not take it to heart and assume that she is a terrible person. This remark seemed helpful because Jody then recalled from her childhood that in her family's church, she had to go along with authority or be cast out. Sam said, "I didn't know that. I won't cast you out."

Their relationship seemed to improve. Their fights temporarily lessened. Sam liked the fact that she stopped taking his criticisms so much to heart. We talked about Sam's concern about her cigarette smoking. I observed that Jody was playing the role of a rebellious teenager and Sam was playing the punitive parent. This allowed them to relax and feel closer.

In the following session, they reported that everything fell apart again. They had another fight at home. Sam was critical. She withdrew. He attacked her more fervently. She threatened to leave. They stopped the fight for about an hour and then resumed antagonisms again. I observed that, despite the relapse, this was still an improvement in their relationship; they were able to avoid slipping into the fight as easily as they had previously, and then they were able to stop fighting for an hour. I worked with them to reconstruct how and why each of them slipped back into this old pattern.

After three months of therapy, Jody offered to stop drinking. Sam said that wasn't necessary, she should only cut back. I had spelled out how destructive alcohol was to both of them and that they might have to stop drinking completely. I now used this opportunity to encourage complete abstinence from alcohol for both of them. In the next session, Sam said, "We're not going anywhere. Drinking is still going on." Jody said, "That's not true.

I stopped. I just drank once when you unfairly accused me of drinking." He said, "I can't trust you," at which point she got up and left the office despite my asking her to stay.

After she left, I spoke to Sam about the necessity for both of them to stop drinking and for Sam to stop worrying, berating, and treating her like a child. I encouraged him to pursue individual therapy in addition to the couples work. Jody came back in the next session and apologized for walking out but reaffirmed her right to protect herself against Sam's criticisms. In the discussions of abstaining from alcohol over the next month, Jody did not agree to stop but only said she wanted to cut back, a reversal of her previous position. Sam agreed with that plan, but I strongly recommended she stop drinking and contact Alcoholics Anonymous.

A Turning Point

During a session in the fifth month of therapy, in which the couple fought over their repetitive issues—Jody's drinking and Sam's criticism—I realized for the first time that neither partner was going to allow themselves to gain control of their own behavior while the other was out of control.

I interpreted this to them, saying, in effect, that each felt guilty of outdoing the other. This created a self-perpetuating system since each was waiting for the other to be in control before they would change their own behavior. Jody agreed enthusiastically with the interpretation.

This was a turning point in the therapy. In the next session, Sam came alone because Jody had checked herself into a thirty-day inpatient alcohol program. Sam said, "I took to heart the discussion last week," following which he described acting differently in response to Jody's provocations. He didn't "bite," and he didn't really get angry. He offered her the telephone number of the inpatient alcohol program, and she threw it out. Later she asked for it again, and he gave it to her. They had both shifted in their behavior.

In that session, Sam spontaneously explored his past for the first time. His history and dynamics seemed clearer to both of us. Jody played his father's role. Sam remembered that once before, when Jody was drunk, she wanted to go into an alcohol program, but he had opposed it, saying that he wanted her to take care of herself. I interpreted this as his having felt pulled to reexperience and maintain the same alcoholic tensions with Jody that his mother had with his father. Because he felt badly that his parents never solved this issue, he wouldn't let himself gain control of a problem that they couldn't.

Sam's identification with his mother became clearer. He began to see how he harassed Jody like his mother harassed his father. I pointed out that the purpose of acting like his mother was to keep from being aware how unpleasant and pathetic she was. Acting like her served to justify her behavior to himself and to protect her from his disappointment and scorn. This line of interpretation allowed Sam to disconnect from his compulsive critical behavior toward Jody. Sam eventually entered his own therapy and developed a more pleasant demeanor even at work, where he had been a tyrannical boss.

Jody became more self-confident and happier in her relationship with Sam. She had quit her therapy with her previous therapist and started working with an alcohol counselor. When I asked whether she was getting enough therapeutic support, Jody replied she felt "greedy" if she let herself get too much. She had several relapses requiring hospitalization during our couples therapy and continued to test whether Sam would ultimately reject her.

The therapy lasted a total of nineteen months. As it came to a close, they dealt with the ability to ask for things from each other, saying no, and such other issues as differences in handling the checkbook and how to have a more satisfying sex life. Significantly, they agreed to move from an "open" to a monogamous sexual arrangement in their marriage.

In a follow-up contact twenty months after the therapy ended, the therapist learned that the couple was still together, though

Jody was still struggling with alcoholism. Sam was not sure whether they were going to stay together. However, the miserable cycle of blame and provocation had been broken. Both partners were dealing with their considerable issues from a different vantage point, no longer locked in their previous patterns.

THE THERAPIST'S STANCE

The therapist's role is not simply one of diagnostician and interpreter. We are inevitably drawn into the psychology and experience of the couple as a member of the system. Besides being an initial diagnostic indicator, the therapist's countertransference is an opportunity to empathize with each partner's feelings about the other. When Jody relapsed in her drinking, I felt worried and frustrated like Sam. When he continued to be verbally abusive and threatening to Jody, I felt angry and considered giving up on him.

Countertransference is also a window into the past to see how each partner experienced a version of this drama as children. When Jody repeatedly acted irresponsibly self-destructive, I felt worried and disdainful, a paler version of the way she felt as a child toward her severely dysfunctional parents. Likewise, Sam's repeated attacks on Jody triggered my feelings of disappointment and irritation toward him, which paralleled his childhood feelings. Sam's seeming inability to change his behavior, despite my best efforts, frustrated me just as it frustrated Sam when his father continued to drink and his mother continued to be inappropriate no matter what he did. My experience of anger, helplessness, and despair in response to Sam and Jody's behavior was a cognitive and emotional glimpse into their experience as children.

The therapist, unwittingly and painfully pulled into the maelstrom, is thereby positioned to help the couple find the way out. We can take stock of our own feelings and understand what the couple feels—depressed and despairing. We feel responsible for helping the couple and are poignantly aware of failing to do so, a situation that may cause us to be angry at people who seem bent on self-destruction. Having such feelings for people we are supposed to be helping can easily provoke our guilt. All these feelings directly repeat those each partner has for each other and are the same feelings each partner had for their parents during childhood.

Consequently, the therapist's emotional and behavioral response can be powerfully therapeutic for both partners. These patients are intensely interested in how the therapist manages his or her internal state, struggling with despair, blame, guilt, and omnipotent responsibility, which can serve as a new model with which each partner can identify. If the therapist's behavior is different from theirs and different from their parents', it can challenge each person's convictions that they have to be miserable and treat each other badly.

If the therapist resists the invitation to believe, feel, and behave as the couple does, they can take heart. Jody may have an intractable drinking problem, but I don't have to panic and attack. Sam may be impossibly critical, but I don't have to get depressed and develop a drinking problem. Just maintaining a thoughtful, helpful demeanor in the face of this drama is an immense achievement that no one in the family has been able to achieve so far.

The content of the therapist's interpretations may be useful and structuring to the couple, but the process is equally powerful. In the case of Sam and Jody, the line of interpretation was accurate and probably helpful, but it was not enough. The couple was stuck. The fights were repetitive and ugly despite months of therapeutic work. I felt silly and worthless at times but didn't give in to that feeling and kept trying to find the cutting edge of the therapeutic work. I was daunted but not crippled by the dynamics. The partners could each take heart and identify with my capacities for energy and ingenuity in the face of their painful intransigence in order to "break the spell" they had woven.

Remembering that patients repeat past relationships is the most orienting asset in the therapist's possession. Naive therapists and patients automatically jump to the conclusion that the patients' behavior directly reflect their underlying capacities. This leads to the therapist accepting patients' own distorted self-concept. Patients may believe they are defective, immoral, or monstrous and then initially act that way to see whether the therapist believes it too. Often, therapists prematurely diagnose their patients as defective or empty based on their initial compelling presentation.

Difficult patients almost always believe this about themselves. A patient once described himself as a Dr. Jekyll and Mr. Hyde because he found that as he pulled up the driveway to his home, he felt himself transform into an abusive nasty stepfather to his wife's teenage sons. He confided that since his mother was of German extraction, he believed he had "Nazi genes." This patient acted as a tyrant toward his subordinates at work and was challenging and critical to me in therapy. When I challenged his view that he was genetically defective and strongly suggested that his behavior represented repetitions of the way his father treated him, he eventually changed his behavior with his subordinates and slowly shed his self-image as a monster.

Omnipotence and Guilt

The process of doing therapy with difficult couples often revolves around the experience of omnipotent responsibility, worry, and guilt. This is a universal experience for people who witness or experience gut-wrenching trauma. It is at the heart of the "spell" that binds difficult couples and ensnares the therapist. For the therapist to deal with this omnipotence requires establishing an appropriate therapeutic distance. Difficult couples invite the therapist to take exaggerated, polarized positions, either to run screaming from the room or to jump into the enmeshed system and drown in an attempt to save everyone.

The therapist has to find a way to stay emotionally connected yet not become overwhelmed by feelings of compassion and longing to help.

The therapist's experience of omnipotent responsibility is powerfully triggered by the couple's seeming intractability. The therapist has to maintain a balance between helping and not helping. The therapist can't force the couple out of its pathologic pattern, nor should the therapist turn away from a couple who seem impossible to help, two clear impulses engendered by the difficult couple.

A powerful alternative approach is for the therapist to invite the couple out of their pathological repetitive behaviors. Such an approach demonstrates clarity of thought, affective attunement, caring, and resisting becoming overwhelmed, panicked, or guilty. The therapist plays the role of expert consultant, who can influence but not control the process, acting out of thoughtful understanding of what the couple is trying to do and what obstructions are getting in its way. This is a capacity that a difficult couple doesn't usually have but can gain by paying close attention to the therapist and identifying with his or her demeanor.

Feelings of omnipotence can distort the therapist's assessment of how to conceptualize goals for treatment. It's important for the therapist to have a rational method for assessing goals for couples therapy. Some therapists invariably try to save the relationship as their primary goal. Others try to ascertain whether the relationship is troubled and, if it is, try to "save" one or the other partner by convincing that person to leave the relationship. Both of these automatic strategies are problematic.

In my opinion, the therapist should always try to assess what the psychological goals are of each member of the relationship and then assess what role or potential role the relationship plays in attaining those goals. When couples come into therapy, the therapist should not assume that the relationship should be saved no matter what. Similarly, if the couple comes in miserably stuck in an unhappy marriage, the therapist shouldn't conclude the relationship should end. It is possible the partners are very invested in working on their individual issues in the context of that miserable relationship. Ending the relationship might not be useful because each partner might repeat the same dynamics in the next relationship. The therapist needs to meet each partner where that person is, help each discover where they want to go, then help each either change the relationship or get out of it depending on what furthers each person's goals.

Since guilt is such a central and destructive force in the experience of difficult couples, its role should be openly explored and discussed. In the case of Sam and Jody, it was the interpretation of how each felt too guilty to be in control while the other was out of control that turned the entire therapy. Talking about guilt with difficult patients can help explain and relieve hopelessness, depression, self-destructive behavior, failure to improve, and inhibitions in self-assertion. Talking about intense worry and omnipotent feelings of responsibility for each other and their families helps put in perspective why these patients are so tormented by guilt. Interpreting the connection between their destructive behavior and their guilt helps give hope and direction out of their repetitive behaviors.

Other Considerations

The case of Sam and Jody illustrates many of the complicating factors that plague difficult couples, including disturbed childhoods marked by parental loss, abuse, and neglect. Both partners also had significant depression and substance abuse. These factors play a destructive role in the life of the couple but often cannot be adequately addressed in the couples therapy alone.

After an initial evaluation, it's often wise to recommend individual therapy for one or both members, refer for a medication evaluation, or recommend Alcoholics Anonymous or other substance abuse interventions. It is to be expected, however, that these recommendations may not be followed, since difficult patients feel undeserving of help and typically eschew rational treatment plans. They also test to see whether being "bad" patients will provoke the therapist to dislike or reject them. The therapist has to retain the same balance described earlier between wanting to help and tolerating frustration when the patient doesn't permit it.

It's also important to remember that difficult patients don't enter individual therapy easily. Often, partners will allow coming to treatment for the couple but not for themselves. The old maxim that patients can't get better unless they want to is not completely true. Some patients are not healthy enough to "want" to get better for themselves. They might feel guilty getting too much and would not be able to initiate or sustain individual therapy. Some difficult patients feel unsafe facing a therapist one on one because of the patient's transference expectations that the therapist would be as dangerous as their parents were. Such a transference expectation is weakened in the couples setting where the therapist can be seen as an ally to each partner. After an initially successful experience early in couples therapy, patients may feel safer and more deserving, and dare to pursue further help that they may have felt too "greedy" to ask for initially.

The couples therapist, like any therapist who works with difficult patients, needs to be able to tolerate the patients' self-destructive behaviors and their slowness in getting better without rejecting them. It would be an error if therapists, in their zeal to be helpful, insisted on adjunctive treatment or no treatment. Some therapists will refuse to see a couple if one partner refuses needed adjunctive treatment. Such a proscription would eliminate many difficult patients from getting any help. The therapist should follow the rule of meeting the patient where that person is, which may necessitate an incomplete and inadequate treatment at first. As therapy progresses, however, the partners can begin to feel more entitled to appropriate help and act less self-destructively.

In the case of Sam and Jody, the therapist tolerated harmful behaviors between the partners for many months. Even though

I strongly recommended they stop drinking, join AA, and get into individual therapy, I did not make it a precondition of our continued therapy since I didn't believe they would have been able to follow through and succeed initially. Working through each partner's guilt and feelings of omnipotence toward the other eventually allowed each to pursue individual treatment. I did not interpret "resistance" but instead interpreted the legitimacy of their needs and the guilt that undermined their ability to meet their needs.

Taking Heart

What helps the therapist keep from getting as discouraged as the couple? What keeps the therapist from being another casualty, dragged into the partners' repetitions rather than staying poised to lead them out? Certainly the therapist needs to be alert to his or her own countertransference feelings and, at the first eerie chill, begin to wonder what tragedy is being subtly replayed. Remembering there are spells and repetitions helps snap the therapist out of the role of victim into that of an agent for therapeutic change.

But more than holding this awareness, the therapist must make peace with the task and maintain a perspective of what is and what is not possible. The most common cause of professional distress or burnout in any field is when the person's goal regularly exceeds his or her reach. Therapists must temper their natural omnipotent wishes to help clients and stay grounded in what is realistically possible. Difficult couples from dysfunctional families regularly struggle with their inability to set appropriate goals and resist irrational guilt. Therapists must be able to do this to maintain their own sanity and to set an example for their clients.

Therapists need to stay centered and positive in order to achieve maximal effectiveness. In order to do that, therapists have to achieve a balance between helping and not helping, paying equal attention to process and outcome. It would be nice if

Jody stopped drinking, Sam stopped harassing, and they both found happiness together. But if the therapist tied his or her task to those goals, the therapist would experience despair along with the couple. The therapist's task has to be maintaining his or her own equilibrium and effectiveness whatever the couple does, which is the soundest way to help the couple eventually approximate their potential.

The therapist can shoot high, be blatantly optimistic, hoping for and designing a plan that tries to address all of the couple's problems. But one's self-esteem and sense of accomplishment should not be too tied to the difficult couple's apparent progress lest it be dashed against the rocks.

The therapist should be mindful of progress, so that strategies that result in gain can be expanded and strategies that don't work can be relinquished. Couples need to be reminded of what is working and when things are better, even if very slightly.

The therapist should remember that doing one's best is a tremendous achievement during the treatment of the difficult couple and in itself is very therapeutic to the couple. Doing one's best means retaining the ability to see and speak, and maintaining the ability to respect and care about the partners as human beings. Knowing that you've done a respectable job under difficult circumstances can be very rewarding, even if you can't relieve all the suffering and solve all the problems. If the therapist can retain balance and stay positively engaged, the difficult couple's spell can be broken. The work itself can be rewarding, and the couple can benefit from a refreshing experience that may offer a completely novel opportunity for change.

FOR FURTHER READING

Foreman, S. A. (in press). The significance of turning passive into active in control mastery therapy. *Journal of Psychotherapy, Practice and Research*.

Weiss, J. (1993). *How psychotherapy works*. New York: Guilford.

Weiss, J., Sampson, H., & the Mount Zion Psychotherapy Research Group. (1986). *The psychoanalytic process*. New York: Guilford.

CHAPTER

7

DOMESTIC VIOLENCE

Susan E. Hanks

Differences of opinion exist concerning the most effective ways
to intervene in domestic violence cases. Given the fact that
domestic violence occurs in the context of an ongoing relationship between a man and a woman, couples therapy would seem
to be a logical mode of clinical intervention. However, the role
of psychotherapy, let alone of couples therapy, is often challenged, if not vigorously opposed. Some of the strongest opposition toward couples therapy is based on the experiences of
battered women who have been retraumatized as participants in
couples therapy.

Couples therapy in domestic violence situations has come to
be viewed as not only clinically contra-indicated but politically
incorrect for some good reasons. Many psychotherapists dismissed the social-political dimensions of family violence and
failed to see the gendered aspects of its causes and consequences.
By doing so, they underestimated the traumatic sequelae of
abuse and victimization.

Clearly, couples therapy is not appropriate for *all* couples in
which a man batters his female partner. Couples therapy should
never imply that the battered woman is equally responsible for
her partner's violence or perpetuate a false hope that she can
control his violent behavior by merely altering her own. It
should never convey a false sense of security to a battered
women who might be endangered by prematurely unleashing
her pent-up rage and anger toward the man who battered her.

However, politically correct or not, couples do request such therapy and psychotherapists do practice it. I have found that couples therapy can be a useful and effective adjunctive treatment modality for *some* relationships in which domestic violence has occurred. To be conducted in a clinically competent manner, such couples therapies must be based in the existent knowledge regarding domestic violence, sensitive to the unique interpersonal and intrapsychic dynamics of wife battery, and grounded in knowledge of the dynamics of victimization and psychological trauma.

I believe that, as psychotherapists, we should never allow our desire to appear politically correct to overshadow our obligation to engage in scholarly dialogue. To this end, I trust this chapter will provide psychotherapists with guidelines for what I believe are effective clinical strategies for intervening in relationships in which women are battered. Specific assessment criteria and a typology of violent couples will be outlined. Modifications of therapeutic techniques and appropriate clinical stances unique to the treatment of wife battery will be discussed.

BRIDGING CLINICAL THEORIES

Psychotherapists' theoretical orientations directly inform their understanding and influence their functioning within the clinical hour, determining their assessment, language, and interventions. Psychotherapists who are effective in working with cases of domestic violence are aware of the range of current theories that explain domestic violence, apply these theories flexibly according to the needs of their clients, and resist pressures to become either immobilized or polarized by the diversity of thought in the field.

The literature is flooded with a host of presumed causes, predictors, and theories explaining marital violence and challenging the appropriateness of various psychotherapeutic interventions.

- *Intrapsychic theories* focus on individual characteristics that make men prone to batter and women prone to be battered.

- *Interpersonal theories* focus on the interaction of situational and relationship variables that might produce violent interactions, explain why violence occurs in some families and not others, and why it occurs when it does in the history of specific families.

- *Socio-cultural theories* focus on historical, legal, cultural, and political factors that legitimize intrafamilial violence and explain why violence occurs within a given society or sector of society.

- *Feminist theories* understand wife abuse as the oppression of women as a class of people by a patriarchal culture in which male power dominates and supports societal norms and values that have historically condoned marital violence.

Feminist Critique

Feminist theorists are highly critical of traditional intrapsychic and interpersonal conceptions as applied to domestic violence. Psychodynamic formulations run the risk of minimizing abusive male behavior by interpreting it as individual psychopathology or by euphemistically reformulating it as an ineffectual attempt to meet ordinary human needs for recognition and acceptance, or when a man's cravings for domination and control are reinterpreted as ordinary masculine needs for mastery. Objections to systemic formulations arise from its view that men's violence toward their partners may be seen as repetitive, reciprocal interactive loops.

Traditional psychodynamic and systemic approaches hold the dubious, although well-deserved, distinction of being historically most responsible for promulgating "victim-blaming" notions that make a battered women's actions the cause of the battering man's violent actions. A feminist approach to understanding the dynamics of domestic violence shifts the responsibility to men for their own violent behavior and focuses on understanding the characteristics of men that contribute to their violence toward women.

My position is that it is essential for the couple's therapist to hold men who batter solely responsible for their own violent behavior and to view the violence as initially emanating from the man's psychology. This stance is not incompatible with acknowledgment of their intrapsychic or interpersonal dynamics. It does assert that most men who chronically batter their female partners would batter *any* women with whom they shared an intimate relationships.

One of the concrete issues that confronts the battered women's movement today is resisting the mental health profession's tendency to disavow a feminist analysis. The report of the Task Force on Male Violence Against Women of the American Psychological Association concurred with this perspective by "emphasizing that the problem of violence against women cannot be fully understood, let alone solved, by focusing exclusively on individual psychology. Only by changing the social and cultural institutions that have given rise to the problem can a lasting solution be achieved."

Politics Influences on Psychotherapy

Domestic violence coalitions, armed with the feminist perspective and fearful of the "reprivatization" of domestic violence, have direct influence on social policy, legislation, and clinical practice. In some states, California for one, psychotherapists are currently precluded from offering couples or family therapy to men who are diverted into a domestic violence men's treatment program by the courts. Domestic violence laws do allow men arrested for spouse abuse to enter an intervention program either before or after entering a plea of guilt or innocence. Some laws require the courts to order such men to participate in perpetrator treatment programs and when they do so prohibit them from concurrently participating in either couples or family counseling. The rationale behind such prohibitions is that to allow couples work conveys the message to the man that the battered woman has contributed to his violence.

Such legislative trends require therapists to remain appraised of the influence of feminist and political theory on clinical practice in the field of family violence. I advise all psychotherapists to stay abreast of the continuously evolving legislative and political trends in their own states and localities. This can easily be accomplished by contacting your local shelters for battered women or your local domestic violence coalitions.

DIFFERENTIAL DIAGNOSIS AND ASSESSMENT CRITERIA

In spite of trends to restrict couples therapy, many couples request couples therapy. In some of these couples, the man may not be involved in the legal justice system; in other couples, the man may have completed his legal requirements. In deciding whether to provide couples therapy in these cases, therapists should know how to assess whether a particular couple is, or is not, clinically appropriate for conjoint therapy.

In making a clinical assessment and ultimate treatment recommendation, it is important to remember that domestic violence describes behaviors, or clusters of behaviors. It is not a psychological syndrome unto itself, nor does it necessarily qualify for a psychiatric diagnosis.

The men and women caught up in the web of domestic violence are a diagnostically varied lot. Some men and women do have character disorders or other diagnoses. But not all men with character disorders batter their partners, and not all women with psychiatric diagnoses are battered. Also, many of the symptoms of battered women are the consequences rather than the cause of abuse.

Men who batter and women who are battered differ in their intrapsychic functioning, in their functioning as marital pairs, in their families' abilities to function as a unit in spite of the violence, and in the social-cultural contexts in which they live. The type, severity, frequency, meaning, and impact of the violence differs from couple to couple.

The criteria presented later may help you assess the history, dynamics, and impact of violence on the life of the couple and on each partner as an individual. They can be integrated with standard diagnostic criteria for evaluating the interpersonal dynamics of the couple, and the mental functioning, characterological makeup, impulse control, and affective disposition of each individual. The criteria also differentiate between the various types of domestically violent couples and help the therapist determine the appropriate combination and sequencing of environmental, legal, and psychotherapeutic interventions.

History of Violence in Relationships

Ask each partner about the history of any violence in the current and past relationship(s) with intimate partners, authority figures, friends, relatives, and strangers. Obtain this by inquiring about the first, the last, and the worst episodes of violence in this or other relationships.

Observe whether the couple is knowledgeable about one another's history. It is an indication of a couple's degree of psychological enmeshment if the woman volunteers to be the spokesperson for the man, as is typical of a Type II couple as described later. Note whether the woman is unaware of the man's past violence toward others, since that may signify a Type III couple.

Questions to Ask Men Who Batter:

In which relationships in your life have you been violent?

Are you only violent toward loved ones?

Have you ever been violent to persons outside of the family context?

Why do you believe you resort to violence?

How do you feel (guilty, remorseful, justified) about your use of violence as a strategy for handling situations?

What have been the consequences of your violent behavior (for instance, loss of relationships, loss of jobs, legal sanctions, injuries to victims)?

Do you believe you have control over your behavior?

Why do you choose to be violent rather than handle situations in a different manner?

What alternatives have you tried to avoid behaving violently?

What strategies do you have in your behavioral repertoire to avoid violence in the future?

Where do you predict your violent behavior will lead?

What are the possible negative or positive consequences if you continue to behave violently?

At what stage in the relationship's development did your violence begin or escalate: courtship/dating, coupling/marriage, pregnancy/childbirth, child launching, or retirement?

Why do you think your violence began at that time?

Questions to Ask Women Who Are Battered:

Are you aware of your partner's violence toward others outside this relationship?

When did you become aware of this?

Why do you believe he resorted to violence in these relationships?

Why do you believe he becomes violent toward you?

What impact has his violence toward others had on you?

How do you believe he feels (guilty, remorseful, or justified) about using violence as a strategy for handling situations?

How do you feel about his use of violence as a strategy for handling situations?

What have been the consequences of his violent behavior toward you on your feelings toward him?

What have been the consequences of his violent behavior toward you on the quality of your relationship?

What has been the outcome or consequences of his violent behavior toward you on the children, on other friends, or on extended family?

In which relationships in your own life have you been abused? Have you been physically or sexually abused by other persons as well?

Do you believe he has control over his behavior?

Why do you believe he chooses to be violent rather than handle situations in a different manner?

What alternatives have you tried to manage his violence?

What strategies do you believe he has in his behavioral repertoire to avoid violence in the future?

What strategies do you believe you have in your behavioral repertoire to avoid violence in the future?

Where do you predict his violence toward you will lead?

Do you think it will get worse?

What will prevent this?

What do you predict will be the long-term effects of violence on the relationship?

Do you believe there will be any negative consequences for him, for you, or for the relationship if he continues to behave violently?

At what stage in the relationship's development did the violence began or escalate: courtship/dating, coupling/marriage, pregnancy/childbirth, child launching, or retirement?

Why do you think it began at that time?

History of Violence in Families of Origin

Both partners should be asked such questions about violence in their families of origin as these:

> Did you witness, receive, or perpetrate physical or sexual violence toward other family members as a child, an adolescent, or during adulthood?
>
> Did you witness your mother being battered? By whom?
>
> How did you respond to your mother's abuse?
>
> What beliefs do you have about why your mother was abused?
>
> What were the consequences of your mother's abuse (that is, loss of relationship(s), legal sanction(s), injuries to victim)?
>
> Did either of you witness your sibling(s) being physically abused or sexually abused? By whom?
>
> What was the impact on you or on them?

Types of Violence

Fundamental to the differential typing of men who batter and focus of any type of treatment is the delineation of the different types of these behaviors. For instance, the co-occurrence of several types of violence in a relationship, and the increase in frequency and severity of these types of violence, heighten the toxicity of the climate of intimidation and control that pervades many domestically violent couples. This may increase the level of danger and potential for lethality in the couple and has implications for using or avoiding couples therapy. Therapists can identify and categorize the types of violence by carefully listening to the detailed descriptions of the episodes of violence.

Physical Violence. This sort of violence includes hitting; slapping; pushing; pinching; throwing objects at someone; pulling hair; burning; shoving; grabbing; choking; stopping partner from moving or leaving; shooting; stabbing; spitting; cutting; throwing or locking someone out of house; locking someone in a room; depriving of food; biting; pushing; pinning to ground or wall; restraining; hitting with object(s) or fists; using or threatening to use a weapon; running over with vehicle, driving recklessly while sober or intoxicated; violently interrupting sleep; forcing sex, forcing the use of drugs or alcohol; stalking.

Psychological Abuse and Violence. This type of abuse and violence includes the use of put-downs; name calling; mind games or gaslighting (that is, making someone think they are crazy); humiliation; making someone feel bad about themselves (intimidation through looks, actions, or gestures); destroying property or hurting pets; threats to harm, physically abuse, and/or kill someone; threats with a weapon to partner; threats to harm, physically abuse, or kill friends, relatives, or children; threats to or actions that interfere with, partner's work or reputation; drunken driving; pathological jealousy; keeping partner prisoner in home; blocking exit from room or house; suicidal threats or gestures for purpose of compelling partner's compliance; the chronic level of intimidation, fear, and/or terror prevailing in relationship's or family's emotional climate.

Verbal Abuse and Violence. Such abuse includes extreme insults or denigration, alone or in the presence of others; threats to leave or abandon the partner; threats to report partner to the welfare agency, the IRS, employers, and the like; verbally raging, cursing at, or haranguing the partner.

Economic Abuse and Intimidation. This type entails preventing the partner from getting or keeping a job; making the partner beg for money; restricting knowledge of and access to communal funds; financially depriving children in retaliation for the partner's behavior or for the purpose of compelling the partner's compliance.

Sexual Abuse. Sexual abuse includes coercive or assaultive sexual activity; lying, withholding information, or pressuring someone in order to gain sexual access; the partner's acquiescence to sexual demands out of fear of a violent outburst if sexual advances are declined; pressuring, badgering, or coercing the partner into agreeing to have sex; marital rape; exposing the partner to sexually transmitted diseases without their knowledge.

Property Violence. Such violence includes destroying the partner's possessions; punching or knocking holes in walls and windows; tearing doors off hinges; entering premises without permission; breaking locks; burning down houses; wrecking cars.

Violence to Pets. This violence includes threats to harm, abandon, or give away the partner's and/or children's pets; physically abusing, tormenting, or killing of pets, especially in the partner's or children's presence; depriving pets of food in order to seek the partner's compliance.

Severity of Violence

The severity of violence may escalate over time. It is assessed by the degree of the battered woman's physical and psychological impairment and the type of medical or psychological treatment required as a result of her abuse by her male partner.

Severity of Physical Injury. This can be rated according to (1) no visible marks and mild pain; (2) bruises or cuts not requiring sutures; (3) severe pain from contusions, cuts requiring sutures, or the loss of teeth; (4) internal injury, severe burns, or fractured bones; (5) wounds from a weapon or the loss of consciousness secondary to choking; and (6) severe injury requiring hospitalization for more than twenty-four hours.

Severity of Psychological Injury. Psychological injury is determined by the extent of psychological care or medical treatment received by the spouse for stress-related disorders, such as anxiety, depression, sleeping disorders, and phobias secondary to battering.

Escalations in Severity of Violence. Increasingly severe injuries and increases in the frequency of physical assault accompany increasingly controlling behaviors, psychological abuse, intimidation, and threats. Isolation of the woman from friends, family, and social supports on the part of the man is common.

Stages and Frequency of Violent Cycles

Some domestically violent couples define episodes of violence as aberrations in their usual mode of relating. Sometimes this view is accurate; frequently it is not. In reality, most domestically violent couples have a typical pattern of cycling through episodes of violence with spiraling frequency and severity. Families suffer cumulative trauma as family interactional patterns become unwittingly structured around episodes of violence.

Anticipating Violence. This tension-building stage is characterized by the man's escalating intimidation, denigration, irritation, controlling behavior, and jealousy. Family members often assume their typical roles vis-à-vis the upcoming episodes of violence. The battered woman may respond by withdrawing, placating, cajoling, or provoking the man's inevitable violent outburst in an effort to control its timing, if not its ultimate occurrence.

Coping with Violent Assaults. The acute episode, which may last anywhere from a few seconds to a few days, is characterized by the man's self-absorbed rage and use of single or multiple forms of physical assaults directed toward the terrified, injured woman. Often, the dynamics and ultimate resolution are influenced by intervention from outside sources such as police, medical personnel, family members, or acquaintances.

Short-Term Recovery. For the woman, post–violent phase reactions can range from withdrawal and distancing to posttraumatic stress numbing, passivity, depression, and exhaustion. There might be an immediate reduction of tension and fear in the relationship as the man's rage, controlling behavior, and violent assaults turn to contrition and acquiescence as he attempts to prevent his partner from withdrawing and distancing from him. Often, the couple can be numbed, or subdued, or emotionally exhausted by the tumultuous disruption of daily life patterns, the intensity of the emotions generated by the violent episodes, and the recovery from the severity of the outcomes of the violence.

Long-Term Aftermath. At this point the woman decides whether her distancing will be either temporary or permanent. If she decides to continue to distance herself from the man, he is likely to escalate his efforts to cajole, charm, threaten, control, or intimidate her into reuniting with him. If the woman ultimately decides not to reconcile with her battering partner and the battering man realizes that his attempts to reconcile with her are futile, a very dangerous time in the violent cycle ensues.

Alcohol and Drug Use and Changes Over Time

Alcohol and drug use often coincides with episodes of violence. The therapist should obtain information about addictive, recreational, and/or prescription drug use. Men who batter often need to work concurrently on gaining control over their use of both drugs and violence. Severely battered women may often be heavily medicated for stress-related symptoms and not be aware their symptoms are somatic reactions to the ever-present tension within the relationship.

Level of Danger

The level of danger in a relationship can be assessed by asking the individual partners directly about their perceived degree of risk and by assessing historical factors known to increase risk in domestically violent relationships. A woman who has been battered can be asked about the degree of intimidation and terror she has experienced and the degree to which she experiences the felt risk of being seriously injured or killed. Such self assessments should be taken seriously as some battered women may underreport rather than overreport their degree of fear. Similarly, a man who batters can be asked directly about the degree to which he feels at risk for further injuring and/or killing his partner. A history of verbal threats to kill the spouse or others, the presence of weapons in the home, a history of threats with weapons, an escalation in the man's isolating behaviors directed toward his partner, the use of drugs or alcohol, and, obviously, previous attempts to kill the partner heighten the level of dangerousness.

 ## Utilization and Response of Support Systems

Previous attempts by the couple to solve their problem will influence their expectations about the potential usefulness or futility of couples therapy. Both members of the couple should be asked about the impact the helping attempts of others have had on the violence. Many individuals have been retraumatized by family and friends, police, and mental health and social service providers whose "help" often made the man's violence worsen.

Women who are battered typically have "burned out" a variety of helping sources or have been abandoned by others because they failed to ultimately prevent the man's violence or to leave the relationship, further compounding their own social isolation. Sometimes, if members of the extended family also have a history of violent behavior, their involvements may have served to condone and escalate, rather than limit and contain, violent episodes.

Police intervention, arrest, court appearance, diversion, and prosecution may serve as a deterrents for some, but not all, men who batter. Men who have no previous history of involvement with the criminal justice system are most likely to be intimidated by arrest and prosecution.

TYPOLOGY OF DOMESTIC VIOLENCE COUPLES

A one-size-fits-all approach to intervention and universal pre-scriptions or proscriptions ill serve the complexities of the lives of the individuals who seek our counsel. After you have taken a careful history, use the following criteria to make a differential diagnosis in order to determine which couples might benefit from which specific treatment modality.

Type I: Acute, Situationally Reactive Violence Directed to Partner Only

The man's violence is acute, situationally reactive, and only occurs within the couple's relationship. A cyclical pattern of vio-lence does not typically develop. He is often alarmed and appalled by his loss of control and feels genuine guilt at having injured someone else, particularly someone he loves. He is able to verbalize and consciously tolerate guilt feelings without retal-iating against his partner. The battered woman is able to respond from a self-protective stance and experience a sense of appro-priate outrage and unambivalently communicate that she will not tolerate being abused again and has the emotional capacity to live separately from the man if necessary.

The violence occurs at a particular juncture in the relation-ship and reflects the man's failure to master a developmental stage or to cope with external life stressors. Both partners' description of the violence is mutually congruent and both assume the man is responsible for his behavior.

Clinical Impressions. Although the man may have little insight into his violence, his guilt and his belief in his partner's deter-mination to leave him if he is violent again serve to contain his behavior and motivate him for change. The woman may suffer from acute anxiety, reactive depression, and an acute posttrau-matic stress reaction. She is unlikely to suffer from long-term emotional trauma, however, as she is clearly able to perceive her partner's violence as inappropriate, out of her control, and not her fault.

Treatment Implications. Couples therapy is often appropriate and effective, focused on preventing any further episodes from occurring, repairing the traumatic emotional sequelae of the violence, reinforcing the couple's determination to prevent wife battery from becoming a pattern within the relationship, and reducing the long-term traumatic impact the violence might have on the relationship. We can help such a couple understand the situational precipitants to the man's violence, develop alternatives to handling life stressors, support the battered woman in doing all that is possible to assure her future safety, and assist the man in owning and apologizing for his behavior. Couples therapy may be combined with individual psychotherapy.

Our countertransference reaction must be monitored to prevent collusion with the couple's tendency to minimize the impact of the violence. Clinicians must guard against a tendency to focus prematurely on other aspects of the relationship in a misguided attempt to alleviate the man's compelling self-acknowledged culpability and self-punitive guilt or to facilitate the battered woman's "forgiveness" of her partner in a self-sacrificing disavowal of her own experience of trauma.

Type II: Cyclical Violent Affective Storms Directed to Partner and Family

Some couples of this type can benefit from couples therapy as adjunctive to psychoeducational groups for men who batter, support groups for battered women, or individual therapy. Women often utilize shelters for battered women.

This man's violence is chronic, cyclical, and expressive of his affective storms. His violent behavior is directed primarily toward family members. The man's violence may have begun during the courtship period and occurs in repetitive cycles, which, over time, may include psychological and sexual violence and violence toward property and pets. The level of dangerousness increases as life threats and weapons become involved, and the battered woman becomes increasingly isolated and estranged from family and friends.

The man's violence is egosyntonic, and he has a limited ability to accept responsibility for his actions. He sees his partner as withholding, controlling, and manipulative, and after a violent episode, he experiences temporary remorse rather than true guilt. He struggles with chronic dysphoric affective states, ranging from depression, anxiety, frustration, rage, jealousy, envy, fear, and shame. He batters his partner in a futile attempt to coerce her into restoring his elusive feelings of well-being.

The battered woman in these relationships is frightened and angered by her partner's violence but not fundamentally outraged by having been abused. She remains attached to her partner in spite of his violence toward her, not because of it.

The relationship of such couples typically fluctuates between states of psychological fusion and enmeshment, with each partner longing for primitive empathy from the other, and states of harsh disengagement, with each partner hating and fearing the other. Outside attachments, autonomous activities, or independent decision making are limited. Both partners fear abandonment and dread being alone.

In a state of psychological fusion, the battered woman suppresses her fears and anxiety and is empathically attuned to the man whose often sad history of childhood deprivation or abuse she can poignantly describe. Likewise, the man seductively idealizes his "one and only"—that is, the only woman capable of "soothing his internal savage beast."

In a state of temporary separation, both partners denigrate the other. The man denigrates the woman he has brutally battered as a "nagging, withholding bitch" deserving of abuse; and the woman pleads with friends, family, and professionals for protection from the omnipotently destructive terrorizing man.

The acute episodes of violence in the lives of this type of couple are often interspersed with times of closeness and reconciliation. The affect of rage itself serves as an efficient way for internally remobilizing the man's fragmented, vulnerable self states. The man's violence may be reinforced if, in fact, the battering results in a restoration of the battered woman's emotional attunement with him during the reconciliation phase of the repetitive cycle of violence. The man who batters his female partner becomes emboldened by the battered woman's attachment to the relationship in spite of his abuse. His violence becomes more frequent, more severe, and more pervasive because of his perception that his violence results in no negative consequences.

Clinical Impressions. This type of violent man has little capacity for psychological mindedness. His ego functions of judgment, memory, and affective regulation are impaired. He often suffers from severe depressive states and states of internal self-fragmentation characterized by intermittent paranoid, suicidal, or homicidal ideation. Narcissistic and borderline character disorders are prevalent.

These men have often witnessed their mothers being abused or were abused themselves as a child. They were chronically and prematurely exposed to the "too-much-ness" of overwhelming affects, which impaired their development of the internal psychological structures necessary for appropriate adult affective regulation.

The chronically traumatized battered women in this type of relationship often suffer from chronic, complex posttraumatic stress disorders as described by Judith Herman in *Trauma and Recovery.* They are particularly vulnerable to the development of such disorders if they had been previously abused as a child, had witnessed abuse as a child, or had been previously abused as an adult.

Treatment Implications. These men who batter often enter treatment involuntarily after police involvement and arrest. A court mandate provides these men with the initial impetus for psychotherapy that they would not muster on their own. These men benefit significantly from participation in a men's group focused on stopping violent behavior. As anger is an affect and only one of the myriad of intrapsychic, interpersonal, and psychosocial problems with which these men struggle, an effective men's group must incorporate a focus on a intrapsychic, interpersonal, and group process issues.

If these men enter treatment voluntarily, it is usually because their female partner has separated from them, and therapy is seen as a prerequisite for reconciliation. A couples therapist should be wary of such motivation. It may quickly dissipate as the battered woman's ambivalence dissolves. Agreeing to see such a man in couples therapy should be predicated on the man's concurrent participation in a domestic violence men's group.

Similarly, a battered woman's motivation for treatment may be high when she is estranged from the relationship but difficult to sustain when she is reenmeshed in the relationship. She, too, may by fooled by the man's temporary "flight into health and nonviolence." I recommend that such a battered woman concurrently participate in either individual therapy or a battered women's support group in which she is encouraged to maintain a reality-based impression of her partner's capacity for change and capacity for danger.

Pragmatically speaking, couples therapy with this type of domestically violent couple can be very helpful, particularly because these couples repeatedly separate and reunite. However, couples therapy will only be effective if the man is able to make a clear commitment to being responsible for and stopping his violence. Similarly, the battered woman must be able to make a clear commitment to preserving her own safety.

Type III: Habitual Instrumental Violence Directed to Partner and Others

Psychotherapeutic interventions for this type of violent man are ineffective in curtailing his violence. Couples therapy is futile and strongly not recommended. It might contribute to the woman's risk for battering by erroneously giving the woman the impression that there is a possibility couples therapy could make the relationship nonviolent.

The violent man in this type of relationship habitually utilizes violence for the purpose of intimidation and control. He is violent and intimidating toward any frustrating person—family members, acquaintances, and strangers. His violence is instrumental; that is, it is used as a means to an end or for the expressed purpose of intimidation and control. He utilizes all types of violence—physical, sexual, emotional, verbal, economic, and violence to property. The level of dangerousness is high as weapons, threats to life, and often alcohol and street drug use are involved. This type of violent man often has a history of involvement with the criminal justice system by whom he is not intimidated. Relationships for this type of violent man are often characterized by sadistic domination or exploitation. The women whom they batter are often severely injured and raped. These women are often dependent on the battering man for housing, money, drugs, social status, and the like.

The battered woman in this type of relationship should be supported in safely withdrawing from the relationship rather than futilely engaging in trying to improve it. Such women are well advised to utilize the supports of shelters for battered women in order to protect themselves and their children while separating from the man. Individual therapy can be helpful in supporting her in extricating herself from a lifestyle of exploitation and the resultant propensities to form traumatically bonded relationships, and in overcoming the effects of the cumulative traumas she has experienced throughout her lifetime.

Type IV: Acute or Chronic Secondary Violence Directed to Partner and Others

For the violent man who engages in this type of violence, couples therapy is strongly not recommended. A domestic violence men's group would also not be an appropriate treatment modality and certainly not a substitute for other forms of medical and psychotherapeutic intervention.

The violent man in this type of relationship suffers from a severe mental disorder (such as paranoid schizophrenia or manic-depressive disorder), or his violence is secondary to a drug or alcohol addiction. The violence is directed to multiple people—most frequently toward their household members due to their sheer physical proximity. The violence is physical and may be accompanied by destruction of property but is usually not accompanied by other forms of violence. The violent incidents are often impulsive, spontaneous reactions to immediate frustrations and do not emanate from the ongoing interpersonal dynamics of the relationship.

Men whose violence emanates from a major drug or alcohol addiction should be referred for treatment for their substance abuse prior to, or concurrent with, participating in a domestic violence men's group. Men whose violence results from their suffering a severe mental disorder should be referred for out-patient psychotherapy combined with psychiatric evaluation, appropriate hospitalization, or medication.

Women who may have been battered by these individuals can often best be assisted in individual therapy or psychoeducational family groups focused on educating family members about the mental or substance abuse disorder.

Additional Couples Therapy Caveats

Couples therapy is also strongly not recommended in the infrequently seen cases of mutual violence and with men who are extremely psychologically or physically sadistic. In mutually violent couples, *both* the man and the woman are *primary* initiators of violent behavior toward one another. (These couples are to be differentiated from those in which the woman's violence is simply a reactive and self-protective response to the man's abuse.) Mutually violent couples are easily recognized by the pervasive "uproar" that characterizes their sessions. Their interactions are filled with loud, argumentative, vituperative, mutual accusations and blame and often also by verbal threats to retaliate or harm the other. In these sessions, the therapist is at best a referee and, at worst, merely an audience for the couple's chaos and unrestrained, mutually abusive tirades.

Conjoint therapy is also not recommended in cases in which the man's violence has escalated to the point of being frequent and severe; the man neither demonstrates nor verbalizes any capacity for empathy for his partner, and he has little motivation to change. This type of abusive man utilizes the subtle but potent psychological tactic of "gaslighting," or trying to convince his battered partner she is crazy. This type of abusive man is likely to increase his coercive and manipulative tactics if the battered woman attempts to make any changes. He will abruptly polarize with the therapist if his coercive and manipulative tactics are challenged in any way. The woman in this type of relationship often has no financial independence, few or no social supports, and demonstrates little autonomy of will. She will inevitably position herself on the side of her abusive partner and against the therapist, as she cannot risk engendering the man's rage and abuse by an independent display of alliance with a therapist who challenges her spouse.

UNIQUE ISSUES IN TREATMENT

What are the requisite and appropriate clinical stances on the part of the therapist in relation to the difficult treatment issues that arise? How can they be managed in the initial assessment stage of couples therapy?

Stages of Therapy: Triage, Preliminary Consultation, and Assessment

Intervention and assessment begins with the *initial telephone triage*. This is followed as soon as possible by a *preliminary consultation session*. If deemed appropriate, the couple is invited to participate in an *assessment phase* of up to four sessions. After an evaluation is completed, the couple is offered the opportunity to participate in a number of *time-limited conjoint sessions*, usually six to eight sessions at a time. This structure ensures that periodic reevaluations of the effectiveness of conjoint therapy will occur between the therapist and the couple. If the man's violence has not significantly abated or has increased, other treatment options will be recommended.

I view the initial sessions of conjoint psychotherapeutic work as an opportunity to educate the couple about the dynamics of their behavior, the battered woman about the legal and environmental resources available to her, and the man about the potential negative consequences of his behavior if he chooses to remain violent. I believe it is legitimate and appropriate to evaluate the couple together in order to evaluate the dynamics of the violence and make a differential treatment recommendation. The range of interventions and treatment recommendations may include couples therapy only; couple therapy contingent on one or both partners concurrently participating in group therapy, individual therapy, substance abuse treatment or obtaining a psychiatric evaluation for medication; or brief conjoint intervention to refer the individuals to more appropriate intervention programs.

Telephone Triage. Clinical interventions may begin at the point of the initial phone contact. It serves as an opportunity for triage and, at times, crisis intervention. Typically, the couple is in the short-term recovery stage of their violent cycle, providing a window of opportunity for the therapist to intervene in the couple's system.

During the initial telephone conversation, I explain to the caller that I never agree to see couples in ongoing couples therapy until we have met in person. I offer couples an appointment for a preliminary consultation session as soon as possible, before the couple cycles into the long-term aftermath stage of the cycle of violence.

Preliminary Consultation Session. The preliminary consultation session ranges from, at least, one hour and ten minutes to, at most, one hour and thirty minutes. The usual fifty-minute session is inadequate for a preliminary consultation. Given the potential for violence and danger, it is essential to leave time for individual crisis intervention if an unforeseen, volatile situation should unexpectedly arise during the first meeting. I explain that the three of us will actively work together to determine whether the couple can benefit from further couples work based on my assessment that conjoint sessions will have a good chance of improving, rather than worsening, their situation.

Assessment Phase. During the assessment phase, there will likely be several "choice points" that the couple and I will encounter. It also allows for one or both members of the couple to demonstrate to the other that they are not yet ready for, or perhaps capable of, the level of change needed for stopping the violence in the relationship. I explain that change cannot occur unless both members of the couple are actively involved. For instance, men who are reluctant participants in couples therapy and attend solely to placate their ambivalent partner must actively demonstrate a desire to stop their violent behavior.

During this time, I will meet separately at least once with each partner. Although I do not explain my reasoning to the couple, I do so for the purpose of privately discussing issues of safety with the woman and making certain she is neither secretly fearful nor participating due to coercion.

If I determine that the either one or both members of the couples are not appropriate for couples therapy, I will discuss my impressions and tell them that their relationship is currently too brittle or too dangerous to treat at this time in conjoint therapy mode. If I do so, I will offer alternative treatment recommendations to the man and the woman. Or, I may offer couples therapy but only contingent on one or both members demonstrating their commitment to the change.

I firmly believe, and hopefully convey, that no couple "flunks" the assessment phase. Their participation has enhanced their understanding of the violence in their relationship, their capacity for change, and community resources.

Must the Violence Stop Before Couples Therapy Begins?

A predominant point of view in the field of domestic violence is that conjoint therapy is inappropriate unless the man has stopped being physically violent. While I agree that there are many cases in which conjoint therapy is inappropriate if violence continues to occur, I also believe that there are some situations in which couples therapy can facilitate the man and woman working together to end his violence. Requiring that *all* violence cease in *all* cases prior to therapy expects the client(s) to resolve their problem for which they sought therapy prior to coming to therapy and, paradoxically, may be expecting the psychologically impossible of them.

I believe that conjoint therapy can provide a container in which the couple and the therapist can work together to stop the man's violence, to empower the woman to keep herself safe, and mutually to join together in keeping their children physically and psychologically safe. In order for conjoint therapy to be effective, the following conditions must be met:

- The violence must not be frequent and severe.
- Both members of the couple must be willing to participate.
- The man must indicate some genuine capacity for assuming responsibility for his violence and make a commitment to not react violently to any material that arises during the course of the therapy.
- The woman must feel safe and not be fearful of his retaliation, be capable of demonstrating some autonomy of will in his presence, and have some degree of financial independence and a social support system.

Conjoint therapy can be effective in these cases because issues of power and control can be equalized. This potential for equality in the couple's relationship makes it possible for the therapist to form an equal although differentiated therapeutic alliance with both partners in the couple. It is this alliance, and the transferential authority invested by the man and woman in the therapist, that make the construction of the metaphorical psychotherapy container possible.

Stating Goals and Defining Violence

During the preliminary consultation session, the couple's therapist should discuss with the couple the goals of couple therapy as follows:

- To stop the man's violent behavior
- To ensure the safety of the woman and the children
- To repair the cumulative trauma experienced by all family members, including the children

In order to accomplish these goals, the man must assume responsibility for both controlling his own violent behavior and also for ensuring the safety of his wife and his children. The woman must assume responsibility for keeping herself and her children safe, and she must recognize that she cannot omnipotently control her male partner's violent behavior. Achieving these goals will create opportunities for emotionally reparative experiences to occur in the life of the couple and improve the general quality of life within the relationship and the family.

Clearly stating the goals of couples therapy clears the way for the issue of violence to become a central focus of conjoint therapy and to be addressed straightforwardly and consistently throughout the therapy. A discussion regarding the definition of domestic violence is also necessary. I often share with the couple a printout of the types of violence and their associated behaviors and a copy of the state law, which has its own definition of domestic violence. Incorporating the legal definition into the conversation enables me to point out to the man that society, not just myself, defines his behavior as not only inappropriate but also criminal. Articulating the goals of couples therapy and clearly defining domestic violence provides the couple and me with a platform for beginning a conversation about the violence in their lives.

Engaging the Voluntary But Reluctant Client

I try to avoid power struggles with domestically violent men, particularly those who are prone to narcissistic injuries. I tell an abusive man who is ambivalent about commencing therapy that he is perfectly free to wait to participate in therapy for his violence until after he is arrested, after his wife is severely injured, after the marriage disintegrates, or after his children become symptomatic. The choice is totally his own. Although I believe that it is in his best interest to receive help voluntarily at the present time rather then waiting until an unfortunate incident occurs, I am confident that at least one if not more of these tragedies will occur. It is in his future legal best interest to change his behavior now, when he has control over his fate, rather than to wait until the courts have control of his life. I also inform him that if he is arrested, the state law will prohibit his participating in couples therapy if he is ordered by the court into a men's treatment program. I suspect he would prefer to have control over his life rather than have the judge control his choice of therapist, choice of program, and choice of treatment modality. I also point out that psychotherapy is a less expensive alternative to being arrested, posting bail, losing income, hiring an attorney, and paying court fines and costs. Hence, if he has any interest in changing his behavior, now is the time to capitalize upon it.

Gender Bias, Linguistics, and Straight Talk

The absence of "straight talk" in conjoint therapy with domestic violence diffuses issues of responsibility and guilt, and it obfuscates issues of gender. For instance, words like *victim* and *perpetrator* are legal terms, and, while they draw attention to the criminal nature of the violence, they nevertheless obscure the gender of the "victim" and the "perpetrator." Likewise, calling the battering of women by men "spouse abuse," "marital aggression," "conjugal violence," "domestic disputes," "abuse between husbands and wives," and the like, implies a diffusion of responsibility.

Couples therapists must understand the gendered aspect of domestic violence without being polarized into extremes of shamefully blaming men or overzealously rescuing women. We must keep the sobering gender-based realities in mind so as not to collude with the man's tendency to minimize and deny the extent and consequences of his violence, or with the woman' desire to suppress the undercurrent of fear with which she chronically lives.

Gender-neutral phrases do not reflect the fact that women are at a greater risk of assault from their intimate male partners than they are from a stranger or than men are at risk for assault from their intimate female partners. It is essential that psychotherapists keep these disquieting gender-based realities in the forefront of their thinking when they treat cases of wife battery. I suggest they read, at a minimum, the references cited at the end of this chapter.

Linguistic Constructions. An important component of conjoint therapy in domestic violence cases is to provide clients with a vocabulary for discussing their behaviors, feelings, observations, and experiences. Our vocabulary and linguistic constructions clearly reflect our beliefs about issues of responsibility, blame, safety, danger, and the like.

Therapists who are reluctant to utilize the language of domestic violence and to verbalize clear linguistic constructions that connote who behaves violently toward whom, and who is responsible for what behavior, risk colluding with their clients. Timid psychotherapists miss the opportunity for role modeling how to talk about violence in clear, assertive, reality-based, non-inflammatory language.

Talking About Safety. The fundamental stance of a couple's therapist must remain neutral regarding the dissolution or continuation of the marriage or relationship. It is the clients' marriage to save, to terminate, or to try to improve, if they choose to do so.

However, psychotherapists cannot be neutral regarding issues of safety. The question as to whether it is safe for either one or both of the partners to live together should be continually raised by the therapist, particularly if there are recurrences of episodes of violence over the course of treatment. The couples therapist must clearly state in the beginning of therapy that couples therapy will stop if the process appears to be endangering the safety of the woman. In addition, the therapist may also work with the couple in separating, either temporarily or permanently, in a nonviolent manner, if safety is an issue. If either partner wishes to separate from the other, his or her wishes are always respected and supported. The couples therapist should also state to both that the most effective preventive measure for avoiding injury is for the couple to avoid being in one another's physical proximity. If a couple states that they cannot be together without the man becoming violent, I question whether they should remain living together at the current time.

This questioning of the safety of the couple's cohabitating provides a perfect opportunity for discussing with men their belief that their violence "overcomes them" and is out of their control. I believe that most men who are violent toward their female partners can choose not to behave violently unless they have a major mental disorder or are under the influence of mind-altering substances. I also know that most men who batter initially believe that they are out of control of their own behavior.

For example, I might ask a man why he decided to destroy some property in the house but not all the property in the house. Why did he only assault his wife in a particular place? Why did he choose not to kill his wife? This type of questioning alerts the man to the fact that he does in fact make decisions about the target, timing, and intensity of his violence.

Activity Versus Passivity

Working with a couple who has a history of violence requires a significant amount of active structuring of the clinical hours on the part of the therapist. The therapist is a role model for active listening, empathic responding, education about basic social interactional skills, and limit setting. Basic communication skills, such as listening without interrupting, thinking before reacting, modulating voices, eliminating vulgar and insulting name calling, eliminating threats, using "I" statements rather than blaming and shaming, and the like, are basic components of the work.

Attention to body language is also crucial. Men who batter are often either unaware of or manipulatively coercive in their utilization of intimidating postures, voice levels, stares, clinched fists, shifts in seating positions, sighs, and the like. It is important to label these behaviors for the man in the session, inquire as to the man's awareness of them, and ask about his intent in using them. Oftentimes, men are astonishingly oblivious to the visual and interpersonal impact their intimidating behaviors can have on other people.

The following vignette, an example of a preliminary consultation session, illustrates many of the points made earlier.

CONNIE AND JOHN

Connie Smith, an articulate but tearful thirty-four-year-old woman, made the initial phone call. She and John, her husband of two years, had had an episode of violence two days before. Connie said they were OK at the moment, but she had promised her obstetrician that she would seek counseling if it happened again. Connie was six months pregnant, afraid John would leave her, and, as she "had already failed one marriage," she was desperate to preserve this one. I asked whether she had been injured. Connie had seventeen stitches in her leg just below her knee.

John Smith, a thirty-eight-year-old university physics professor currently up for tenure, reluctantly took time out of his busy schedule to come to the preliminary consultation session. He sat in a chair by himself, starring impatiently at Connie who was slumped wearily in the corner of the sofa. Makeup covered the dark circles under her puffy eyes. Slacks covered the bandage on her leg.

John initiated the conversation, explaining that Connie's obstetrician was concerned about her. She had been depressed for the past year because of her mother's death, a miscarriage, and being laid off from her job as a lawyer. "I've tried really hard, but I'm at the end of my rope. I'm very pressured myself. I'm rushing to publish before my competitor does. I can't get a good night's sleep because Connie has been coughing a lot all night due to allergies. I hated to do this, but I had to tell Connie to sleep on the living room sofa. I can't risk any delay in my work due to loss of sleep."

I said that it sounded like John was very busy and felt very pressed. I was glad he was able to come. His marriage must be very important to him.

I asked Connie to talk about her phone call with me and why she had come today. Connie elaborated on her depression, feelings like she had failed as a wife, a lawyer, and now as an expectant mother. Asking Connie's permission, I asked about her injury. "I noticed no one mentioned this, but I wondered whether there had been an episode of violence that resulted in Connie's leg being seriously injured and requiring medical attention?"

John defensively retorted, "Connie cut her leg on broken glass. I know what you're thinking. I'm not one of those men who go around beating their wife. I just lost it the other night . . . a mistake . . . that's all. . . . It won't happen again. I'm here today to make sure of that. I'm here to make sure Connie gets all the help she needs to get over her depression. If she'd only stop clinging to me, I won't have to get angry to get some space." John explained that when he came home from work at 11:00 P.M. two nights ago, "after losing sleep for the last three nights and working hard all week, Connie wanted *me* to feed myself. But that's all she has to do all day!" Feeling hungry and deprived, he retreated with a beer to his study to work. Connie wouldn't leave him alone, standing by the door "whimpering." John suddenly felt furious: "We're just lucky the computer didn't get smashed." He swung open the door, pushed past Connie, went into the kitchen, and began to fix his dinner. "Just what she wanted me to do." When he discovered that the dishes in the dishwasher were still dirty from breakfast, he threw a dish of reheated lasagna on the tile floor. "I didn't know Connie was standing there. It's not my fault. It was an accident. The glass cut her leg by mistake." John, turning to Connie, said "You knew about my moods before we got married. Don't complain now. You're the one who wanted a baby—not me. You just have to learn to stop pushing my buttons!"

John explained to me he wanted Connie to come to therapy by herself. He'd be too busy traveling. In fact, Connie's eleven-year-old daughter had problems too. Connie needed help handling her. She had a lot of stomach aches, often came home sick from school, or, because she couldn't fall asleep at night, was too tired to go to school the next day.

I commented to John, "It sounds like you're doing very well at work. That must feel great—but you're under a lot of pressure and you're very concerned about Connie and her daughter. Sounds like you become violent when you feel pressured."

I turned to Connie, heretofore silent. With gentle questioning, Connie elaborated on the events of the evening two nights ago, reluctantly describing her perception that "sometimes John just snaps." After opening the door to his study, he flew out of the room, pushed her forcefully against the wall, and stormed to the kitchen. She followed, fearful of his mood. As she entered the kitchen, he threw the hot lasagna dish in her direction, yelling, "Now look what you've made me do. I'll never be able to concentrate tonight." He grabbed Connie by the arm, forced her to her knees, yelling at her and at her daughter who had by then been awakened by the noise and come into the kitchen. I asked, "What did he yell?" Connie, looking sadly at John, tearfully said, "Clean it up, you bitch!" John also yelled at her daughter, who stood frozen in fear, to "get the f___ out of here, go to your room, don't come out, or you can clean it up, too." Connie was terrified and silently, compliantly started to clean up the mess. John locked himself in his study. I asked at what point did her leg get cut. Connie hesitantly replied, "When he pushed me down, the glass went into my leg. My daughter screamed at him. 'Don't hurt my mommy!' Then he left." Connie later sat outside the study door, softly weeping. John came out. He collapsed into her arms when he saw the bandage, berating himself, "I'm such a shit, I'm such a shit." Connie reassured and comforted him. They felt close again.

I turned to John and asked how he felt right at the moment, hearing about this scene. John avoided the question and responded by saying, "I feel it will not happen again as long as she stops pushing my buttons. I won't let it happen again."

I told John that I was glad he had decided that he was not going to be violent toward Connie again and that he and I agreed that his violence must stop. However, our opinions differed as to the solution to stopping his violence. I believed that John himself must learn how to be nonviolent when his buttons are pushed.

Talking to both Connie and John, I said that the scene they described sounded very familiar to me. It was typical of couples in which the man assaults the woman. I knew John does not want to think of himself as a wife batterer or Connie of herself as a battered wife, but I knew the state of California would consider his violence as wife battering.

More important, I was concerned for Connie's safety. Pregnancy often heightens tension in a relationship. Injuring Connie posed a danger not only to Connie but also to their unborn baby.

I asked Connie what she meant by "sometimes John just snaps" and John when he described himself as "moody." Had episodes of violence happened before? John said no. I asked Connie whether she had ever felt frightened of John before. She said yes, and then described enduring episodes of his verbal tirades, door slamming, pushing and shoving, and reckless driving. I commented that the violence was repetitive and increasing in frequency, and Connie's injuries were becoming more severe.

In summary, I commented to John that it sounded like his career was going very well and that must be very gratifying after all his hard work. I could see why he wouldn't want anything to happen to impede it. I wanted to help him with managing his behavior at home so that nothing would happen that might interfere with his career.

I could also understand the urgency to help Connie get some relief from her depression. However, I thought John's abuse of Connie was a major cause of her depression. I, too, shared John's concern about his stepdaughter. She clearly had the classic symptoms of a daughter who had witnessed her mother being abused.

I pointed out to John that we agreed on many things. I asked John whether I could have his permission to share something with him that might be hard for him to hear. I had the impression that he was someone who valued talking straight about things and getting to the point without wasting time. He didn't need to agree with my point of view, but I hoped he would be willing to hear it and think about it. He hesitantly agreed.

I got the impression that John was much more violent and intimidating that he believed himself to be. I suspected that he must silently struggle with his own feelings of rage a lot; it might even feel to him that he suddenly "snaps." However, I believe he actually made decisions to let himself become violent, just as he made a decision not to destroy his computer.

"But only Connie makes me do it. It's not a problem elsewhere," John retorted. I said I knew that was a typical perception of men who batter their wives, although I believed that John would probably have this problem in any close, intimate relationship with a woman.

I was concerned that John seemed unconcerned that he might damage his own reputation, impair his career, and possibly jeopardize his own tenure appointment. I asked whether he had ever been arrested before and explained in detail the humiliating process of arrest, police transport, booking, strip searching, jail time, arraignment, and so forth. I wanted very much to help John avoid these hassles and humiliations in his life.

John, irritated, defended himself. He disagreed with me. California laws were "just a bunch of liberal laws made by liberal women." I told John I could tell that this was a very difficult conversation for him. It would be for me also if I were in his shoes. I appreciated his willingness to hang in with me. He didn't have to agree with me. We didn't have to arrive at any consensus of opinion today. I hoped he would be willing to return and talk some more, although I felt certain that without his getting counseling, his rages would only get more severe and more frequent. But only he could decide if he wanted counseling now. It was totally under his control. If he decided he wanted to wait until he got arrested, until his professional peers found out, until he injured Connie again, or until he injured his unborn baby, I would be willing to see him then. However, I just didn't think it was in his best interest to wait. It certainly wasn't in Connie's best interest to live with a violent man who was delaying his work on controlling his violence and who might injure her or their unborn baby.

I proposed that we meet four more times, and then he could make a well-informed decision for himself to be in counseling or not. In the meantime, we could get Connie some help with her depression.

I asked Connie what she wanted. She said she'd like to work on the marriage. To John I said, "You deserve a good marriage. You deserve to protect yourself from being damaged by your violence. Let's work together so you can learn to be nonviolent, so Connie and your unborn child can be safe." John reluctantly agreed to one more session. I said I thought they had made a wise choice.

Crisis Intervention and Recurrence

Couples who have a pattern of domestic violence will not be able to change their behaviors immediately upon entering therapy. Many crises may occur, providing us with the opportunity to intervene directly in impending or occurring episodes of violence and possibly to influence the outcome in a nonviolent direction. These crises also provide the couple with opportunities for developing skills in avoiding violent outcomes.

Crisis intervention often occurs over the telephone. We provide an empathic ear for an agitated batterer while giving specific, simple behavioral directives regarding what he should do in order to avoid being violent. The therapist can also assist a potentially battered woman in making immediate decisions based on the priority of keeping herself and her children safe. Remember: the woman is most likely to be injured, and her best protection against physical assault is physical distance. The therapist should work with both members of the couple to achieve physical distance from one another.

The therapist must feel comfortable in soliciting police intervention if necessary. The therapist should never "protect" a man who batters from the legal consequences of his behavior.

These telephone crisis interventions should be followed shortly with an individual meeting with each member of the couple before bringing the couple back together conjointly. A conjoint session at this point may provide an opportunity for further violence to occur. Separate meetings prevent a woman from being retraumatized by being in the man's physical proximity.

If a woman seeks shelter in a battered women's shelter at this time, the therapist should ask the woman to inform the therapist of her safety but not to tell the therapist her location. Therefore, the therapist does not have that information to either share with or withhold from the man. The man should also be informed of the therapist's policy regarding knowledge of the woman's whereabouts.

These episodes also allow the therapist to observe and understand the unique intrapsychic and interpersonal dynamics that occur for each couple. The therapist can use this experience to assist the couple in achieving insight into the dynamics of their episodes of violence and in changing any behaviors that contribute to the occurrence or escalations of episodes of violence. It is expected that behavioral avoidances of violence during these episodes should increase and acts of physical violence should decrease.

Avoiding Violence in the Consulting Room

Physical violence, verbal threats, or intimidating behavior in the therapy hour are absolutely unacceptable. I inform the couple at the beginning of the preliminary consultation session that if this should ever occur, the session will end immediately. I will ask the intimidating person to leave my office and the building. I will interpret any threatening behavior to be an indication to us all that it is not safe for the couple to work in a conjoint therapy modality. This stance accomplishes several things. It models for the battered woman an attitude of "zero tolerance" for abuse. It conveys to the man the expectation that he can volitionally control his behavior. It also provides therapists with a clear, proactive strategy for protecting themselves, guards against clinical omnipotence, and buffers them against the secondary traumatization and narcissistic depletion that often develops in response to overzealous rescue fantasies in work with domestic violence.

LOOKING BACK, LOOKING AHEAD

Twenty years after the term *battered wives* was first coined by the feminist author Del Martin in her seminal book of that title, the protective veil shielding domestic violence from public scrutiny has lifted. Violence in the family has become a conspicuous preoccupation of contemporary American consciousness.

Fortunately, the social science and mental health fields, whose historical obliviousness to wife battery mirrored the then prevailing cultural myopia, have paid increasing attention to this problem over the past twenty years. I am heartened to know that, in contrast to my experience in 1973 when a review of the literature surfaced only two articles related to spouse abuse, there has been a proliferation of research and clinical attention paid to this problem since that time. I hope that this chapter will contribute to the amelioration of this tragic social and family problem and that we can truly become a society with "zero tolerance" of violence toward women.

NOTES

P. 189, *Some of the strongest opposition:* Bograd, M., (1992). Values in conflict: Challenges to family therapists' thinking. *Journal of Marital and Family Therapy, 18*(3), 245–256; Kaufman, G. (1992). The mysterious disappearance of battered women in family therapist' offices: Male privilege colluding with male violence. *Journal of Marital and Family Therapy, 18*(3), 233–244.

P. 189, *sequelae of abuse and victimization:* Goldner, V., Penn, P., Sheinberg, M., & Walker, G. (1990). Love and violence: Gender paradoxes in volatile attachments. *Family Process, 29*(4), 343–363; Herman, J. (1992). *Trauma and recovery.* New York: Basic Books; Moltz, D. (1992). Abuse and violence: The dark side of the family, An introduction. *Journal of Marital and Family Therapy, 18*(3), 223.

P. 190, *Psychotherapists who are effective:* Hanks, S. (1992a). *An exploratory study of psychotherapists' biases in the treatment of domestic violence.* Unpublished doctoral dissertation, California Institute of Clinical Social Work, Berkeley, CA.

P. 191, *Objections to systemic formulations:* Avis, J. (1992). Where are all the family therapists? Abuse and violence within families and family therapy response. *Journal of Marital and Family Therapy, 18*(3), 225–232; Herman, J. (1990). Sex offenders: A feminist perspective. In W. L. Marshall, D. R. Laws, & H. E. Barbaree (Eds.), *Handbook of sexual assault: Issues, theories, and treatment of the offender* (pp. 177–193). New York: Plenum.

P. 191, *A feminist approach to understanding the dynamics:* Hotaling, G., & Sugarman, D. (1986). An analysis of risk markers in husband to wife violence: The current state of knowledge. *Violence and Victims, 1,* 101–124.

P. 192, *The report of the Task Force:* Goodman, L., Koss, M., Fitzgerald, L., Russo, N., & Keita, G. (1993). Male violence against women: Current research and future directions. *Journal of the American Psychological Association, 48*(10), 1055.

P. 194, *The criteria also differentiate between the various types:* Hanks, S. (1992b). Translating theory in practice: A conceptual framework for clinical assessment, differential diagnosis and multi-modal treatment of maritally violent individuals, couples and families. In E. Viano (Ed.), *Intimate violence: Interdisciplinary perspectives* (pp. 157–176). Washington, DC: Hemisphere.

P. 199, *Severity of Physical Injury:* Stuart, E., & Campbell, J. (1989). Assessment of patterns of dangerousness with battered women. *Issues in Mental Health Nursing, 10*(3–4), 245–260.

P. 203, *After you have taken a careful history:* Hanks, S. (1992b). *op. cit.*

P. 206, *The chronically traumatized battered women:* Herman, J. (1990). *op. cit.*

P. 215, *Likewise, calling the battering of women:* Lamb, S. (1991). Acts without agents: An analysis of linguistic avoidance in journal articles on men who batter women. *American Journal of Orthopsychiatry, 61*(2), 250–257.

P. 216, *Gender-neutral phrases:* Browne, A. (1993). Violence against women by male partners: Prevalence, outcomes, and policy implications. *Journal of the American Psychological Association, 48*(10), 1077–1086; Dobash, R. E., & Dobash, R. (1979). *Violence against wives.* New York: Free Press; Novello, A., Rosenberg, M., Saltzman, L., & Shosky, J. (1992). From the surgeon general, U.S. Public Health Service. *Journal of the American Medical Association, 267*(23), 3132.

P. 216, *the references cited at the end of this chapter:* Koss, M., Goodman, L., Browne, A., Fitzgerald, L., Keita, G., & Russo, N. (1995). *Male violence against women at home, at work, and in the community.* Washington, DC: American Psychological Association.

P. 225, *Twenty years after the term* battered wives: Martin, D. (1976). *Battered wives.* San Francisco: Glide.

THE PARENTING COUPLE

Vicky A. Johnson

This chapter addresses a critical but neglected aspect of couples therapy, namely, the influence of children on their parents' relationship. Most couples—regardless of age, marital status or previous relationships—are preparing for, involved in, or have completed some form of parenting. The impact of parenting is often at the very center of couple's issues.

In the first section of the chapter, I argue that attending to a couple's basic assumptions about the meaning of parenting and to their responses to the challenges and stresses of parenting may be critical in dealing with their relational dynamics. The second section of the chapter extends this argument and explores the possibility that parenting offers untapped resources for the therapist to draw on in helping the couple construct a more meaningful and satisfying relationship with one another.

The relational issues couples bring to the therapist's office often are so compelling and complicated that it is difficult to consider simultaneously the further entanglements of parenting, much less the neglected resources and healing opportunities that might exist in the couple's day-to-day lives. To recognize these entanglements, resources, and opportunities, the therapist needs to approach each case with pragmatic flexibility. I have found a grounded pragmatism to be far more effective with most parenting couples than the more formal, logical, and internally consistent theories of therapy and human behavior developed from systematic research.

This is not to say that therapists should be atheoretical in their work with parenting couples. I often bring several theoretical perspectives into service as I attempt to understand the dynamics of a relationship and to devise a plan of action. In dealing with parents, therapists must draw on research findings and the theoretical constructs of many different fields, including child development, psychology, anthropology, sociology, and at times even ethology. These constructs and findings can be useful in stimulating hypotheses, speculations, and insights, but only if they are recognized as specialized and limited tools, to be used briefly and then set aside before they blind the therapist to the pragmatics of the particular case being confronted.

I must confess I have not always been as suspicious of formal theories of therapy or of human behavior and development as I am now. Especially in my early days of practice, I preferred theory to the rather more grimy image of the therapist as an explorer of healing resources. But the latter image fits the effective therapist far better and helps us remain open to the possibilities that children offer our therapeutic efforts with couples.

This chapter is an effort to broaden the focus of couples therapy to include the impact of parenting on the couple's relationship. The major focus will be on the issues and therapeutic opportunities raised by couples as parents.

THE CHALLENGES AND STRESS OF PARENTING

Many couples arrive at therapy unable to state what they want out of either therapy or their relationship. Usually they identify frustration as the prime reason for seeking therapy. Often when goals are voiced, they are in terms of generalized expectations of the marriage—desires for a soul mate, spiritual union, unconditional love, and acceptance of their physical needs. Only rarely do they openly identify their frustrations with their own or their partner's parenting and their need for help in that area.

Your job as their therapist is to inquire about that issue and discover whether that is one of the reasons they are coming to see you. If the couple has young children or troubled adolescents, gritty basics come into focus quickly.

Making the Transition to Parenting

Transitioning into the parenting role, whether of a newborn or of an older child, can be an overwhelming experience. When such parents enter therapy, they are likely to be desperately interested in the basics of survival—that is, getting enough sleep with a demanding, often noisy infant in the house; possibly juggling two jobs with the ever-present needs of growing children; coping with adolescent insecurity, resistance, and anger; manipulating multiple schedules to free one evening a month for a dinner rendezvous with one another.

As I begin to work with parenting couples, I look for small, attainable goals, giving high priority to basic health and relationship needs, such as food, sleep, and time alone together. The reality of both parents employed outside the home having to confront the daily twenty-four-hour dependency of an infant must be recognized, and their positive and negative feelings as well as the basic principal for survival need to be addressed. As we work on these goals the basic dynamics of the relationship also come into play.

Often just reassuring a couple that their experience is predictable and that it will pass reduces the tension and allows further progress. However, there is more to the pressures and tensions that most couples feel in the transition to parenting. The loss of valued pleasures, problems of budgeting, confusions of self-identity and value, and a host of other stresses may conspire to impoverish the couple's relationship so that the child is experienced as a burden or divisive responsibility. These concerns and needs are real, and they must be dealt with before other therapeutic issues.

Consider the case of Peter and Cathy:

PETER AND CATHY

This couple separated under the strains of their transition to parenthood, each overwhelmed with the burden of establishing new roles and identities. When he called, Peter seemed ambivalent about coming to see me, so I asked whether they had tried therapy before. He said that they had before they separated, but the experience was discouraging:

> We went to a psychiatrist for eight sessions, two as a couple, two each individually, then we did two more as a couple. He would only work with us in this pattern, and we got no help out of any of the sessions. All he ever said was, "How do you feel about it?" He didn't offer any suggestions or statements or tell us anything that we could do. So we stopped.

Both Peter and Cathy wanted to end their separation and rebuild their relationship, but they clearly needed flexible and responsive treatment strategies. In the first session two things became clear almost immediately. First, they needed to recognize that the stresses they were feeling were part of the parenting transition and not caused by their mates. Second, they needed to realize that they were attempting to cope with this transition with far fewer supports and resources than most new parents enjoy.

When Cathy became pregnant, the couple stopped their usual socializing with their cadre of friends, much of which centered around after-work drinking and dining. Although the choice to stop using alcohol during the pregnancy was laudable, it did leave them feeling out of phase with their friends, most of whom were childless. They lost the only peer network they had known together, the anchoring point for their identity as a couple.

They needed help in developing a new reference group as well as new social supports and community resources. I gave them an abundance of specific suggestions for shaping new supportive networks, a diversity of referrals, and continuous encouragement and input. Using a diversity of community resources, about which they knew very little or thought to be inappropriate or unavailable to them, they made a successful transition from a childless couple to parenthood.

Mundane therapy, perhaps. But it worked. When they left therapy a few months later, they were reunited and felt competent and confident in their newly crafted abilities to be "help-finders."

They still had a good deal of work ahead on feelings, boundaries, and early childhood experiences, but they showed themselves that they could work together to solve their problems. Now they would have time together to build their relationship, and it seemed clear that they could do most of that work themselves.

Few issues in couples therapy so clearly hinge on parenting issues, however. Usually it is necessary to spend some time in the ordinary but invaluable process of assessing the role that parenting plays in the problems the couple brings to their first therapy session.

Assessing the Importance of Parenting Issues

Assessing the role parenting plays in the couple relationship helps the therapist decide whether to address parenting issues during the therapy. A concrete assessment plan may be helpful, because at the beginning of therapy many couples are confused or unsure whether their couple issues involve conflict around parenting roles. Some couples may not at first be able to take into account the impact of the child or children on their relationship; others may unduly focus on problems that involve their children.

Initial assessments of the role that parenting plays in the couple relationship are simple and straightforward, concerning the presence of children currently in the household and their origin. For example, here are some questions you might ask:

- Are children currently living in your home?
- What are their names and ages?

- Who is primarily responsible for the child or children?
- Do they spend significant time with other related adults outside the home?

Depending on the specific situation of the couple, answers to these questions will shape those that follow. For example, it might be useful to identify how these children came to be part of the household:

- How are these children related to the two of you?
- How did you two go about deciding to have children?
- Who wanted them the most?
- Were grandparents interested in the decision?

If a couple has partial custody of children or responsibilities for children from other relationships, try to find out how the decision was made to include these children in the household and who was involved in the decision. Attempt also to find out about financial issues concerning children in the household and those not in the household.

Couples parenting children from previous relationships may be interacting with previous spouses concerning child care, child support, and other parenting issues. These interactions can be problematic for the new spouse. Questions such as the following may be helpful in determining the extent to which the parenting role is confused by the previous spousal relationship:

- How is it working out to have shared custody?
- Are the weekend visits successful?
- Does your ex-spouse often change plans for child care and visits?
- How does this work out for the two of you?

The couple's parenting situation may have changed in the past and perhaps will change again during the course of therapy.

Finding out what the couple's early expectations were about parenting children from previous relationships may be helpful in determining the history of any particular conflict.

After asking about the history of parenting, find out about the couple's expectations and hopes for their children's future and about plans for additional children. Pursuing these questions in some detail provides opportunities for hurts, conflicts, or confusions related to parenting issues to emerge.

In discussing these questions, I also listen for their family histories of children and parenting. With little direct probing, the individual and couple perspectives will usually emerge concerning themselves and their families of origin. While the factual data often are useful, I listen for the personal meaning ascribed to the activity of parenting.

I want to know whether parenting is viewed as an adventure or a chore, a creation or a limitation, a mode of expression or a mode of repression. I listen for surprise, irritation, betrayal, fear; for tenderness, intimacy, fulfillment, hope; for feelings of entrapment, inadequacy, dependency, duty. These expressions or their absence help the therapist discover the couple's perspectives on parenting. If these perspectives are filled with internal or interpersonal conflict, I include them in the couples therapy, exploring how these conflicts are expressed in other aspects of their relationship.

Exploring the Meanings of Parenting

How the couple "decided" to become parents or to be childless and the meaning each partner attaches to those processes may hold important clues to the couple's dynamics. Therapists might miss this information unless they remain conscious of the meanings given by the couple to parenting or not parenting. The issues inherent in these meanings can be complicated. One or both spouses may have reversed their positions about becoming parents or may be tangled in ambivalence. They may have grown desperate to become parents or be increasingly fearful of it. The misperception of the other's understandings or feelings is quite common. The following example is a case in point:

RICK AND AILEEN

I met Rick and Aileen in the way I often meet couples for the first time: they brought their child in to be fixed. Sarah was indeed troubled, and, as prudent, caring parents, they were anxious to do whatever was required to help their child, as long as their couple relationship was not included in the therapy. I soon realized that to move forward in therapy we would first have to deal with Sarah's problems, even if they were grounded in her parents' issues.

Sarah was ten when I met her, and Aileen was most concerned about her lack of interest in personal grooming. She wouldn't bathe or wear appropriate clothes to school. Rick was more concerned about her lack of friends and her physical inactivity. After about a year of weekly and biweekly therapy, Sarah was taking pride in her appearance, was getting some needed tutoring, was participating in sports, and had given a party for her friends. She had learned to ignore her parents' constant bickering and to isolate herself in less damaging ways. Her parents, however, seemed to become more agitated and sharp with one another as Sarah improved. After I completed my work with Sarah, I invited them to come in for a few sessions about parenting, in order to tie things up.

I led off by referring to something that I expected them both to deny, even though Sarah and I saw it clearly—that though it was hard to raise an "unwanted child," especially one as bright as Sarah, at least they were more than halfway through the process. Both parents did take exception to my observation that Sarah was unwanted, but not quite in the way I had expected. Each said that the other parent had wanted the child and that they had just gone along with it.

To my surprise, both recognized their own intense feelings that, even though they loved Sarah, they themselves hadn't really wanted a child and didn't like living with one. What they had missed all these years was that the other parent felt the same way. They had never admitted their feelings to one another out of fear that it would hurt the other and Sarah. Each felt that they were a terrible person, because of their terrible secret.

Slowly in couples work they began to appreciate one another in a different way. Each had become a parent for the sake of the other and had stayed the course, trying to do the right thing for Sarah, despite their own feelings. The unhappiness they shared became a symbol of their commitment to one another. In raising Sarah they learned that they could trust the other, and as their empathy grew, they were able to support one another's efforts at parenting.

Exploring the Meanings of Not Parenting

It is easy to see how conflicting assumptions about children and child rearing can erode the relationship of a parenting couple. However, the fact that a couple is childless does not limit the possible impact of "the child" on them, as witnessed in the riveting play *Who's Afraid of Virginia Woolf?* The avoidance of parenthood or the inability to become a parent for whatever reason (for example, infertility problems) can result in enduring and, at times, destructive conflict among couples.

Even couples who are childless by mutual and conscious choice may experience unanticipated consequences of this decision later on in their marriages. For example:

JAN AND MIKE

From the beginning of their marriage, Jan and Mike agreed to remain childless, and during the eleven years of marriage they never reconsidered their decision. Yet, in individual sessions, they both reported that during their fights they were often reduced to mutual despair by the other saying that they had created nothing together, not even a child. They began to feel that their time together had been worthless and that without a child they shared nothing in common. They both worked, had very different hobbies and recreational interests, and often found that they had little to talk about together. At times they felt bored in one another's company.

During therapy they came to see one another differently and to recognize that they had created something real and deeply valuable in their marriage, a relationship that was not there eleven years ago. They invented ways of being together, and in doing so, each changed. Together they created a relationship that altered the ways that each thought about parenthood. In their discussions about what it would be like to choose parenting in some form, they discovered that they had many hopes and fears in common. Eventually, they mutually renewed their decision to remain childless, but in the process their deepest existential issues were opened naturally for discussion. And in discussing them their relationship became deeper and more durable.

SALLY AND FRANK

In another case, Sally and Frank, a couple in their thirties, married for seven years and childless by apparent default, had never even alluded to the possibility of becoming parents. Both came from and were still very involved with dominant, controlling families of origin, which to an important degree cut them off from one another, emotionally and physically. Even their fights seemed to lack engagement, and both reported them to be more like rituals than emotional battles.

After a number of frustrating sessions dominated by the same kinds of ritualistic, emotionally flat interchanges, Sally came to a session alone, because Frank was ill. In this session I learned that they had enjoyed an active premarital sex life until Sally became pregnant. With little discussion, Frank helped her arrange for an abortion, insisting that she keep it secret from his parents. Since premarital sex and abortion were strictly prohibited by her family's religious beliefs, she was isolated from all support except Frank's. They married soon after and never discussed the abortion again.

As therapy progressed, we identified the trauma of the abortion and the resulting fracture of their relationship as the organizing principal of their misery. Real closeness or happiness had to be avoided for fear it would result in another trauma. Real fighting had to be avoided for fear it would renew the old trauma.

Understanding this, the couple learned to tell their story to one another in our sessions and then alone at home. In time, they were able to recount it to some family members as well as to their priest. Released from their painful secret and freed from the depths of its shame, they began to interact with their nieces and nephews and discussed their sexuality, contraception, and the possibility of becoming parents.

Listening for What's Missing: Challenging Parental Assumptions

In the course of therapy, it is critical that the therapist listen for what is omitted as the couple tells their story. Shifting perspectives between what is told and what is left out, between what may be known but cannot be said and what may not be known at all often helps therapists generate interventions uniquely suitable for a particular couple.

For example, parenting couples often present their children as a generic excuse for their own behavior. I frequently hear, "We are getting a divorce because it's best for our children" or "We are staying together because of our children." "Everything got better when we had children." "No, everything fell apart." It's a challenge to untangle these statements without shifting the focus to the child.

Before resorting to something more exotic, I usually explore the possibility that these general statements express an ambivalence or conflict between parental and spousal roles. For example:

1. "We are getting a divorce because it's best for the children" may translate into "My spouse is OK as a spouse but lousy as a

parent" or perhaps into "My suffering doesn't count, but my children's suffering does."

2. "We are staying together for the kids" may mean "My spouse is a lousy spouse but a good parent" or perhaps "I'm afraid to be alone raising the kids."

3. "Everything changed for the better after the children came" may mean "I'm not much interested in being a spouse any more. I'm interested in being a parent."

4. "Everything changed for the worse after the children came" may mean "Enough of this parenting stuff; I want (to be) a spouse again."

Translations such as these can be helpful in therapy, for they convey a good news/bad news message, which is that although one role is troublesome, the other is not. Admitting to multiple feelings and multiple roles is often a first step in teaching couples to experience the whole range of their relationship in such a way so that one disagreeable part doesn't automatically dominate their daily life or relationship. This creates a resilience that allows the couple to adapt to the unpredictable changes that parenting brings to the relationship.

At times, it is useful to draw attention to a couple's inherent conflicts between the multiple feelings and roles in their relationship. For example, when a couple comes in assuming that the true worth of their relationship as a couple is measured by their children's "success" (however defined), the therapist might ask how long their relationship will survive the impact of their parenting. The couple's responses may reveal aspects of their relationship that they might have overlooked.

In our reverence for measurable outcome variables and bottom-line planning, we readily assume that a couple's functioning can be assessed by the duration of the relationship and the success of its product, the children. The identification of the child as a definitive outcome variable is so basic to our thinking that it is almost sacrilegious to question whether the couple has a legitimate function beyond the reproduction of genetic codes and prevailing mores. The question plagues both therapist and couple: can the couple be seen as successful if the child is unsuccessful?

Posing this challenging question may open the way to vital revelations and timely action. For example:

GENE AND MARY

When Gene came to see me in a last-ditch effort to save his fourteen-year marriage, he stated that his wife, Mary, wanted a divorce because they had been unsuccessful in raising her two children by a previous marriage. Mary felt their failure as parents was making everyone unhappy, and she simply couldn't take it any longer. Gene, a fairly kind, gentle, and very intelligent man, had to agree that no one in the family was happy.

Both were at a loss for ideas on how to make the changes that Mary needed. Gene saw no way to make Leon, his sixteen-year-old stepson, and Beth, his thirteen-year-old stepdaughter, into what Mary and he had hoped for. Leon was especially difficult and had been in and out of treatment facilities for years. Beth stayed away from home as much as possible to avoid Leon. Over the past three years, all four members of the family participated in various therapeutic modalities, but they always revolved around Leon's difficulties and dealt with ways to fix him. The plans and programs they tried worked, at best, for only a few weeks before Leon brought trouble to the family once again.

In our second session, after conferring with Leon's psychiatrist and other professionals familiar with the case, I suggested that we work on damage control before anything else. I put it something like this:

"I'm not so much interested in Leon at this point. I'd like to help the two of you find ways to get what you want for yourselves. What you both clearly want is a satisfying relationship with each other. So your first task is to do emergency damage control. You have to limit the impact of Leon's behavior on your relationship with each other and on Beth."

This advice was rather shocking for both of them. Helping professionals had always focused on Leon, as the least functional family member and therefore the one needing the most help. The couple relationship, everyone assumed, would get better after Leon's behavior improved. It was a reasonable assumption: helping the child can reduce the burdens on the couple, and they can take credit for improving the child's behavior. However, Leon had made it impossible to put the assumption to the test, and there was little reason to believe that he would soon change.

The idea that we would limit Leon's impact, rather than try once again to help him, was especially difficult for Mary to accept. Eventually, however, she recognized that she was still trying to prove that she was a good mother. Her first husband—who drank, used drugs, and physically abused both her and Leon—always blamed her for his problems and their divorce. Mary wanted Gene to help prove she was a good mother.

We set up three rules that seemed to focus this couple's efforts and make sense to them. First and always, "Control the damage." This rule included both damage to people and objects as well as damage to relationships, particularly the couple relationship.

Gene and Mary became quite efficient at this, and Leon gave them considerable practice by setting the house on fire, "borrowing" a neighbor's car and driving it into their fence, and harassing Beth's friends when they came over. In working through Gene and Mary's principles of damage control, they learned to stay in the here and now and not get into "why-ing" or blaming. They learned to stay with the potential life-and-death consequences of Leon's behavior. Finally and perhaps most important, they learned to make up rules for themselves concerning how to respond to Leon's actions.

At the center of their collaboration was their second rule, "Anticipate problems and establish boundaries to contain them." For example, if they saw white powder and a razor blade in Leon's room they called the police to identify the substance. If Leon used vulgar and abusive language to them on the phone, it was an "automatic hang-up." If Leon stole the neighbor's car, it was an automatic "call police and encourage the neighbors to press charges."

Their third rule was "Do not allow the family to decline to Leon's level." Mary and Gene enjoyed the theater, so I asked them to read the powerful family dramas of O'Neil and Pinter to help them understand that theirs was a common problem with rather predictable dynamics. They came to recognize that unless other family members think clearly and consistently about what they are doing and facilitate one another in their efforts, the most dysfunctional member quickly gains the most power and sets the level of functioning for the entire family. Mary and Gene were bright and motivated, and so was Beth, who dearly wanted to come in out of the cold. Together they were able to change the ways they made sense of Leon's behavior and of their situations and roles. They were learning that they could be a successful couple even with a child like Leon.

Now the therapeutic challenge was to keep focus on the new rules and to explore ways in which they could be honored. It was tempting to turn the therapy at this point back to Leon's problems, for by now our sessions had uncovered a legion of possibilities for exploring the etiology of his problems—the abuses of Leon's first father, the birth of a rival sibling, Mary's remarriage, the connection of Leon's drug use with his father's substance abuse. But following these or any of the many other compelling leads would have quickly undermined the constructions of new meanings of parenting and family life that Mary and Gene had established and were establishing.

PARENTING AS THERAPEUTIC RESOURCE

The realities of raising children can change almost everything between a couple. When the initial phases of parenting are navigated successfully by a couple, that success paves the way for feelings of effectiveness and competency, which, in turn, help deepen their relationship. Therapeutic facilitation of even small successes, such as helping them accept the limitations parenting imposes on their relationship, often helps couples achieve greater successes later on.

By embracing the changes that parenting brings into one's life, a couple can find new mutually enhancing constructions in their relationship. This opens the possibility of discovering that parenting offers the couple new opportunities: that they can share the most tender parts of themselves through their reflections in the growing children, that in seeing one another with their children they can know and understand one another in new and deeper ways, that in the relationships they construct with their children, as a couple, they disclose who they are to one another.

Using Parenting Skills to Enhance Couples Therapy

Couples who are confused and limited in their child-rearing skills often experience feelings of shame and guilt that erode their relationship. Helping these parents with basic parenting skills can relieve some of the shame and increase their therapeutic connection, allowing them to speak more openly of their own fears and inadequacies.

For example, confusion concerning who is in charge will generate issues of authority and security for the child. Through a range of disruptive behaviors the child asks, "Does anyone know what they are doing here?" Parents who fail the child's implicit test tend to feel inadequate and become depressed or blame the spouse. Help in identifying the roots of the problem and in teaching the parents some parenting skills can dramatically change the couple's pattern of interaction.

It is important to put this sort of parental coaching in language that keeps the focus on the couple rather than on the child. Many couples are only too willing to shift attention from themselves and their relationship and will even ask to bring the child into therapy, turning the couples therapy into family therapy, centered on parent-child relationships. Since family therapy with another therapist can be a natural follow-up to couples therapy, I rarely discourage the interest in the family dynamic. But I do carefully avoid shifting the ongoing couples therapy into family therapy.

The fact that there are children in the family sometimes can be used to give couples a chance to experiment with new response patterns in their couple relationship. For example:

NEAL AND MARIE

Neal and Marie came in with a bevy of issues. Neal believed that everything could be fixed with logic and that therapists were somewhere between voyeurs and parasites. Marie's attempts to talk about her feelings were usually aborted by Neal, who, appearing agitated, would tell her how to fix the problem. My efforts to help Neal listen rather than playing "Mr. Fix-It" to Marie's feelings were futile.

Fortunately, Neal and Marie had a child, Jeff, a seven-year-old, who was "causing a lot of trouble." Only Marie could handle him. I gave Neal clear directions on how to talk to Jeff about the latter's feelings, without fixing or judging them. After considerable practice in my office—with Marie pretending to be Jeff—Neal was able to learn to just listen. He then tried his new skills with Jeff, and they worked. After that he began to try them with Marie, and once again they worked. This small success rescued our couples therapy. Neal learned to experiment with his communication style with Jeff, who gave him clear feedback, and he took pride in reporting his experiments to Marie. She, in turn, began to feel more hopeful about the relationship.

When helping couples with their parenting skills, it is useful to first find out whether one of the partners is inhibiting their parenting role. This may occur, for example, when the couple is part of a blended family with "his, hers, and ours" offspring. In such cases it may be difficult to establish clear rules and understandings about who is in charge and what authority each person has to make decisions and to help maintain the household.

❧

Inhibited parenting may also occur if one or both parents refuse to assume parental authority. In such instances, the underlying factors need to be explored, exposed, and removed before the partner can assume their role as a parent.

One young knowledgeable couple managed to raise their three-and-a-half-year-old child defending themselves all along from assuming their parental roles. The mother could not bring herself to draw a line and discipline the child, and the father would not step in for fear of criticizing the mother's abilities. Consequently, the child became more and more unruly and a burdensome embarrassment to both of them. After some therapy, however, the mother was able to give herself permission to discipline the child and to recognize that she could still be a loving mother. This allowed the father to participate in setting limits, and with time the couple was able to assimilate a range of new parenting practices.

I have found that by helping couples expand and develop their parenting skills they are more likely to exert joint parental authority. This, in turn, usually leads to improvements in other areas of their functioning. For example:

One couple in a blended family with three children—one his, two hers—dreaded going to Disneyland because of the inevitable conflicts over who would sit where, who would go together on which rides, and so forth. The parents anticipated that they would be arguing with the kids the entire time and, sooner or later, would fall apart as a couple, because they might be "forced" to take the side of their own kids.

I spent considerable time helping them realize that by negotiating rules of control in advance they could take charge of the trip before it even began. The next night, the five family members sat down after dinner to decide whether they could all agree to a plan for the trip. It was made clear that unless they could came to an agreement, the trip would not take place.

The parents presented the plan they worked out together with me in therapy. Each morning the parents would agree on which of them would be in charge and the children would be told before breakfast. All pairing-up and seating arrangements would be decided by the parent in charge. Any child behaving in an unacceptable way would be given a warning from that parent, and if the behavior was repeated, everyone would get a five-minute time-out, wherever they were. If it was repeated again, everyone would go back to the hotel for two hours. After discussing some of the details, the plan was accepted by all the children.

After the trip, both parents reported that the trip had been a smashing success and that everyone had a great time, the best ever as a family. No one even had a five-minute time-out, and the authority of neither parent was ever challenged or questioned. Clearly, in this parenting success, the couple felt empowered in their relationship to one another.

There is something akin to "self-esteem" for couples. When tasks like this are accomplished successfully, the couple's perception of themselves and each other is enhanced, which makes it easier to act more effectively and with greater confidence in the future. The strength of their partnership amplifies their "couple esteem" and is reflected in their parenting.

Discovering the "Here and Now" of a Couple Relationship Through Parenting

Becoming parents can deepen a couple's awareness of one another's everyday anxieties about life, opening new possibilities for mutual understanding. In opening to the child, parents can discover or regain an ability to *be* with one another. From within the womb the baby inspires the deepest of anxieties, forcing its parents to confront the realities of their aloneness. At the same time, the newly created being evokes a sense of awe in the parents, evoking wonderfully tender bondings, not only to the child but also of the partners to one another. If they are lucky and sensitive to one another, it can even open new realms of mutually affirming togetherness between them.

As the child grows, parents are offered one of the greatest gifts of parenting: the chance to act together as a couple with their child in constructing anew the meanings of life, death, and everything in between. The opportunity that couples have to sort out and understand the relationship between love and death is greatly enhanced by the predictable questions that young children have about death: "Will I die?" "Will you die?" "Why do you have to go to work when I want you home with me?" "Don't you love me?" Confronting and sharing these questions, the couple can explore their own and one another's feelings and fears. In helping their children confront their wondrous vulnerabilities, parents may recognize the seamless bond of their own lives to their own deaths and the infusion of their loved ones' lives and deaths with their own.

Parental openness to the sensibilities of their children is thus rich in potentials for advancing couples therapy. For example, it is often useful in therapy to encourage couples to keep their focus on the construction of meaning in the *here and now* rather than in a past "there and then" or a future "when and if." This focus is not easy to maintain, however, nor is it easy to help the couple appreciate the importance of such a priority. By approaching the idea through the couple's parenting concerns, however, the therapist's task might be greatly eased because the interaction of meaning, perspective, and perception of reality is present in the parents' daily interactions with the child.

If encouraged to think about those interactions and to imagine it through their child's eyes, the couple can learn the essence of being present in the here and now. When asked to identify their child-rearing objectives, for example, many couples say that their first priority is to prepare the child for the future. This translates into "helping my child develop a 'when and if' approach to life," reflecting their own responses to the uncertainties of modern life. Therapy that encourages them, individually and together, to spend more time in the here and now of the child's life can begin to alter these priorities, sensitizing them not only to their parenting but also to their couple relationship.

One couple in their early forties came to my office simply not knowing where else to turn. They didn't know what was wrong with them, individually or as a couple:

ELLEN AND PAUL

Ellen was crying all the time, and Paul was starting to drink more than was comfortable for either of them. They had good jobs and a beautiful home. They loved each other and had two healthy little girls. Yet, they were miserable. They felt unsure of their decision to come for help because they always associated couples therapy with fighting. In fact, they didn't fight. They were very considerate and sympathetic toward one another.

I decided to not focus on what was "wrong," since that's what they had been doing together for almost a year. Instead, I asked, over and over, what they wanted. This unleashed considerable emotion and frustration, which continued to build until, through his tears, Paul said, "I just want to be together and feel good with each other. I just want to feel the depth of appreciation and thankfulness that we are together, safe, well, and with each other, right now. That's everything to me." It was a riveting statement.

Ellen immediately admitted how deeply she, too, wanted that. But she was afraid. She said that she really loved what he said but didn't know how to do it. As the therapy progressed, I learned that she came from a home with a father who was an abusive alcoholic and a mother who treated the children as objects, as she struggled to keep up the appearance that everything was in control. Paul and Ellen had tried for seven years to become pregnant. Finally, they decided to adopt an infant girl, whose arrival was followed, eighteen months later, by the birth of a baby sister. Ellen was a talented manager and organizer. Each parent had assigned jobs at home, and Paul helped with everything. Even though both had demanding jobs away from home, they missed hardly a step as they expanded their family from two to four within a year and a half. On the surface everything was perfect. But beneath that surface, both were miserable.

After two years of parenting, there still was no time for them together, as a couple. They were experiencing their children not so much as children but more as objects needing maintenance and constant vigilance. Raising the children right was a moral issue involving rigid routines and constant monitoring and assessment. Clearly, if they were to ever again "feel good with each other," as Paul had expressed it, they would have to shift their perspectives on parenting.

When Ellen called to say that she and Paul had allowed the girls to miss the first bath in their entire lives, we both laughed. In the next session, they proudly showed me how they entered the event in their baby books as the baby's first "nonbath." With time they learned to do less and be more. They learned how to shift to children's time when they got home from work and to hang out together. They learned how to let the kids get dirty and how to feel proud of it. They accepted their own competence as parents and their ability to deal with whatever came up. As they learned all of this, they also discovered they had more energy to spend on being a couple and appreciating what they had accomplished together.

It is especially difficult for some couples to tap into the shared sense of fulfillment and well-being that can go hand and hand with parenting, since this is a relatively passive task that requires reflective time together. The latter is generally an unfamiliar relaxation for parents who tend be in the more active, problem-solving mode, so common to middle-class parents today. But, discovering these quieter qualities of parenting can be a moving experience for couples, especially when they are introduced at the right time and in the couple's own language.

Therapeutic Possibilities in Parenting Adult Children

As the couple matures, they will find that mutually enhancing their parenting roles and gaining satisfaction from that enhancement can renew and strengthen their relationship. Recognizing that they continue to accomplish together what neither could accomplish independently offers a bonding that maturing couples can experience in parenting their adolescent and adult children. This recognition can give the therapist enormous leverage in dealing with the issues of mature and aging couples.

In most cases, adult children provide important resources for therapy of the parental couple. Children tend to enhance the latter's lives by direct interaction, by helping them find access to other people and community resources, and by sharing their experience in ways that may allow the parents to enjoy vicariously the careers, caprices, and joys of their children and grandchildren.

But even the most supportive and successful young adults also bring arguments, pain, and misery into the lives of their maturing parents. Here, too, in most cases it is necessary to emphasize the primacy of the couple's relationship, encouraging them to firmly defend the living conditions and the access to activities that support and enhance their life together. With clear boundaries, the couple's relationship can continue to unfold into the couple's final years of life, as new parenting issues change over time.

Couples who learn how to share with one another the little things that tickle them and irritate them about their children develop a mutual appreciation that may strengthen their relationship in later years. By sharing this intimate knowledge and feelings about their children, couples may find a lifelong source of revelation and renewal in their own relationship.

In therapy the things couples share about what is most irritating or amusing in their older children may reveal who they are as a couple and how they feel about themselves and their life together. Perhaps, most importantly, couples who share these feelings of delight and irritation will not be emotionally bored.

Couples entering the grandparenting stage of parenting often need explicit help in maintaining boundaries with their mature children, especially around issues of illness, money, and residence. Many couples, who have for years given their own needs second place to those of their children, need help in recognizing that their adult children may be unaware—even lack the experience to be aware—of the vulnerability of their aging parents. Although keeping one's health and freedom of movement are critical to the aging couple, adult children, even in late middle age, are rarely sensitive to these issues until it is too late.

As in the earlier phases of parenting, adult children, even when they also become parents, bring both problems and possibilities into the lives of their parents and provide both therapeutic difficulties and healing resources. Couples therapists sensitive to the specifics of these intertwining issues and resources can more readily limit the negative encumbrances of the aging couple and engage the positive possibilities.

The negativities of parenting for couples who seek therapy, and the array of destructive effects of children on couple dynamics, are well established in the literature on couples therapy. Much of the advice to couples offered by mental health professionals and by the popular media seems to tell them to act as if they don't have the kids that they do in fact have. It is almost as if parenting is viewed as a disease, that with luck (enjoyed, it seems, by a diminishing number of parents) goes into remission after eighteen or twenty years.

Throughout this chapter, I have attempted to bring attention to the impact of the child on the couple, to the usefulness in couples therapy of direct interventions that help the couple cope with the child, and to the healing resources of parenting. My suggestions and case illustrations are meant to encourage other therapists to actively consider these perspectives and resources in their frame of reference and choice of interventions.

What a therapist feels and believes about children and parenting makes a difference to the parenting couple in treatment, and particularly to the couple grasping for some validation of their difficult roles. It is far too easy to trivialize these roles, limiting them within caretaking and efficiency models. Unfortunately, such a simple model rarely provides the strength required for parenting. Similarly, in issues of roles, gender, housework, and responsibilities, what a therapist feels and believes makes a difference.

Embracing and treasuring the awareness called out by a child's concerns can enrich and renew a couple's relationship. To discount such processes in our therapy, as we so often do, is to lose a precious therapeutic resource. Regrasping that resource, we may be able to help couples connect more closely with one another. In their interactions with children we may be able to help them design a relationship that allows for the construction and reconstruction of meaning, and the interpretation of problems against a horizon of good faith and hope.

I have found that when they are offered the viewpoints represented in this chapter along with the possibility of some joy in the parenting process, most couples, while perhaps not fully understanding or agreeing with everything, seem to like their work in therapy and to feel happier and more hopeful.

NOTES

P. 229, *neglected aspect . . . the influence of children:* Any random selection of titles from couples and marriage therapy literature will demonstrate this neglect. Consider the following works, which represent various approaches to couples therapy; each offers an excellent treatment of its focal subject: Bornstein, P. H., & Bornstein, M. T. (1986). *Marital therapy: A behavioral-communications approach.* New York: Pergamon: (the word *child* is never mentioned); Weeks, G. R. (Ed.). (1989). *Treating couples: The intersystem model of the marriage council of Philadelphia.* New York: Brunner/Mazel: (this is the complete list of entries under "children" in the subject index: ". . . and extramarital sexual crisis; . . . knowledge of, about secret extramarital sex; . . . separation and divorce effects on; . . . sessions including, in separation and divorce therapy"); Beach, S. R. H., Sandeen, E. E., & O'Leary, K. D. (1990). *Depression in marriage: A model for etiology and treatment.* New York: Guilford: (the words *child, mother, father,* and *parent* are not mentioned in the index); Greenberg, L. S., & Johnson, S. M. (1988). *Emotionally focused therapy for couples.* New York: Guilford: (emotions are seen as "complex syntheses of all that is being experienced" [p. 3] by persons "embedded in a social context that is highly influential in determining their behavior" [p. 227], yet children are given no mention, either as part of "all that is being experienced" or as active in the embedding context).

P. 231, *Transitioning into the parenting role:* Michaels, G. Y., & Goldberg, W. A. (Eds.), (1988). *The transition to parenthood: Current theory and research* (pp. 114–154). New York: Cambridge University Press; Cowan, C. P., & Cowan, P. A. (1992). *When partners become parents: The big life change for couples.* New York: Basic Books.

P. 231, *confusions of self-identity:* Cowan, C. P. (1988). Working with men becoming fathers: The impact of a couples group intervention. In P. Bronstein & C. P. Cowan (Eds.), *Fatherhood today: Men's changing role in the family* (pp. 276–298). New York: Wiley.

P. 235, *family histories of children and parenting:* Paul, N., with Paul, B. B. (1990). Enhancing empathy in couples: A transgenerational approach. In R. Chasin, H. Grunebaum, & M. Herzig (Eds.), *One couple, four realities: Multiple perspectives on couple therapy* (pp. 83–105). New York: Guilford.

P. 239, *what may be known but cannot be said:* Polanyi, M. (1963). *The tacit dimension.* Garden City, NY: Doubleday.

P. 240, *reverence for measurable outcome variables:* Hansen, D. A. (1991). The child in family and school: Agency and the workings of time. In P. E. Cowan, D. Field, D. A. Hansen, A. Skolnick, & G. E. Swanson (Eds.), *Family, self and society: Toward a new agenda for family research.* Hillsdale, NJ: Erlbaum; Bernstein, R. J. (1983). *Beyond objectivism and relativism: Science, hermeneutics and praxis.* Philadelphia: University of Pennsylvania Press.

P. 243, *parenting . . . navigated successfully . . . paves the way for feelings of effectiveness:* Cowan, C. P., & Cowan, P. A. (1992). *op. cit.*

P. 244, *Couples . . . limited in their child-rearing skills often experience feelings of shame:* Fisher, J. (1993). The impenetrable other: Ambivalence and the oedipal conflict in work with couples. In S. Ruszczynski (Ed.), *Psychotherapy with couples: Theory and practice at the Tavistock Institute of marital studies* (pp. 142–166). London: Karnac Books; Cowan, C. P., & Cowan, P. A. (1992). *op. cit.*; Hansen D. A., & Johnson, V. A. (1979). Rethinking family stress theory: Definitional aspects. In W. R. Burr, R. Hill, F. I. Nye, &

I. L. Reiss (Eds.), *Contemporary theories about the family* (pp. 581–603). New York: Free Press.

P. 248, *constructing anew the meanings of life, death, and everything in between:* Yalom, I. D. (1980). *Existential psychotherapy.* New York: Basic Books; Becker, E. (1973). *The denial of death.* New York: Free Press; Erickson, E. (1963). *Childhood and society.* New York: W.W. Norton; Fromm, E. (1963). *The art of loving.* New York: Bantam Books.

P. 249, *the uncertainties of modern life:* Giddens, A. (1991). *Modernity and social identity: Self and society in late modernity.* Palo Alto: Stanford University Press; Bruner, J. (1987). *Actual minds, possible worlds.* Cambridge, MA: Harvard University Press.

ABOUT THE AUTHORS

Joel Crohn, Ph.D., author of *Mixed Matches: How to Create Successful Interracial, Interethnic, and Interfaith Relationships*, is a clinical psychologist, co-director of the Cultural Competence Consultation Center, and is on the faculty at the Asian Family Institute in San Francisco. He has researched, written, and lectured nationally about intermarriage for over fifteen years and was the director of a major research project on interfaith marriage for the American Jewish Committee. He is a past president of the Marin County Psychological Association and is in private practice in Kensington and San Rafael, California.

Steven A. Foreman, M.D., is on the faculty at the University of California, San Francisco, and has a private practice of child and adult psychiatry in San Francisco. He does child psychotherapy research with the San Francisco Psychotherapy Research Group, where he sits on the board of directors and serves as chairman of the Curriculum Committee. Dr. Foreman is a member of the Society of Psychotherapy Research and formerly was director of child psychiatry at Pacific Presbyterian Medical Center in San Francisco. He received his B.A. degree (1975) as a College Scholar, graduating with distinction in all subjects from Cornell University, and received his M.D. degree (1979) from Thomas Jefferson University. He finished his residency training in psychiatry (1983) and his fellowship in child psychiatry (1985) at the University of California, San Francisco.

Susan E. Hanks, Ph.D., has been in independent practice offering psychotherapy to children, adults, and families with specialties in family violence, divorce, traumatic stress, and dissociative disorders since 1975 in Berkeley, California. She provides social policy, research, and organizational consultation to numerous private and governmental organizations; forensic consultation in criminal, civil, and immigration cases related to psychological trauma, violence against women, and child custody mediation. Dr. Hanks has been the founding director of The Family & Violence Institute at the California School of Professional Psychology, Alameda, California, since 1983. She received her master's degree (1972) from the Simmons College School of Social Work in Boston and doctorate in clinical social work (1992) from the California Institute for Clinical Social Work in Berkeley. Dr. Hanks is board certified as a Diplomate in Clinical Social Work by the American Board of Examiners in Clinical Social Work and also holds a NASW Diplomate in clinical social work.

Vicky A. Johnson, Ph.D., is a clinical psychologist in private practice in the San Francisco Bay area. The author of numerous articles and chapters on families, child development, education, and animal behavior, she holds a Ph.D. from the University of California, Berkeley, and has taught and studied in Europe, Mexico, and New Zealand. Before entering private practice, she served as a clinical and research psychologist in the Department of Psychiatry in the Stanford Medical School and as a research psychologist at the University of California, Berkeley. She lives with her husband, Don, sons, Michael and Cole, and mother, Naoma. Together they raise Lipizzans and provide a home for many animal friends.

Hilda Kessler, Ph.D., has been a practicing clinician in the San Francisco Bay area for the past twenty-five years, specializing in couples therapy and couples groups. She has been a lecturer at San Francisco State University and San Jose State University and is on the clinical faculty of the Wright Institute, Berkeley, California. Her interests in group phenomena include thought reform and psychological trauma. She consults with corporate law firms on workplace stress.

Seymour Kessler, Ph.D., is a licensed clinical psychologist and an associate clinical professor in the Department of Pediatrics at the University of California, San Francisco. He has published numerous articles dealing with the psychological impact of health issues. He edited a book, *Genetic Counseling: Psychological Dimensions* (Academic Press, 1979) and has recently published *Heart Bypass* (St. Martin's Press, 1995), a book on preparing for coronary bypass surgery and dealing with its psychological impact.

Jack Schiemann, Ph.D., works with individuals, couples, and groups at the Berkeley Therapy Institute in California. Additionally, he has a private practice in Kensington, California. Dr. Schiemann received his Ph.D. in clinical psychology from the Wright Institute in Berkeley. He has over twenty years of experience in helping professions both as a parish priest and psychotherapist.

Margaret Thaler Singer, Ph.D., is a clinical psychologist and an emeritus adjunct professor, Department of Psychology at the University of California, Berkeley. She has received numerous awards for her research extending over the past fifty years on families, couples, cults, stress, and schizophrenia. Her book *Cults in Our Midst* was published by Jossey-Bass in 1995.

Wendy L. Smith, Ph.D., has a private practice in Albany, California, working with individuals and couples. She received B.A. degrees (1986) in psychology and women studies from San Francisco State University, and M.A. (1989) and Ph.D. (1994) degrees in clinical psychology from the Wright Institute, Berkeley, California.

INDEX